# ASPECTS OF THE POETRY OF
# DAFYDD AP GWILYM

# ASPECTS OF THE POETRY OF DAFYDD AP GWILYM

*Collected Papers*

RACHEL BROMWICH

CARDIFF
UNIVERSITY OF WALES PRESS
1986

© Rachel Bromwich 1986

**Cataloguing-in-Publication Data**
Bromwich, Rachel
  Aspects of the poetry of Dafydd ap Gwilym.
  1. Dafydd ap Gwilym—Criticism and interpretation
  I. Title
  891.6'611    PB2273.D3

  ISBN 0–7083–0905–4

Printed in Great Britain at The Bath Press, Avon

Er cof am Syr Thomas Parry,
gan ddiolch iddo
am roi inni destun
gwaith y bardd

# PREFACE

THE six chapters contained in this book are revised versions of articles which were written over a period of nearly twenty years, each one commissioned independently for a specific purpose. Ch. 1 reproduces my booklet on 'Dafydd ap Gwilym' published in the 'Writers of Wales' series (Cardiff, 1974). This chapter was originally conceived in order to give a brief general account of the poet for the benefit of the uninformed reader: all the other chapters are of a more specialist nature, and are addressed to an informed audience having a first-hand knowledge of the poet's work in the original Welsh. Ch. 2 on 'Tradition and Innovation' originated as a lecture delivered to the Honourable Society of Cymmrodorion in 1963, and published in the Society's *Transactions* for the following year, with a subsequent reprint as a booklet by the University of Wales Press (1967, 1972). Chs. 3, 4, and 5 were first written in Welsh and are here translated; ch. 3 was contributed to *Dafydd ap Gwilym a Chanu Serch yr Oesoedd Canol*, ed. John Rowlands (Cardiff, 1975); ch. 4 is an expanded version of a chapter published in *Ysgrifau Beirniadol*, ed. J. E. Caerwyn Williams, vol. X (Denbigh, 1977), and ch. 5 appeared in *Ysgrifau Beirniadol*, vol. XII (1982). Ch. 6 reproduces one of two chapters which were commissioned by A. O. H. Jarman and Gwilym Rees Hughes, editors of *A Guide to Welsh Literature*, vol. 2 (Swansea, 1979). The Introduction to the present volume reproduces a part of the companion chapter in the same volume on 'Dafydd ap Gwilym', but I did not avail myself of the kind permission of the publishers of *A Guide to Welsh Literature* to reproduce this chapter in its entirety, since it corresponds closely with my account of the poet in the 'Writers of Wales' volume. In revising my work for this re-issue I have taken trouble to avoid such overlaps in subject-matter, in so far as it has been possible, and this has necessitated excisions here and there of passages which appeared in the original texts.

I am grateful to Christopher Davies, Swansea, for permission to re-issue the substance of my two chapters in *A Guide to Welsh Literature*, and also to use in my Introduction a part of my contribution to *Poetry Wales: Special Dafydd ap Gwilym Number* (vol. 8, Spring, 1973); to Messrs. John Rhys and Iwan Llwyd Williams of the University of Wales Press for their care in guiding this work through the press, and to the printers of the Bath Press for their skilful work.

RACHEL BROMWICH

*September, 1985*

# CONTENTS

*page*

PREFACE                                                         vii

INTRODUCTORY                                                     xi

ABBREVIATIONS                                                  xvii

1. DAFYDD AP GWILYM                                              1

2. TRADITION AND INNOVATION IN THE POETRY OF DAFYDD AP
   GWILYM                                                       57

3. THE SUB-LITERARY TRADITION                                   89

4. DAFYDD AP GWILYM AND THE BARDIC GRAMMAR                     105

5. ALLUSIONS TO TALES AND ROMANCES                             132

6. THE EARLIER *Cywyddwyr;* DAFYDD AP GWILYM'S
   CONTEMPORARIES                                              152

   INDEX                                                       172

# INTRODUCTORY

POETA NASCITUR, NON FIT, it has been said, 'a poet is born, not made'. Nevertheless, it is tempting to speculate as to how far genius may not receive its initial stimulus from a rare combination of circumstances peculiarly congenial to its flowering. The birth of Dafydd ap Gwilym coincided, appropriately enough, with an unprecedented opportunity to mate the new with the old, the foreign with the national idiom, and to draw Welsh poetry, if only briefly, into the mainstream of contemporary European literature. It is because of Dafydd ap Gwilym that we look back upon the fourteenth century as a major turning-point and a fresh beginning in Welsh poetry, just as it is because of Chaucer that we regard the fourteenth century in England in a similar light. Without doubt, these were the two giants of the fourteenth century, in so far as the poetry of the 'Island of Britain' is concerned. To explore their similarities and their differences may prove unexpectedly rewarding for the light which it casts upon the literary climate in which each grew to manhood. Both poets were favoured in their birth, having been born and nurtured in just those areas of England and Wales which were most accessible to influences from without: for Geoffrey Chaucer the south-east midlands and the ambience of the royal court in London, for Dafydd ap Gwilym those very areas in south and west Wales into which Norman-French influences had been penetrating for two centuries before his birth. It is hardly a coincidence that there existed for both poets, beyond these spotlighted areas to the forefront, which readily received influences from abroad, a hinterland to the north and west, which in England, as in Wales, was the surviving stronghold of earlier poetic modes. North-west England was the home of the 'Gawain' poet and of the aristocratic alliterative tradition derived ultimately from court-poetry in Old English: in a comparable manner the ancient kingdom of Gwynedd in North Wales was the stronghold of classical bardic panegyric as fostered from the earliest times until 1282 by a rich succession of court poets attached to the Gwynedd princes. (The validity of the long entrenched standards inculcated in traditional bardic panegyric is the subject of the poetic controversy which took place between Dafydd ap Gwilym and the Anglesey poet Gruffudd Gryg.) Outstanding differences between the two poets are immediately apparent: when Chaucer wrote, the English language as a literary medium had only comparatively recently consolidated its victory in the fight for survival against the language of the conquerors, having been deprived of what has been described as the 'cultural superstructure'[1] of Old English by the Norman Conquest, and only by degrees was it in process of evolving a new and radically altered literary medium. In contrast, Welsh had at this time suffered no comparable deprivation, so that Dafydd ap Gwilym inherited as his medium an old and mature speech, richly endowed with the kind of poetic nuances that are only acquired by the passage of time, and by the continuous and selective use of a language by an unbroken succession of poets. He drew richly upon the tradition of bardic eulogy which lay to his hand, going back to the sixth century Taliesin and to the poetry of the 'Old North'—the lost ancestral territories which, though they might be only dimly remembered in a geographical sense, were still powerfully evocative in their literary associations. (In this respect the difference between Chaucer and Dafydd ap Gwilym is epitomized in the fact that Chaucer evinces no comparable recollection of the poem of *Beowulf*.)

Yet by the benefit of hindsight we can see that among so much that is different in the national idiom inherited by the two poets, they nevertheless possessed some significant features in common. Neither was a professional poet, and the relatively 'amateur' status with respect to their art which both enjoyed in consequence, gave to them both a privileged freedom to experiment and to break with earlier tradition, so that these two became the first poets of their respective nations to take full account of certain foreign literary modes and to assimilate them, each into his national medium, and in this way to create a new synthesis. And it so happens that it was the same literary works from abroad which were paramount in their influence upon the work of both—the Latin poet Ovid and the French poetry of *amour courtois*, which found its supreme expression in the *Roman de la Rose*. Both poets also responded in their highly individual fashion to the continental *genres* of romance and *fabliau*. Though Dafydd ap Gwilym is no narrative poet in the manner of Chaucer, yet within the brief compass of his *cywyddau* (which rarely exceed sixty lines in length) he can on occasion prove himself to be an adapt narrator of incidents, and one no less skilled than Chaucer in introducing colloquial dialogue and even idiomatic asseverations with apparent effortlessness into the confined

---

[1] D. S. Brewer in D. S. Brewer (ed.) *Chaucer and the Chaucerians* (London, 1966) 9, 26.

limits of his intricate verse-form. Both poets portray themselves as characters in their own poems, both in addition make references to their living contemporaries, and both adopt attitudes of irony and self-depreciation in their poetic *personae*. Both employed a 'relaxed' and relatively informal style of writing, which Dafydd shares, remarkably, with the English poets who came to the fore in the latter part of the fourteenth century—with Chaucer, Gower, Langland, and the 'Gawain' poet, and which a recent English critic has termed a 'Ricardian' style.[2]

As a result of both Chaucer's and Dafydd's unprofessional status, we may also suppose that the original audience (a listening audience) of both poets was a small and intimate one, composed of individuals who were well-known to them, and to whom they themselves were familiar companions. With such an audience it was possible to introduce innuendos and topical allusions of a kind which would have been unintelligible outside their immediate intimate circle—and for this reason we can only regret that many of the implications of their verse must inevitably be lost to us, their readers, at this distance of time. Finally, the unprofessional status which both poets enjoyed with respect to their art must undoubtedly have facilitated the climacteric changes to which both contributed with regard to the metrical systems of their two countries. Yet as an afterthought, were not both of these poets equally peripheral to the European poetic tradition on which both so richly drew? Both were equally incapable of paying back, out of their own rich contributions to their national literatures, any reciprocal influence upon the literature of Europe. It is solely as a *grant translateur* that Chaucer's French contemporary Eustache Deschamps commemorates him.[3] And even upon her nearest neighbour, let alone upon the literature of Europe, the impact of Welsh poetry has at no time been other than barely minimal. Yet upon the literatures of their own countries the influence of both these poets has been permanent and irreversible.[4]

A contributory reason for this neglect is to be found in the recognition of the fact that poetry is virtually untranslatable, except at the cost of so great a loss as to call in question the reason for ever attempting it. Dafydd ap Gwilym's poetry is an extreme example of the validity of this interdiction, since his *awdlau* and *cywyddau* made their primary appeal to the ears of their original audience: rarely—if ever—did these audiences see his poems in writing. Such impact as his poetry made

[2] J. Burrow, *Medium Aevum* xlv (1976), 240; ibid. *Ricardian Poetry* (London, 1971).

[3] 'Grant translateur, noble Geffrey Chaucier' is the refrain of the *ballade* which Eustache Deschamps (1936–*c*. 1406) addressed to his English contemporary, *The Oxford Book of French Verse* (1931), 11–12. For him, Chaucer's fame rested upon his translation into English of the *Roman de la Rose*.

[4] Cf. P. Sims-Williams 'Dafydd ap Gwilym and Celtic Literature' in Boris Ford (ed.) *Medieval Literature, Part 2, The European Inheritance* (*The New Penguin Guide to English Literature*, Harmondsworth, 1983), 301.

upon their understanding must have been made at levels which varied according to the circumstances and capacity of the individual listeners: for instance, it has been observed that such a device as that of *dyfalu* ('likening') presupposes an audience familiar with this convention.[5] By intricate innuendo and often by intentional ambiguity arising from the nuances of his traditional vocabulary, and by his figurative use of the new words of French origin which in his day were flooding into the language, Dafydd evolved for himself a poetic medium of a degree of complexity never previously envisaged in Welsh, and one which by its very nature defies all attempts at adequate paraphrase, let alone the far more difficult task of transposition into another language. It follows that very often there is no single 'right' meaning for a line or a passage, and since the full range of meaning possessed by the words in any one language does not possess the same nuances as the words which come nearest in meaning to it in another language, the translator is too often obliged to opt for a single meaning out of a choice of equally valid but never completely satisfactory alternatives. Any attempt to translate Dafydd's poetry must therefore come to terms with two main problems, the difficulties presented by his syntax, and the straight-jacket which the requirements of *cynghanedd* (rhyme combined with alliteration) imposed upon his choice of vocabulary. Dafydd inherited from his professional predecessors a traditional syntax which belonged essentially to poetry. This was highly condensed and often imprecise, admitting of an inverted word-order which allowed for ambiguities in the relationship of substantives to each other, made frequent new compounds of either nouns and adjectives in combination, or of two substantives or two adjectives with each other, and could on occasion dispense with pronouns, prepositions, and conjunctions, and even with certain forms of the verb 'to be'; and which frequently employed 'verb-nouns' (i.e'. nouns denoting the verbal act, a characteristic of the Celtic languages) in place of the more precise finite forms. The frequent counterpointing interjections enshrined in Dafydd's *sangiadau* (interpolated phrases) further enhance the difficulties for the translator.

The formidable difficulties which thus have always faced any would-be translator of Dafydd ap Gwilym's verse, with its intricate interplay of sound with sense, has resulted in the virtual neglect of Dafydd's high standing among the foremost poets of the European Middle Ages, except in his own country. Yet it was solely on the basis of reading the poet's works in translation that Peter Dronke remarked with astonishment· not long ago[6] on the breadth and versatility of the poet's

---

[5] D. J. Bowen, 'Dafydd ap Gwilym a Datblygiad y Cywydd', LlC viii (1964), 23, n. 163.

[6] P. Dronke in John Rowlands (ed.) *Dafydd ap Gwilym a Chanu Serch yr Oesoedd Canol* (Caerdydd, 1975), 1–2.

*repertoire*, and to demonstrate that this covers the complete span of the types of verse practised by the court poets of medieval Europe, whether in Latin or in the vernaculars; that is to say: (i) religious verse; (ii) secular praise-poems (i.e. formal elegies and greetings to patrons); (iii) satire and controversy with rival poets; (iv) informal addresses to friends, and greetings to fellow-poets, together with the whole range of love-poetry, comprising (v) subjective verse (i.e. reflections on love and poems addressed to the loved one—though the latter are rare in Dafydd), and (vi) objective verse (poems of dialogue and incident).

Of course the first three categories listed above represent Dafydd's indigenous inheritance from native Welsh tradition (they include his controversy with his rival Gruffudd Gryg): it is in the final three categories that Dafydd added to Welsh poetry a new dimension, and one which had only been foreshadowed in quite minor ways by any of the poets who were his predecessors. Nothing at all resembling his highly personalized love-poetry had previously been known in Welsh, neither his 'subjective' complaints on his plight as a lover, nor his 'objective' poems of fanciful incident, which include both his *fabliaux* and his *llatai* or love-messenger poems, with their inimitable descriptions of wild nature and of forest creatures.

It is paradoxical that the circumstances which were so conducive for the nurture of Dafydd's exotic genius arose from that very state of traumatic flux in society and in politics, with all their disruptive implications for Welsh culture, which followed the conquest of 1282. The traditional bonds of poetic patronage became loosened at the very time when ideas and influences from the outside world were flooding into Wales as never before: this was a time, as a Welsh historian once remarked[7] when Wales held her windows wide open to the outside world, and yet retained, in spite of all, an assured confidence in her individual national identity. French loan-words were at this time flooding into the Welsh language, both directly and through the medium of English: they seem to have been borrowed at all levels of society, and there is a good deal of evidence that the upper classes—men like Dafydd's uncle Llywelyn, the constable of Newcastle Emlyn, who taught him and may have strongly influenced him—were thoroughly conversant with French. Here, too, there are grounds for a valid comparison: behind Chaucer there lay two-and-a-half centuries of social, literary, and linguistic disruption consequent upon the Norman Conquest of England; behind Dafydd ap Gwilym a much shorter but comparable period of disruption following upon the Edwardian Conquest of Wales, some forty years before his birth. The clash of cultures brought with it effects which were comparable, and in certain respects similar—for it meant that both poets composed in a milieu in which a very high

[7] R. T. Jenkins, *Y Llenor* xiii (1934), 142.

standard of knowledge of a second language, other than that of their own nation, could be assumed on the part of the aristocratic audiences whom both addressed. And French was at this time the dominant key-language in Britain, both culturally and for the purposes of administration. It follows that in the work of both poets it is impossible to be certain in every instance whether they were introducing a French loan-word directly, knowing at the time that it would be perfectly comprehended and recognizable by their bi-lingual audience, or whether they were using one which was already acclimatized in their own vernacular. This linguistic background offered exceptional opportunities for creating particular kinds of effect by the employment of such loan-words, each of which would have subtly differed in its degree of familiarity or strangeness. And the fact that the earliest attested occurrence in Welsh of many of the loan-words used by Dafydd is to be found within the *corpus* of his own poetry suggests (though it cannot be proved) that he was himself frequently responsible for the individual transplantation of a number of foreign words into Welsh in this manner.

For Dafydd ap Gwilym this post-conquest atmosphere was one which proved more stimulating than it was depressing (though undertones of personal sadness and—possibly—of national frustration are from time to time made manifest in his work), enabling him to achieve a highly original and personal synthesis between the new modes and the metrical and linguistic expertise which he had inherited from a long line of poetic forebears. Here again, fortune favoured Dafydd's birth, for Dyfed on the western sea-board where he was born and which had been the home of his ancestors, and Morgannwg in the south-east which was the home of his later patron Ifor ap Llewelyn, were just those areas where assimilation of Norman-French cultural influences had been taking place since the early years of the Norman Conquest of England. In the south these influences had long been gaining ground, and to a degree quite unparalleled in independent and culturally conservative Gwynedd. Here, too, there existed a society which was more than ready for a poet or poets who could give fitting expression to a perplexingly altered world, with its new ideas and widened horizons. The traditional maxim that in Wales 'the South initiates and the North conserves'[8] has in no instance been more fully realized than in the unique phenomenon of Dafydd ap Gwilym.

---

[8] *Y Gogledd sy'n cadw, y De sy'n cychwyn* was the dictum enunciated by W. J. Gruffydd in contrasting Dafydd ap Gwilym and Williams Pantycelyn from the south, with Dafydd ab Edmwnd and Goronwy Owen from the north; *Llenyddiaeth Cymru o 1450 hyd 1600* (Lerpwl, 1922), 68.

# ABBREVIATIONS

| | |
|---|---|
| *Arch. Camb.* | *Archaeologia Cambrensis* (London, 1846–). |
| *As.H.* | *Astudiaethau ar yr Hengerdd: Studies in Old Welsh Poetry*, ed. R. Bromwich and R. Brinley Jones (Cardiff, 1978). |
| B | *The Bulletin of the Board of Celtic Studies* (Cardiff, 1921–). |
| BBC | *The Black Book of Carmarthen*, ed. J. G. Evans (Pwllheli, 1906). |
| BD | *Brut Dingestow*, ed. Henry Lewis (Cardiff, 1942). |
| BDG | *Barddoniaeth Dafydd ap Gwilym*. O grynhoad Owen Jones (Myfyr) a William Owen Pughe (London, 1789). |
| *Braslun.* | Saunders Lewis, *Braslun o Hanes Llenyddiaeth Gymraeg* (Cardiff, 1932). |
| CA | *Canu Aneirin*, ed. Ifor Williams (Cardiff, 1938). |
| CD | *Cerdd Dafod*, J. Morris-Jones (Oxford, 1925). |
| Chotzen | T. M. Chotzen, *Recherches sur la Poésie de Dafydd ap Gwilym* (Amsterdam, 1927). |
| CLlH | *Canu Llywarch Hen*, ed. Ifor Williams (Cardiff, 1935). |
| *Contribb.* | *Contributions to a Dictionary of the Irish Language* (Royal Irish Academy, 1942–). |
| CPWP | J. Lloyd-Jones, *The Court Poets of the Welsh Princes* (Proceedings of the British Academy, 1948). |
| CRCy | T. H. Parry-Williams, *Canu Rhydd Cynnar* (Cardiff, 1932). |
| *Cy.* | *Y Cymmrodor* (London, 1877–). |
| DGG² | *Cywyddau Dafydd ap Gwilym a'i Gyfoeswyr*, ed. Ifor Williams and Thomas Roberts (2nd ed. Cardiff, 1935). |
| EEW | *The English Element in Welsh*, T. H. Parry-Williams (London, 1923). |
| EWGT | *Early Welsh Genealogical Tracts*, P. C. Bartrum (Cardiff, 1966). |
| G | *Geirfa Barddoniaeth Gynnar Gymraeg*, J. Lloyd-Jones (Cardiff, 1931–63). |

| GDG | *Gwaith Dafydd ap Gwilym*, ed. Thomas Parry (Cardiff, 1952, 2nd edn. 1963). |
|---|---|
| GDG² | ibid. (2nd edn. 1963). |
| GP | *Gramadegau'r Penceirddiaid*, G. J. Williams and E. J. Jones (Cardiff, 1934). |
| GPC | *Geiriadur Prifysgol Cymru: A Dictionary of the Welsh Language* Cardiff, 1950–). |
| H | *Llawysgrif Hendregadredd*, J. Morris-Jones and T. H. Parry-Williams (Cardiff, 1933). |
| HLl | *Hanes Llenyddiaeth Gymraeg*, Thomas Parry (Cardiff, 1945). |
| HW | *A History of Wales from the Earliest Times to the Edwardian Conquest*, J. E. Lloyd (London, 1911; 1948). |
| IGE² | *Cywyddau Iolo Goch ac Eraill*, ed. H. Lewis, T. Roberts and Ifor Williams (2nd edn. Cardiff, 1937). |
| LBS | *Lives of the British Saints*, S. Baring-Gould and J. Fisher (London, 1907–13). |
| LLC | *Llên Cymru* (Cardiff, 1950–). |
| Mab. | *The Mabinogion*, Gwyn Jones and Thomas Jones (London, Everyman edn. 1949). |
| MA² | *The Myvyrian Archaiology of Wales*, ed. Owen Jones, Edward Williams and William Owen Pughe (2nd edn. Denbigh, 1870). |
| Meistri. | Saunders Lewis, *Meistri'r Canrifoedd*, ed. R. Geraint Gruffydd (Cardiff, 1973). |
| NED | *The New English Dictionary* |
| NLW | The National Library of Wales |
| OBWV | *The Oxford Book of Welsh Verse*, ed. Thomas Parry (Oxford, 1962). |
| PBA | *Proceedings of the British Academy* (London, 1903–). |
| PKM | *Pedeir Keinc y Mabinogi*, Ifor Williams (Cardiff, 1930; 2nd edn. 1951). |
| Principality | R. A. Griffith, *The Principality of Wales in the Later Middle Ages*: vol. I, *South Wales 1277–1536* (Cardiff, 1972). |
| PRO | Public Records Office |
| RP | *The Poetry from the Red Book of Hergest*, J. G. Evans (Llanbedrog, 1911). |
| RWM | *Report on Manuscripts in the Welsh Language*, J. G. Evans (London, 1898–1910). |
| SATF | *Societé des Anciens Textes Français* |
| SC | *Studia Celtica* (Cardiff, 1966–). |
| Selections | *Dafydd ap Gwilym: A Selection of Poems*, R. Bromwich (Llandysul, 1982). |
| THSC | *Transactions of the Honourable Society of Cymmrodorion* (London, 1892–). |

| TYP | *Trioedd Ynys Prydein: The Welsh Triads*, R. Bromwich (Cardiff, 1961; 2nd edn. 1978). |
| UWP | University of Wales Press, Cardiff. |
| YB | *Ysgrifau Beirniadol*, ed. J. E. Caerwyn Williams (Denbigh, 1956–). |
| YCM | *Ystorya de Carolo Magno*, ed. S. J. Williams (Cardiff, 1930). |

# 1. DAFYDD AP GWILYM

## I

*Bald heads forgetful of their sins,*
*Old, learned, respectable bald heads*
*Edit and annotate the lines*
*That young men, tossing on their beds,*
*Rhymed out in love's despair*
*To flatter beauty's ignorant ear.*

*. . . Lord, what would they say*
*Did their Catullus walk that way?*

Some such thought as Yeats expressed ironically in his poem 'The Scholars' is likely to beset with uneasiness anyone beyond the years of early youth who undertakes to write of the poetry of Dafydd ap Gwilym. Life in fourteenth-century Wales is so hard for us now to apprehend, so remote in its way of thought and in all its circumstances, that it is almost as difficult for us to believe in it as a living reality as it is for us to apprehend the world of the Latin love-poet Catullus, who was born in Verona in the century before Christ. Nevertheless, it is of the nature of the higher forms of art that they can transcend cultural barriers, and can communicate perennial human experiences— love's frustrations and youth's passionate perplexities, the transitoriness of all earthly beauty and of life itself—in language which retains its vitality across the long intervening centuries. It is, however, with Ovid, rather than with Catullus, that Dafydd ap Gwilym has been most frequently, and indeed more appropriately, compared: the classical inheritance of eighteenth-century scholars prompted the Morris brothers and William Owen Pughe (co-editor of the first collected edition of Dafydd's poetry in 1789) to label him 'the Ovid of Wales'. But the validity of the comparison with Ovid is limited to certain aspects alone of Dafydd's poetry—that is to say, to the poems of incident and situation, in which he treats of his amatory adventures in a fanciful and self-depreciatory vein, and with a light irony which recalls not only Ovid, but also the

medieval French *fabliaux*, and the Latin poets who composed in the
'Goliard' tradition.  It is significant, however, that Dafydd himself
claimed Ovid as his master and his instructor; he describes himself
as *dyn Ofydd* 'Ovid's man', and for him *ofyddiaeth* and *cerdd Ofydd* 'Ovid's
song' were comprehensive terms which described love-poetry in general.
By his own confession

> *Nid gwas, lle bo gwyrddlas gwŷdd,*
> *Llwfr wyf ar waith llyfr Ofydd* (GDG 58, 19–20).

*(Wherever there may be fresh green trees/I am no coward in the work of Ovid's book.)*

On the one hand, Dafydd's avowed allegiance to Ovid—who is the
only foreign poet to whom he ever so much as alludes—implies a significant awareness on his part of the existence of a literary tradition beyond
Wales and differing from that of Wales, and it is this which places
Dafydd in the mainstream of contemporary European poetry in a way
that no previous Welsh poet had ever been.  On the other hand, there
is hardly a theme or motive or antecedent convention which had
appeared in Welsh literature before his time, which does not find some
kind of echo or reflection in his work.  To particularize: he is alike conversant with the conventions of orthodox bardic praise-poetry, going back
to the beginnings of the Welsh tradition in the poetry of the old British
northern kingdoms; with the nature-descriptive, gnomic and proverbial
*englynion* which were cultivated by the more popular and less 'established' poets; with the world of the romances, *Mabinogi, Bruts* and Triads
(with many allusions to tales and folk-lore and folk beliefs which have
since become lost to us); with the traditions of the native saints; and
with the precepts and terminology of the Bardic Grammar and of
*Cyfraith Hywel*, the native legal system.  The European stream of tradition
was rooted, with Ovid and Catullus, in classical antiquity, but it had
become blended and fused with other national elements in the course
of its transmision down through the centuries: as, for instance, with
the erotic poetry of the Provençal troubadours, whose influence ultimately reached Dafydd through the intermediary of the poetry of northern
France; while this French poetry in its turn introduced a variety of
new elements into the European tradition.  Dafydd ap Gwilym accomplished a daring and original synthesis by integrating selected elements from this European tradition with the equally ancient and
indigenous tradition of Celtic poetry in these islands (for many of the
most characteristic features of his style and imagery and technique
are significantly paralleled in early Irish poetry, no less than in Welsh).
By enshrining his new subject-matter in a new verse-form—the flexible
and cursive fourteen-syllabled couplets of the *cywydd* (to which his genius

gave a lasting and decisive prestige)—in the mid-fourteenth century Dafydd ap Gwilym effectively added a new dimension to Welsh poetry. His themes cover a wide spectrum: a group of bardic praise-poems and elegies (with a satire, which is the conventional opposite of a praise-poem) exhibit in varying degrees both formality and strong personal feeling, and demonstrate Dafydd's thorough mastery of the metrical techniques of the court poets who were his predecessors, while a group of more personal praise-poems in the *cywydd* metre combine traditional elements with striking new imagery and ideas. There are in addition a handful of sincere and self-revelatory religious verses. The episodic or *fabliaux* poems, such as *Trafferth mewn Tafarn* (GDG 124) ('Trouble at a Tavern'), *Y Pwll Mawn* (GDG 127) ('The Bog-hole') and *Merched Llanbadarn* (GDG 48) ('The Girls of Llanbadarn') adopt the device of causing amusement by raising a laugh at the poet's own expense. The greater number by far of Dafydd's surviving poems are concerned with one aspect or another of the theme of love's pursuit; yet often enough this theme is itself only ostensibly to the fore, and is in reality little more than a pretext for giving expression to a quality which is far more striking and impressive in a medieval poet. This is Dafydd's acutely sensitive response to the manifold aspects of beauty in nature as it lay around him, his imaginative presentation of this beauty in detail, and his wonder and delight, combined with reverential awe, before the inexhaustible variety of God's created works.

# II

The forest and all the varied life which it shelters is indeed the focus for Dafydd's most significant poetry, and it is in describing it that his gifts find their distinctive and unparalled expression. The forest is the setting for the poet's *oed* or tryst with his chosen sweetheart 'Morfudd' or—on occasion—with some other girl; hardly less often, however, the forest is described for its own sake at its spring awakening or at its summer meridian, and always as the setting for the busy activities of its natural inhabitants, in particular of the birds. *Gwell yw ystafell os tyf* means literally 'a room is better if it grows', and Dafydd employs the phrase in speaking of the *deildy* or house of leaves and branches which he has constructed to be a shelter for himself with his beloved. The *deildy* is the antithesis of the conventional man-made dwelling; its life, untrammelled by convention, is the calculated opposite of normal gregarious human society. It is thus that he reports the advice which the Cock-Thrush has given to him:

> *Gwyddwn yt gyngor gwiwdda,*
> *Hir ddyddiau Mai, os gwnai, gwna,*
> *Ac eistedd dan fedw gastell,*
> *Duw a ŵyr na bu dŷ well;*
> *A than dy ben gobennydd*
> *O fanblu, gweddeiddblu gwŷdd;*
> *Ac uwch dy ben, fedwen fau,*
> *Gaer loywdeg o gwrlidau* (GDG 36, 9–16).

*(I would give you sound advice/ for the long days of May: do it, if you will./ Sit beneath the birch-tree castle—/ God knows there was never a better house—/ and place beneath your head a pillow/ of fine feathers, the beautiful feathers of the trees/ and let my birch-tree be above your head/ a fair, gleaming fortress of coverlets.)*

At the symbolic centre of the forest-life, indeed, the birds are ever-present, and it is in their contemplation that Dafydd's poetry attains to its heights of inspired expression. They are the poets of the woodland, in whose activities Dafydd discerns the implicit counterpart of his own (just as, in other contexts, he can describe his fellow-poets as nightingales). Nor is any explanation required for the portrayal of the woodland birds as ordained priests who celebrate the Mass and offer thanks and praise to God for His miraculous creation. Such personification is always implicit, since in Welsh, as in many other literatures, birds have always been regarded as *exempla* whose activities parallel those of humans, and from whose example much can profitably be learned by all such as may be ready to learn. The distinctive feature of Dafydd's bird-poetry is that such personification, though implicit, is always counter-balanced by an accurate perception of each bird's individual characteristics. These are frequently delineated with loving detail: of the Thrush he says;

> *Ba ryw ddim a fai berach*
> *Plethiad no 'i chwibaniad bach?*
> *... Pell y clywir uwch tiroedd*
> *Ei lef o lwyn a 'i loyw floedd* (GDG 28, 5–6, 9–10).

*(What sweeter composition could there be than his little whistle?/ Far across the land his voice is heard from the thicket and his clear loud shout.)*

And of the Nightingale:

> *Serchog y cân dan y dail*
> *Salm wiw is helm o wiail.*
> *Deholwraig, arfynaig fwyn,*
> *Da ffithlen mewn diffeithlwyn.*
> *Cloch aberth y serchogion,*
> *Claer, chweg a theg yw ei thôn.*
> *Bangaw fydd ei hunbengerdd*
> *Ar flaen y wialen werdd* (GDG 25, 31–8).

*(She sings lovingly beneath the leaves/ a fair psalm under a covering of saplings./ Exiled one, gentle seeker,/ good is her whistle in the empty thicket./ The sanctus-bell of lovers,/ clear, sweet and pure is her voice;/ eloquent the quality of her unique song/ on the tip of the green branch.)*

Leaving the wood for the sea-shore, the Seagull is:

> *Unlliw ag eiry neu wenlloer,*
> *Dilwch yw dy degwch di,*
> *Darn fel haul, dyrnfol heli.*
> *Ysgafn ar don eigion wyd,*
> *Esgudfalch edn bysgodfwyd* (GDG 118, 2–6).

*(Of the hue of snow or of the white moon,/ unpolluted is your beauty,/ a fragment of the sun, gauntlet of the salt sea./ You are light upon the ocean wave:/ swift, proud, fish-eating bird.)*

Mass is celebrated in the forest by the Thrush and the Nightingale:

> *Mi a glywwn mewn gloywiaith*
> *Ddatganu, nid methu, maith,*
> *Darllain i'r plwyf, nid rhwyf rhus,*
> *Efengyl yn ddifyngus.*
> *Codi ar fryn ynn yna*
> *A frlladen o ddeilen dda.*
> *Ac eos gain fain fangaw*
> *O gwr y llwyn gar ei llaw,*
> *Clerwraig nant, i gant a gân*
> *Cloch aberth, clau ei chwiban,*
> *A dyrchafel yr aberth*
> *Hyd y nen uwchben y berth;*
> *A chrefydd i'n Dofydd Dad,*
> *A charegl nwyf a chariad* (GDG 122, 21–34).

*(I heard prolonged chanting in perfect speech, unfailing;/ and the gospel read distinctly to the parish—no unseemly haste./ A perfect leaf as consecrated wafer/ was raised upon a mound for us./ And the Nightingale, slender, fair, and eloquent/ from the corner of the near-by thicket/ (the wandering poetess of the valley) rang out the Sanctus bell to the assembly with clear whistle,/ and lifted up the consecrated Host/ to the sky above the copse,/ with adoration to our Lord the Father,/ with a chalice of ecstasy and love.)*

In describing the Skylark, his tone approaches nearly to one of mysticism:

> *Dyn uwchben a'th argenfydd*
> *Dioer pan fo hwyaf y dydd.*
> *Pan ddelych i addoli,*
> *Dawn a'th roes Duw Un a Thri:*
> *Nid brig pren uwchben y byd*
> *A'th gynnail, mae iaith gennyd,*
> *Ond rhadau y deau Dad*
> *A'i firagl aml a'i fwriad* (GDG 114, 33–40).

*(Man sees you aloft/ when day is at its longest./ When you come thus to worship./ God Three-in-One has bestowed on you this gift./ No branch of tree high up above the world sustains you/ —you have your own language—/ but the grace of the righteous Father,/ His abundant miracles and His design.)*

Poet and bird are thus felt to be united in a common act of praise and worship to their Creator for His great and small miracles. But the quality in birds which is to Dafydd their most enviable possession is their immunity from all human cares and sorrows. In a skilful paraphrase of an older *englyn*[1] he says of the Blackbird:

> *Chwerddid mwyalch ddichwerwddoeth*
> *Yng nghelli las, cathlblas coeth.*
> *Nid erddir marlbridd iddi,*
> *Neud iraidd had, nid ardd hi.*
> *Ac nid oes, edn fergoes fach,*
> *O druth oll ei drythyllach* (GDG 76, 23–8).

*(The Blackbird, wise and cheerful, laughs/ in the green copse, a mansion of fine song;/ no fruitful soil is tilled for her:/ the seed is fertile, so she does not toil;/ and there is not—little short-legged bird—/ any livelier chatter than is hers.)*

The apothegm is transformed by the last two lines, which bring the Blackbird into instantaneous focus before our eyes. It is Dafydd ap Gwilym's characteristic quality that he can transcend the conventional personification of birds as under-studies for human beings in all their varied activities, widely exemplified as this is in medieval poetry, and endow each bird with a vital and independent existence. A much later Welsh poet whose imaginative and symbolical portrayal of birds may be regarded as in the direct line of descent from Dafydd ap Gwilym is Robert Williams Parry.

[1] See pp. 108, 112 below.

# III

W. J. Gruffydd once observed significantly that 'were it not for the absolute impossibility of adequately translating his *cywyddau*, Dafydd ap Gwilym would rank among the greatest poets of medieval times.'[2] This difficulty of translation arises from the sheer virtuosity of Dafydd's elaborate artistry, in which he deployed all the resources of the linguistic and metrical media which had come to him as the legatee of an ancient and elaborate poetic tradition; while at the same time he adapted and extended them to suit the needs of the new kinds of poetry which were now appearing in Welsh for the first time. The *cywydd* is a couplet of seven-syllable rhyming lines, in which the rhyme must always be between an accented and an unaccented syllable ('men: happen'; :king: liking' may illustrate this in English). Though in a simpler form, known as the *traethodl*, this metre had been used previously by many generations of humble and for the most part unrecorded poets, it rested with Dafydd ap Gwilym and his contemporaries to embellish and adapt it to a greatly extended range of new purposes, including that of sophisticated and aristocratic praise-poetry, for which it had never previously been used. This meant endowing it with full *cynghanedd* (the intricate system of alliterating consonants, balanced stresses, and internal rhyme which had been gradually developing at the hands of the official bards over the previous centuries). This development and the adoption of the *cywydd* by highly-trained and sophisticated poets was the great metrical innovation of fourteenth-century Wales, and whether Dafydd was himself the pioneer who was responsible for so adapting it, or whether there were others who preceded him, is as yet an unsettled question. It is certain, however, that he was the master who moulded the *cywydd* into a medium sufficiently flexible to meet with all the varied demands which he made of it: altering its movement to suit his different purposes, from swiftly-moving narrative to passages of more leisurely reflection or description— even at times moulding it to embrace idiomatic conversation in racy dialogue.

One of the means by which Dafydd increased the flexibility of his poetic medium was by greatly extending the vocabulary of poetry by introducing a large number of new loan-words into the language: words either borrowed directly from French, or else indirectly through the medium of medieval English, in which these words had already been acclimatized. Most frequently, Dafydd employs such loan-words figuratively, and right out of their normal and expected context (for instance,

---

[2] 'Welsh Literature' in *Encyclopaedia Brittanica* 11th edition (1910–11), 641.

the leaves of May are *fflwringod* or 'florins' on the tops of the branches) (GDG 23, 13), thus creating an effect of surprise and novelty. Some degree of comprehension of both French and English must have been widespread among the audiences whom Dafydd addressed, however varied in their character these may have been, so that there is little doubt that he could have relied upon his hearers to understand his borrowings of foreign words; yet the nuances which such words brought with them would have differed subtly on each occasion (and in a manner which it is impossible for us now to re-capture) in the extent to which they either represented startling novelties, or else were words which had already become familiarized in the spoken Welsh of his day.

Another device which gave flexibility to Dafydd's poetic medium was his frequent employment of *sangiad*. This is a *cheville*, or a phrase interpolated in parenthesis, usually of an exclamatory or descriptive kind. In their simplest form such phrases occupy part of a line only, but in Dafydd's poetry they are sometimes continued over one or more lines at a time, running parallel to the poet's main statement, yet always subordinated to it. The linguistic constituents of the *sangiadau* are conditioned by the requirements of *cynghanedd* and rhyme, to which they give obvious assistance; yet as Dafydd employs the device, his *sangiadau* very rarely fail to make an essential contribution to his total meaning, and therefore—however difficult they may often be—they can never safely be ignored.

Any attempt to translate Dafydd ap Gwilym's poetry, therefore, must take account alike of the complex requirements of *cynghanedd* and of the parallel but subordinated statements in his *sangiadau*, as well as of the depths of meaning which may at any time underlie his use of language. By intricate innuendo, and frequently by an intentional ambiguity attained by a complex play upon the richly varied nuances both of his traditional vocabulary and of the new words which were at his disposal, Dafydd evolved for himself a poetic medium of a degree of complexity which had never previously been envisaged in Welsh, and which at times by its very nature defies all attempts at adequate transposition into another language. Except in the case of some of his very simplest passages, only a restricted part of his meaning can be conveyed by translation or by paraphrase. To attempt to do either for his greatest poems can only be compared with the task of attempting to paraphrase some of the more involved passages in Shakespeare: too often it becomes a matter of opting for a single meaning out of a wide choice of equally valid but never completely adequate alternatives. The degree of one's comprehension of Dafydd's poetry is directly commensurate with the degree of one's knowledge of the sum-total of his linguistic resources, so that for any one of us living today, it can never be such as it was for Dafydd's contemporaries. We can no longer recover the actual tones by which the poet imparted much of his intended meaning, and we

also lose immeasurably from our ignorance as to the circumstances
in which Dafydd's *cywyddau* were recited, and as to the nature of their
harp accompaniment.

By illustration and discussion I have now outlined some of the qualities by virtue of which a high estimate has been placed upon Dafydd
ap Gwilym's poetic achievement, and I have indicated some of the
difficulties which his poetry presents. Beyond doubt he was one of the
great medieval poets. He has long been recognized as such, both in
Wales and beyond the borders of Wales, and not only by those whom
Yeats would have classed as 'the scholars', but by all who can respond
to great literature, and who have come to know his poetry at first hand.
Before giving further discussion to his poetry, I must now describe
briefly the circumstances in which Dafydd ap Gwilym lived, and give
the few facts about him which can be established with any degree of
certainty.

# IV

When Edward III came to the throne in 1327, less than half a century after the fall of Llywelyn the Last Prince, Dafydd ap Gwilym can have been little more than a child. Since the few elements in his poetry which can be dated with any degree of assurance fall within the mid-forties and fifties of the century, it has been estimated that he may have been born in or about the year 1320, or possibly a few years earlier. We do not know when he may have died, but it is usually concluded that his voice had become silent before the final quarter of the century. On the sole authority of Gruffudd Gryg's poem to the Yew-Tree above Dafydd's grave 'by the monastery wall of Ystrad Fflur' (OBWV 55) it is generally believed that he was buried at Strata Florida, rather than at Talley Abbey, as a tradition recorded in the sixteenth century would have it.[3]

His original home, it seems, lay in the parish of Llanbadarn Fawr in Ceredigion, within a few miles of the castle and chartered borough which later came to be called Aberystwyth. An ancient tradition gives as his birth-place 'Brogynin', a site which has been identified as lying beside a ford on the river Stewi, close to the modern farm of Brogynin Fach. Until recently there were to be seen on this spot the remains of what must once have been a substantial dwelling-house; this in its turn is believed to have been erected upon the site of an earlier house which may have been partially incorporated into it. The modern bungalow

---

[3] Mostyn MS. 110, p. 188 (RWM I, 25): a list of the burial places of poets, in the hand of Thomas Wiliems, Trefriw. The date of this MS. proves that the tradition of Dafydd's burial at Talyllychau (or Talley) goes back to before 1600. It is supported by a persistent local tradition, recorded in *Arch. Camb.* for 1879 (4th Series, vol. x, 184) as going back to the mid C 18th., and one which is still alive and vigorous at the present time. Yew-trees said to mark the place of Dafydd's burial are shown both at Strata Florida and at Talley. Apart from the fact that the former is nearer to Dafydd's birth-place, the case for Strata Florida has always been firmly based on the evidence of Gruffudd Gryg's 'elegy' to Dafydd, *Yr ywen i oreuwas/ ger mur Ystrad Fflur a'i phlas* (OBWV no. 55). Hence the commemorative plaque placed at Strata Florida in 1951 by the Hon. Soc. Cymmrodorion (THSC 1949–51, 83–8). In ch. 6 (pp. 159–61 below) I have drawn attention to the evidence which suggests that Gruffudd's poem is one of two *marwnadau ffug* or 'fictitious' elegies' by this poet, composed while Dafydd was still living. If this is accepted, the strong and persistent local tradition which claims Talley as Dafydd's place of burial deserves more serious consideration than it has received hitherto. The *englynion* which Iolo Morganwg attributed to Hopcyn ap Thomas (*Iolo Mss.* p. 95) are plainly a forgery, but this does not contravene the fact that not all the assertions of Iolo Morganwg are necessarily without foundation. On the two traditions see J. H. Davies 'The date and Place of burial of Dafydd ap Gwilym' THSC 1906–7, 55–74; GDG xl–xli (= GDG² xxii).

(named 'Tŷ Dafydd') preserves in its front garden a small piece of the ancient masonry. Mr David Jenkins has pointed out a remarkable series of still identifiable place-names in Dafydd's poems—particularly in the *cywydd Taith i Garu* ('A Journey to Woo')—which testify to the poet's close familiarity with places in the immediate neighbourhood of Brogynin.[4] The steep wooded valleys and rolling moorlands between the rivers Rheidol and Leri (which must indeed have been far more densely wooded in the fourteenth century), roughly in the triangle between Tal-y-bont, Aberystwyth and Ponterwyd, may properly be called Dafydd's country, and the scene of his meetings with his Morfudd. (Half-a-mile from Brogynin is the farmstead of Cwm-y-Glo, which two poems suggest may have been Morfudd's home before her marriage.) Pen-y-talwrn near Ponterwyd can perhaps be identified with the *Gwern-y-talwrn* of *Taith i Garu*, and here, as Dafydd tell us, is the place

> *Lle y gwelir yn dragywydd,*
> *Heb dwf gwellt, heb dyfu gwŷdd,*
> *Llun ein gwâl dan wial da,*
> *Lle briwddail fal llwybr Adda* (GDG 83, 47–50).

*(Where there will for evermore be seen/ the shape of our bed beneath a fine sapling,/ without any growth of grass or trees,/ a place of small leaves like Adam's path[5] (i.e. a well-worn path).)*

Among the poems which have close associations with Dafydd's home-neighbourhood may be included the often-quoted *Merched Llanbadarn* (GDG 48) ('The Girls of Llanbadarn'), in which Dafydd reproduces the whispered comments on his personal appearance made by two girls attending divine service in Llanbadarn parish church.

Dafydd ap Gwilym was born into one of the most influential families of *uchelwyr* in south Wales. (No exact English equivalent exists for the term *uchelwr*, which denotes a member of the native landed nobility in the years following the settlement of 1284.) Many such families gained considerably in influence and responsibility after the fall of the princes. Dafydd's genealogy has been thus recorded in a sixteenth-century manuscript (Peniarth 128; the names in brackets are added on the earlier authority of a poem by Dafydd Nanmor):[6]

*Dafydd ap Gwilym Gam (ap Gwilym ab Einion) ap Gwilym ap Gwrwared ap Gwilym*

---

[4] As shown by David Jenkins, B viii (1937), 140–5; R. J. Thomas, *Y Llenor* xxi, (1942), 34–6. See also *Y Traethodydd* cxxxiii (1978), 83–8.

[5] *Llwybr Adda*, 'Adam's Path'. The image derives from *Genesis* 3, 17, which tells how God cursed the ground because of Adam's trangression. For parallel references by Gruffudd ab Adda and Iolo Goch see B xxix (1980), 80–1.

[6] Ifor Williams and Thomas Roberts, *Poetical Works of Dafydd Nanmor* (UWP 1923) 121.

*ap Gwrwared ap Cuhelyn Fardd ap Gwynfardd Dyfed ap Cynan Gerdd Gemell ap Gwran-
gon feindroed iarll Kaer Wyrangon.*[7]

A scrutiny of state papers made by J. E. Lloyd[8] has made it possible
to check the veracity of this genealogy at more than one point. Gwrwared
ap Cuhelyn (Fardd) and his brother were proprietors of land in Cemais,
(Pembrokeshire), Dyfed, during the twelfth century, and this was the
original home of the family. His great-grandson Gwilym ap Gwrwared
(father of Einion) is recorded as having been constable of Cemais in
1241, and from 1260 he was constable also of Cardigan castle, holding
lands by royal gift in recognition of his services. At the beginning of
the fourteenth century this Gwilym's grandson, Gwilym ab Einion,
with his brother Gruffudd, held lands both in Emlyn and in Cardigan,
also by royal gift. Though no documentary evidence has so far come
to light relating either to Dafydd's father Gwilym Gam, or to the poet
himself, yet Dafydd's uncle Llywelyn ap Gwilym is known to have
been constable of Newcastle Emlyn under Gilbert Talbot, and to have
been one among a group of *uchelwyr* who swore an oath of allegiance
to the Black Prince in the year 1343. It is possible, however, that
Dafydd's relationship with Llywelyn was through his mother, and not
through Gwilym Gam, his father.[9]

It would be a misinterpretation of the wholly different circumstances
of the fourteenth century from those of today to regard such families
as these as 'king's men', *Prydeinwyr*, or 'western Britons'; or to conclude
that their existence was wholly centred on their administrative duties
on behalf of the greater power beyond Offa's Dyke. On the contrary,
it was among just such families of *uchelwyr* as these that there were

[7] GDG[1] xxii–iii; xxxii (=GDG[2] xiv); DGG[2] xxv. For Dafydd's genealogy cf. P. C.
Bartrum *Welsh Genealogies 300–1400* (UWP 1974), vol. 3, 496–7; *NLW Journal* xiii (1973),
120; RWM I, 797 (quoting Dafydd's genealogy from Peniarth 128, 733*b*. On this manuscript, which is the sole authority for Dafydd's descent from Gwynfardd Dyfed, see Bartrum, THSC 1968, 81–3). Lewis Dwnn (*Heraldic Visitations* I, 59) gives the genealogy
of the collateral Tywyn family with the epithet *Gerdd Gyn(n)il* 'song-accomplished' or
'expert in song' in place of *Gerdd Gemell* 'song-imposing' and attaches it to Gwynfardd's
grandson Gwrwared in place of the latter's father Kynan. Whichever of these is correct,
there are three names indicative of poetic gifts bestowed upon men belonging to three
generations of Dafydd's remotest ancestors. On Cuhelyn Fardd see R. G. Gruffydd 'A
Poem in Praise of Cuhelyn Fardd' SC x/xi (1975–76), 198–209. The same writer suggests
that Cuhelyn Fardd may have been *pencerdd* to Rhys ap Tewdwr, SC xiv/xv (1979–80)
99–100.

[8] 'Hynafiaid Dafydd ap Gwilym' B viii (1937), 1–3.

[9] P. C. Bartrum, *Welsh Genealogies 300–1400*, vol. 4, p. 674 (see also SC xiv/xv, 99–100,
note). The opinion that Dafydd's uncle Llywelyn ap Gwilym was brother to the poet's
mother Ardudfyl was expressed by William Owen Pughe (BDG p. vi) and by Iolo Morganwg (*Iolo MSS.* 92–3), and was recognised as a possibility by Dr Parry (GDG[1] xxiii).
Bartrum identifies him with 'Llywelyn o'r Cryngae' of which Dôl-goch (mentioned in
GDG 13, 77) may have formed a part. On these places see G. Evans 'The Story of
Newcastle Emlyn' *Cy.* xxxii, 107–8.

to be found the prime supporters of Welsh culture in the years following the conquest. A tradition incorporated in the sixteenth-century 'Statute of Gruffudd ap Cynan' informs us:

*A gwedy'r tywyssogion y cymerth y gwyr bonhedhigion, a hanoedhynt o waed y tywyssogion, y gwyr wrth gerdh attunt . . .*[10]

*(After the (fall of the) princes, the noblemen who were sprung from the blood of the princes undertook the support of the men of art (i.e. poets and minstrels).)*

This separation between culture and politics had been of long standing in south Wales, and goes back as far as the time of Hywel Dda in the tenth century, as Mr Eurys Rowlands has aptly reminded us.[11] Internal evidence suggests that Dafydd moved in local Cardiganshire circles which for several previous generations had been closely associated with Welsh scholarship and with the patronage of poetry. All that we are enabled to deduce about Dafydd's own family suggests that they too would not have been behind, either in culture or in the provision of patronage. Two *awdlau*[12] (one of them an elegy) have come down which Dafydd addressed to his uncle Llywelyn, the constable of Newcastle Emlyn. In complex traditional style, and in the old metres of *englyn* and *toddaid*, Dafydd extols his uncle's wide learning and culture, describes him as poet and linguist (*prydydd ac ieithydd*), and says that he 'knew all knowledge', and comprised in himself a complete *llyfr dwned* or 'book of Donatus' (this is a comprehensive, if inexact, description of the treatise on grammar and metrics which represented a part, at least, of contemporary bardic learning).[13] *Ys difai y'm dysgud* ('faultlessly you instructed me') are Dafydd's words of his uncle. Bearing in mind the official position and high-level external contacts with which Llywelyn ap Gwilym is credited, it is reasonable to conclude that the wide culture which his nephew attributed to him must have ranged much further afield than the contents of the *llyfr dwned* alone, and that he is likely to have been proficient and at ease in both French and English. Not only was Llywelyn Dafydd's bardic teacher to all appearance, therefore, but he was also in a position to have been a likely intermediary in introducing his nephew to literary influences which originated far beyond the borders of Wales—to new poetry, new stories, and by no means least important, to a new vocabulary. Of the very many French loan-words which were taken up into Welsh during this period, and which were borrowed either directly from French or indirectly through the medium of medieval English, the earliest recorded

[10] T. Parry, 'Statud Gruffudd ap Cynan', B v (1931), 27.

[11] *Y Traethodydd* cxxii (1967), 18.

[12] GDG nos. 12 and 13.

[13] G. J. Williams and E. J. Jones, *Gramadegau's Penceirddiaid* (see ch. 4 below).

instances cited in the dictionaries are quoted with impressive frequency
from the works of Dafydd ap Gwilym. How many of these words were
the poet's individual borrowings, and how many were already acclimatized in the colloquial Welsh spoken about him in Dyfed, can never
be known for certain, yet without doubt a considerable knowledge of
French—if not also of English—could have been relied upon on the
part of the intimate and familiar audiences whom Dafydd primarily
addressed. If, as seems probable, the two poems addressed to Llywelyn
belong to Dafydd's early career, the close relationship which they indicate to have existed between uncle and nephew suggest an obvious
channel through which Dafydd may have from an early age familiarized
himself simultaneously with 'the two cultures'. Dafydd's *marwnad* states
clearly that his uncle met his death by the violent hand of an assassin.
We have no direct knowledge of what happened, but there can be no
doubt of the strength of the feeling with which Dafydd reacted to the
event.

The three earliest names in Dafydd's pedigree suggest another consideration which may perhaps be significant. Whether or not the names
of these remote ancestors have been correctly transmitted, it is striking
that each one bears an epithet which proves its holder to have been
a poet. Could these three have belonged to a family of professional
bards in Dyfed during the eleventh and twelfth centuries? It is an intriguing possibility: yet it is difficult to assess the significance of this conjunction of names, since 'Gwynfardd Dyfed' was one of the 'tribal patriarchs'
from whom a number of other families in south and west Wales also
traced descent. Cuhelyn Fardd is known as a patron to whom a twelfth-
century poem was addressed, rather than as a poet in his own right.[14]
Nevertheless, it is tempting to conclude that Dafydd's *expertise* in the
traditional techniques of bardic verse as practised by the court poets
of the preceding centuries was a legacy which was transmitted to him
through his uncle, from a long line of trained bards who were his remoter
ancestors. Such a transmission of poetic skills by word of mouth from
one generation to another is known to have been customary in bardic
families in medieval Wales, just as it was in the closely similar culture
of medieval Ireland.

There remains much which we could wish to have elucidated concerning Dafydd's family circumstances, and those of his early life. We are
on slightly firmer ground concerning his intimacy with members of
a Ceredigion family which had demonstrably succeeded in combining
posts of administrative authority with traditions of poetic patronage
throughout several previous generations: the family of Ieuan Llwyd

[14] A. O. H. Jarman, *Llyfr Du Caerfyrddin, gyda Rhagymadrodd, Nodiadau Testunol a Geirfa* (UWP 1982), xl–xlii. See also R. G. Gruffydd, SC x/xi, 199–200.

of Glyn Aeron. Dafydd composed an *awdl marwnad* to Ieuan's wife Angharad (GDG 16),[15] and he also refers to her in a *cywydd* (GDG 140)
in terms which bespeak an affectionate relationship. He composed a
*cywydd* (which purports to be an elegy, though it is obviously not a
'genuine' one) to Ieuan's son Rhydderch (GDG 17), the owner of the
famous *Llyfr Gwyn Rhydderch*.[16] Since this Rhydderch was also a recognized authority on the native legal system, he could well have been
a prime informant on the technicalities of *Cyfraith Hywel* the 'Law of
Hywel the Good', with which the poet shows his familiarity on a number
of occasions.

Of yet more exalted status was another landowner of Ceredigion,[17]
Sir Rhys ap Gruffudd who was knighted, it seems, for his exploits
at the battle of Crécy (1346). He was the patron of that 'Einion Offeiriad'
whose name is associated with the early fourteenth-century redaction
of the *llyfr dwned*—the remarkable prescriptive treatise on grammatical
theory and on Welsh prosody, illustrated by examples, which has
already been referred to. The poet was related to Sir Rhys ap Gruffudd
through the latter's mother Nest.[18] In one poem (GDG 75, 1–8) Dafydd
refers to Sir Rhys's local activity in recruiting levies for the war in
France.

It is evident that Dafydd was on terms of familiarity with other poets
who were his contemporaries: with Madog Benfras, Gruffudd ab Adda,
and Gruffudd Gryg. The eloquent *marwnadau* which Dafydd and these
poets composed in tribute to each other (whether these are genuine,
or follow what is to us the curious custom of composing 'fictitious'
elegies during their subject's life-time) testify in each case to their high
mutual regard. The circumstances are obscure which surround the composition of Dafydd's *dychangerdd*, a richly vituperative satire (GDG 21)
on a rival poet called Rhys Meigen (about whom nothing is otherwise
known), and who, according to tradition, was actually slain by the

---

[15] GDG¹ lxiv–lxv (=GDG² xxxviii–ix). See also D. Hywel E. Roberts, LlC x (1968)
84. It seems probable—or at least possible—that the same 'Angharad' is also referred
to in some passages of the Bardic Grammar of Einion Offeiriad and in some of the
metrical *exempla* there cited; see ch. 4 below.
[16] On Rhydderch ab Ieuan Llwyd of Parc Rhydderch, Glyn Aeron, Ceredigion, see
R. A. Griffiths, *The Principality of Wales in the Later Middle Ages* 117; Eurys Rowlands
LlC vii, 221–2, and in D. Greene and J. Carney (eds.) *Celtic Studies in Memory of Angus
Matheson* (London, 1968) 139; D. Hywel Roberts, LlC x (1968), 83–9, and ch. 4 below.
Bartrum gives his genealogy *op. cit.* vol. I pp. 178–9.
[17] See R. A. Griffiths, *op. cit.* 99–102; D. J. Bowen, LlC viii (1964) 3–4, and 'Bardd
Glyn Teifi' *Y Traethodydd*, cxxxi (1976), 143–4, Ifor Williams, *Cy.* xxvi (1916) 115ff.
[18] i.e. Nest Fechan, daughter of Gwrwared. See Bartrum, *Welsh Genealogies 300–1400*
vol. 3, 496; vol. 4, 681; and cf. *Bywgraffiadur*, 789. The genealogy given by Ifor Williams
in 'Dafydd ap Gwilym a'r Glêr' (THSC 1913–14), 98 must be amended: Nest's father
Gwrwared was brother to Dafydd's great-grandfather Einion (Fawr).

virulence of the heaped-up abuse.[19] Dafydd also composed an *awdl* in tribute to Hywel ap Goronwy (GDG 15), the dean of Bangor. All this evidence taken together indicates that Dafydd must have lived a life which was rich with human relationships and that he was far from being the rootless and homeless wanderer that is sometimes suggested. It is clear that he must have travelled widely over the greater part of Wales, being familiar with the boroughs of Caernarfon and Rhosyr[20] (which later became Newborough in Anglesey), and with the cathedral city of Bangor, as well as with the homes of *uchelwyr* in Ceredigion and perhaps further south. It is probably no unjustifiable stretch of the imagination to picture him reciting his *cywyddau*, and at times accompanying his own recital on the harp, in the hospitable houses of such *uchelwyr* as provided him with a small and sympathetic audience of familiar friends: an audience whose similarity of tastes and interests he could depend upon for appreciation of his art, and for understanding of his allusions and of his witticisms and of his intentional ambiguities. His genius derived essential nourishment from the response which he would have derived from such familiar audiences. There is no reliable evidence that he ever travelled anywhere beyond the borders of Wales. A chief reason, probably, why we have no manuscript of Dafydd's poems written during his own life-time—or any scrap, indeed, of his own handwriting[21]—is that his *cywyddau* must have circulated originally among such audiences by oral, word-of-mouth channels, both during the poet's life-time and among more widely-dispersed audiences for many years, if not for centuries, afterwards. The oldest fragmentary manuscript, which contains no more than seven of his poems, was written about the year 1450; it is Peniarth MS.48 in the National Library of Wales. No more than eight collections date from a period earlier than 1500: presumably a number of others have been lost.

The following hearsay account of Dafydd ap Gwilym's appearance has come down to us in the form of a note in the 'Book of David Jones'

[19] On Rhys Meigen see ch. 2 p. 62 below.

[20] A number of the (mainly Welsh) burgesses of Llanfaes were moved to Rhosyr (Rhosfyr) in south-west Anglesey, after the establishment of the castle and borough of Beaumaris in 1295. The name was changed to 'Newborough' in 1305. Dafydd ap Gwilym knew of the place by both names (GDG 128, 134). See Hugh Owen, *Hanes Plwyf Niwbwrch* (Caernarfon, 1952); E. A. Lewis, *The Mediaeval Boroughs of Snowdonia* (1912) 52; A. D. Carr, *Medieval Anglesey* (Anglesey Antiquarian Society, 1982) ch. vii, esp. 258–65.

[21] This earlier statement now requires modification in view of the suggestion made by Daniel Huws 'Llawysgrif Hendregadredd' *NLW Journal* xxii (1981) 18 to the effect that specimens of Dafydd's own handwriting may survive in H. (and possibly in the White Book); in particular he makes a case for the *englynion* in H. to the Cross at Chester. The text of the eight poems attributed to Dafydd's composition in Peniarth 48 (of which the last is fragmentary) were printed by T. Lewis, *Aberystwyth Studies* xiv, 35–51; see GDG[1] cix; RWM I, 382.

(vicar of Llanfair in Dyffryn Clwyd, but originally from Meirionydd), which was written in 1587:[22]

*Mi a welais. 1572. hen wraic a welsai un arall a fyssai'n ymddiddan a Dafydd ap Gwilym. hirfain oedd ef a gwallt llaes melyngrych oedd iddo a hwnnw yn llawn cayau a modrwyau arian meddai hi.*

*(In 1572 I saw an old woman who had seen another who had conversed with Dafydd ap Gwilym. He was tall and slender, with long yellow curling hair, full of clasps and silver rings, she said.)*

Belief in the veracity of this tradition is subjected to considerable strain, however, since the span of some two hundred years which must have elapsed betwen Dafydd ap Gwilym's death towards the end of the fourteenth century and the year 1572 obviously requires more than one intervening tradition-bearer in order to fill it in any credible manner.

What else do Dafydd ap Gwilym's poems reveal concerning the external circumstances of his life? He was no less familiar with the use of the bow and of the sword than with the technicalities of the harp, and he was accustomed to hunting and hawking. The world in which he moved was peopled with friars, nuns, pilgrims, hermits, tinkers, drovers, ostlers; the countryside with which he was familiar was one in which there were to be seen red deer and roebuck as well as peacocks, hares and foxes and squirrels; in which small birds were shot with bow and arrow, or snared beside pools with bird-lime, and scared from the growing crops with rattles; oxen were yoked in pairs for ploughing. Taverns offered rich food together with French wines as an alternative to the native mead (vines for wine-making were also grown in Wales). Houses had wooden shutters or glazed windows, and lime-washed interior walls, gilded or painted with coats of arms; peat was used as well as wood for firing. Like us he was not unfamiliar with the sight of hay-cocks, pig-sties, goose-sheds, and domestic cats (ill-treated); and he was acquainted with games played with balls and with nuts. Recently introduced novelties included church clocks with chimes, the organ in Bangor cathedral, wooden hobby-horses, mirrors, 'mangonels' used for hurling stones in up-to-date siege warfare (there was also a smaller kind of catapult for taking pot-shots at straying hens). He was familiar with sailing-ships, with parchment books (or scrolls) in which love-poems were inscribed; he knew the signs of the zodiac, and was fully cognisant with the significance of the influence of these upon daily life.

[22] RWM II, Pt. iv lists the contents of the 'Book of David Johns, vicar of Llanfair Dyffryn Klywd' (= B. M. Addl. MS. 14, 866). This note is found on p. 333 of the manuscript. It is repeated in Gwyneddon MS. 3 (ed. I. Williams, UWP 1931) p. 128, with the slight variant 'Yr oedd...' for 'Mi a welais...' See further D. J. Bowen, LlC vi, 39. Owen Myfyr quotes the note in his introduction to BDG 1789, p. xii.

In one poem Dafydd tells us that he is *gŵr â chorun*, that is, a man who wears a tonsure (a statement which it is hard to reconcile with the description quoted above of his 'long yellow curls'). The implication of this must be that he had qualified at some period of his life for minor religious orders. Mr Saunders Lewis has indeed suggested[23] that Dafydd had received training in early youth in a monastic school, and that in this way he had acquired his evident familiarity with the technical terms of church music. Certainly Dafydd describes himself in several passages in his poems as a member of the *clêr*. This word, apparently borrowed originally from Irish *clíar, cléir*,[24] was semantically influenced by French *clers* 'a clerk', and was used in a sense which corresponds to the *clerici vagantes*, the 'wandering scholars' or *joculatores*[25] of other countries. But it is also capable of retaining an older meaning in which it is a comprehensive and entirely non-committal term for poets in general. What is confusing in Dafydd's use of the word is that he is capable of using *clêr* and *clerwr* in both senses: positively, when he speaks of himself as one of a body of honourable practitioners of the craft of poetry, and negatively and disparagingly when he contrasts himself with the *clêr ofer* or 'vain versifiers' (such as the unfortunate Rhys Meigen) who lack his own high qualifications. Only once, in imagining the Grey Friar's censure of him (GDG 137, 29), does he include himself in this disparaging use of the term. Dafydd also employs the verb *clera* to denote a bardic expedition to solicit gifts for praise-poetry—a custom which grew up in the fourteenth century as a result of the cessation of the princely patronage of poets, and which was to become a regular practice in the following centuries.

[23] LlC ii (1952–53) 204. Re-printed in *Meistri'r Canrifoedd*, ed. R. G. Gruffydd (UWP 1973), 48. For the reference see GDG 35, 10 and T. Parry's note.

[24] GPC 497; GDG 439; both following Chotzen, *Recherches* 76. See R. I. Acad. *Contribb.* 'C' cols 238–9 on early Irish *clíar, cléir*: a collective word denoting a band of clerics or laymen, used especially to denote a poet's following (and, significantly, in a single recorded instance used of bird-song). Dr Parry shows that *clêr* was used by fourteenth-century poets in two distinct senses: for poets in general, and for lower-class poets. Dafydd ap Gwilym uses the word in both of these contrasting senses, though with him the generalized and favourable sense predominates.

[25] Cf. J. Morris-Jones and John Rhys, *Llyfr Ancr Llanddewifrefi* 40, 4 where *Pa obeith yssyd yr glêr?* translates Lat. *Habent spem joculatores?* The text is precisely dated to 1346, a time when Dafydd's career was at its height; see Ifor Williams, THSC 1913–14. It seems likely that the derogatory meaning of *clêr* (un-paralleled in Irish) springs from ecclesiastical usage, and may be no older than the time of Dafydd himself.

# V

A further examination of some of the problems which concern Dafydd's personal relationships and the sequence of events in his career is essential to a just assessment of the range and variety of his poetry. There is a group of seven poems in which the poet expresses his gratitude for the generosity towards him of a patron called Ifor ap Llywelyn, of Gwern-y-clepa, near Basaleg in Morgannwg: *Ifor Hael* or 'Ifor the Generous' is Dafydd's name for him. Whatever the precise nature of the relationship between Dafydd and Ifor may have been (and there can be little doubt but that it was close and affectionate) it is in the terms of one of the *penceirddiaid* in the old society, addressing his princely patron, that Dafydd envisages himself in these poems. Just as, in an earlier generation, Cynddelw Brydydd Mawr had proudly epitomized the mutual dependence which subsisted between himself and his princely patron Rhys ap Gruffudd, each giving to the other as much as they received in turn:

> *Ti hebof, nid hebu oedd tau,*
> *Mi hebod ni hebaf finnau* (RP 1440, 15–16).

*(You without me would lack all utterance/ no more could I on my part speak without you.)*

—so Dafydd endowed Ifor with the epithet *Hael*. This epithet subsequently clung to his name and permanently recorded his generosity to his poet, linking him with the *Tri Hael*—Rhydderch, Nudd and Mordaf, the three proverbially generous patrons of classical Welsh tradition,[26] rooted as it was in the sixth-century northern British 'Heroic Age':

> *Rhoist ym swllt, rhyw ystum serch,*
> *Rhoddaf yt brifenw Rhydderch* (GDG 7, 9–10).

*(You have given me treasure, a pledge of love,/ I bestow on you the great name of Rhydderch.)*

In another poem, it is as Taliesin at the court of his patron Urien Rheged that Dafydd presents himself; it is noticeable, indeed, that there is in these seven poems to 'Ifor Hael' a pronounced concentration of references back to the heroic figures of the 'Old North'.[27]

[26] TYP triad no. 2.
[27] Cf. D. J. Bowen, LlC ix, 53, and ch. 2 below.

In another poem, Dafydd gives this description of the delights of Ifor's court:

> *Mawr anrhydedd a'm deddyw:*
> *Mi a gaf, o byddaf byw,*
> *Hely â chwn, nid haelach iôr,*
> *Ac yfed gydag Ifor,*
> *A saethu rhygeirw sythynt,*
> *A bwrw gweilch i wybr a gwynt,*
> *A cherddau tafodau teg,*
> *A solas ym Masaleg.*
> *Pand digrif yng ngŵydd nifer,*
> *Pennod, saethu claernod, clêr,*
> *Gwarae ffristiol a tholbwrdd*
> *Yn un gyflwr a'r gŵr gwrdd?*
> *O châi neb, cytundeb coeth*
> *Rhagor rhag y llall rhygoeth,*
> *Rhugl â cherdd y'i anrhegaf,*
> *Rhagor rhag Ifor a gaf* (GDG 8, 31–46).

*(Great is the honour which I have received:/ for while I live, I am allowed/ to hunt with hounds—there is no more generous lord—/ and drink with Ifor,/ and shoot a straight course at the stags,/ and cast hawks to the wind and sky,/ and enjoy sweet songs by word of mouth/ and entertainment here at Basaleg./ Is it not pleasant before hosts,/ the aim of poets, to shoot the mark?/ to play backgammon and chess/ on equal status with the mighty lord?/ By mutual consent, if either one should win/ excellent precedence above the other/—with verse I freely him endow—in this I win precedence over Ifor.)*

And Dafydd crowns his gratitude and praise with a memorable hyperbole:

> *Hyd yr ymdaith dyn eithaf,*
> *Hyd y try hwyl hy haul haf,*
> *Hyd yr hëir y gwenith,*
> *A hyd y gwlych hoywdeg wlith,*
> *Hyd y gwŷl golwg digust,*
> *Hydr yw, a hyd y clyw clust,*
> *Hyd y mae iaith Gymraeg,*
> *A hyd y tyf hadau teg,*
> *Hardd Ifor hoywryw ddefod,*
> *Hir dy gledd, hëir dy glod* (GDG 7, 27–36).

*(As far as man may travel furthest,/ as far as the bold summer sun turns on its course,/ as far as wheat is sown/ and as far as fair dew-fall moistens,/ as far as the unclouded eye may see/ —strong he is—and as far as the ear may hear,/ as far as the Welsh tongue is known/ and as far as fair crops grow:/ Splendid Ifor, of sprightly ways/ (long your sword) will your praise be sown.)*

Ifor's praise is 'sown' just as in other poems Dafydd claims to have 'sown' the praise of his chosen sweetheart throughout the length and breadth of Wales.

Doubts which were at first cast on the authenticity of the 'Ifor Hael' poems in the introduction to Dr Thomas Parry's magistral edition of Dafydd ap Gwilym's works (which nevertheless provisionally included these poems as belonging to the previously accepted canon) have subsequently been largely laid to rest by a fresh examination of the evidence, and by the citation of manuscript references not originally available to Dr Parry. These enable us to take back the antiquity of the tradition of Dafydd's association with Ifor Hael and with Morgannwg to a date within a century of the poet's life-time.[28] And further, a close comparison of the vocabulary and imagery of these poems with that which appears elsewhere in poems which are accepted as being Dafydd's work, substantiates the conclusion as to their authenticity.[29] As Eurys Rowlands has emphasized, 'Ifor Hael's patronage of Dafydd ap Gwilym is one of the most important facts in the history of Welsh poetry'[30] and it need no longer be regarded as a matter which is in any serious doubt. One of Dr Parry's strongest reasons for the uncertainty which he expressed concerning them, however, lay in the fact that there is to be found no other reference to Morgannwg anywhere in Dafydd ap Gwilym's extant poetry. And this raises a major and still unsettled question as to the relative chronology of Dafydd's poems. The *marwnadau* addressed to him by his fellow-poets Madog Benfras and Iolo Goch commemorate him as *eos Dyfed* 'the nightingale of Dyfed', *hebog merched Deheubarth*, 'the hawk of the girls of Deheubarth' (the old south-western kingdom which comprised Pembrokeshire, Cardigan, and Ystrad Tywi) and *colofn cerddau'r Deau dir* 'the pillar of song of the southern land'.[31] Much would be explained, however, if as seems probable, these two elegies can be regarded as 'fictitious' and as having been composed while their subject was still living. Dafydd composed *marwnadau* to Madog Benfras and to Gruffudd Gryg: and these two poets also composed *marwnadau* to him (two in the case of Gruffudd Gryg). The fact that these five poems cannot all be genuine elegies casts doubt upon each one individually. They may all belong to an early period of Dafydd's career, and therefore perhaps to a time before he had found for himself a home in Morgannwg. Another sufficient explanation would be that Dafydd's family origins were in Dyfed, and

[28] D. J. Bowen 'Dafydd ap Gwilym a Morgannwg', LlC v, 164–73, with a closing note by G. J. Williams citing the evidence of a poem by Dafydd Benwyn, composed between 1560–1581; also LlC vi, 111–12; vii, 249–51. The genealogy of Ifor Hael is given by Bartrum, *Welsh Genealogies*, I, 200, 202.

[29] See especially D. J. Bowen, 'Agweddau ar Ganu'r Bedwaredd Ganrif ar Ddeg â'r Bymthegfed', LlC ix, 47, 51–2.

[30] In a review of GDG², LlC viii, 109 (trans.).

[31] GDG pp. 422–30.

it is essentially as the poetic representative of Dyfed and of *y Deau* 'the South' that he speaks of himself in his poetic controversy with Gruffudd Gryg, and is similarly alluded to by his antagonist, who represents the older and more conservative traditions of Gwynedd. The Ifor Hael poems do not in themselves contain any evidence which suggests that they were composed early in Dafydd's life: on the contrary, the suggestion that they may belong to a late period is supported by some slight suggestions in them which are indicative of reaction on the poet's part against his previous preoccupation with the pursuit of love. He purposes to 'sow' Ifor's praise, just as elsewhere he claims to have 'sown' that of Morfudd; Ifor is figuratively described as *caeth y glêr* 'the slave of poets' just as Dafydd elsewhere describes himself as *caeth* to Morfudd. Above all the following passage is significant:

> *Duw a'i gŵyr ...*
> *Fy mod es talm, salm Selyf,*
> *Yn caru dyn uwch Caerdyf.*
> *Nid salw na cham fy namwain,*
> *Nid serch ar finrhasgl ferch fain.*
> *Mawrserch Ifor a'm goryw,*
> *Mwy no serch ar ordderch yw.*
> *Serch Ifor a glodforais,*
> *Nid fal serch anwydful Sais,*
> *Ac nid af, berffeithiaf bôr*
> *Os eirch ef, o serch Ifor,*
> *Nac undydd i drefydd drwg,*
> *Nac unnos o Forgannwg* (GDG 8, 8–20).

*(God knows ... that I have been now a while—the psalm of Solomon—/ courting a being near to Cardiff here./ No fortune ugly or perverse is mine,/ no love for slender, smooth-lipped girl,/ but I am overwhelmed with love for Ifor,/ more than the love for any girl it is./ I have celebrated Ifor's love/ which is not like the love of stupid Saxon churl;/ nor will I go, most perfect lord,/ for Ifor's love, if he should ask—/ one single day to wicked towns,/ or pass one night away from Morgannwg.)*

It is easier to believe from the tone of these poems that Dafydd was Ifor Hael's friend and near-contemporary rather than that he was his junior, and though we do not of course know over how long a period of time their composition may have been spread, it is perhaps significant that the opening line of Dafydd's elegy for Ifor and his wife Nest (GDG ll) refers to the poet's own *henaint* or old age. On balance, it seems to me unlikely, that this poem is anything but a genuine *marwnad*, though a statement made in the following century in a poem by Lewys Glyn Cothi to the effect that Dafydd 'went to Heaven before Ifor' gives ground for a contrary interpretation, and the matter must be regarded as incapable of proof.[32] There is a tradition that the similtaneous death of Ifor and Nest was due to *yr haint chwarren*: that is, to 'glandular plague', possibly but not certainly the Black Death, which was at its height in Wales in 1350. Unfortunately this tradition rests on no better authority than that of Iolo Morganwg;[33] but it gains some slight support from what may well be a couple of oblique references to the plague which are contained in the poem. The foundations of Ifor Hael's home, together with surviving fragments of masonry, are still to be seen at Gwernyclepa, though covered by dense woodland undergrowth—*mieri lle bu mawredd.*

[32] On internal evidence Ifor Williams took the poem to be a genuine *marwnad*, and to imply that Dafydd out-lived his friend and patron, DGG[2] xix. But on the evidence of the not-far-from contemporary poem of Lewy Glyn Cothi, *Poems* (1837) 176–7, Dr Parry has argued that Dafydd must have composed his 'elegy' while Ifor and Nest were still living (GDG lxix = GDG[1] xl).

[33] *Iolo MSS*. 93, 486.

# VI

There can be little doubt but that the poems which relate to Dafydd's love for his 'Morfudd' are concerned with a long lasting and deeply-felt experience. A passage in *Y Serch Lledrad* ('Stolen Love') expresses his love at its happiest and most serene:

> Cerddais, addolais i ddail,
> Tref eurddyn, tra fu irddail.
> Digrif fu, fun, un ennyd
> Dwyn dan un bedwlwyn ein byd.
> Cydlwynach, difyrrach fu,
> Coed olochwyd, cydlechu,
> Cydfyhwman marian môr,
> Cydaros mewn coed oror,
> Cydblannu bedw, gwaith dedwydd,
> Cydblethu gweddeiddblu gwŷdd.
> Cydadrodd serch â'r ferch fain,
> Cydedrych caeau didrain.
> Crefft ddigerydd fydd i ferch—
> Cydgerdded coed â gordderch,
> Cadw wyneb, cydowenu,
> Cydchwerthin finfin a fu,
> Cyd-ddigwyddaw garllaw'r llwyn,
> Cydochel pobl, cydachwyn,
> Cydfod mwyn, cydyfed medd,
> Cydarwain serch, cydorwedd,
> Cyd-ddaly cariad celadwy
> Cywir, ni menegir mwy (GDG 74, 21–42).

*(I walked, while leaves were green, and gave/ my worship to my darling's leafy home./ It was sweet, my love, a while/ to live our life beneath the grove of birch,/ more sweet was it fondly to embrace/ together hid in our woodland retreat,/ together to be wandering on the ocean's shore,/ together lingering by the forest's edge,/ together to plant birches—task of joy/—together weave fair plumage of the trees,/ together talk of love with my slim girl,/ together gaze on solitary fields./ It is a blameless occupation for a girl/ to wander through the forest with her lover,/ together to keep face, together smile,/ together laugh— and it was lip to lip—together to lie down beside the grove,/ together to shun folk, together to complain,/ to live together kindly, drinking mead together,/ to rest together and express our love,/ maintaining true love in all secrecy:/ there is no need to tell any more.)*

This passage, a metrical tour-de-force with its alliterating initial consonants throughout a series of eighteen lines, invites contrast with the description of the virile delights of Ifor Hael's home, already quoted.

Morfudd's name occurs in some thirty of Dafydd's poems, and she is surely the un-named subject of many others. In the passing pageant of both named and un-named girls who claimed the poet's attention, Morfudd remains the single object of his permanent love: according to Dafydd's own statement, he composed 'seven and seven score' *cywyddau* to her, which must denote a very large number, even if the number given is itself no more than a fanciful formula.

If we are to believe his story as outlined in his poems, the course of Dafydd's love ran far from smoothly. There are veiled and unexplained allusions to unhappy experiences with other girls, but Dafydd's continual frustrations in the pursuit of love are to be attributed above all to Morfudd's vacillating and exasperating behaviour. She was exceedingly vivacious—he describes her as 'a glowing coal'[34]—and she could at times be sporadically affectionate, but Dafydd dwells with greatest frequency on Morfudd's elusiveness, her persistent trickery and her faithlessness, which culminates in the final betrayal of her marriage to *Y Bwa Bach* 'the little man bent like a bow', or 'the little hunch-back', by whom she became pregnant, and later a mother. Morfudd was fair-haired and dark browed (this combination seems to have been greatly admired in the Middle Ages)[35]—and Dafydd was irretrievably bound under the spell of her *hud* or enchantment:

> Heodd i'm bron, hon a hyllt,
> Had o gariad, hud gorwyllt.
> Heiniar cur, hwn yw'r cerydd,
> Hon ni ad ym, hoywne dydd.
> Hudoles a dwywes deg,
> Hud yw ym ei hadameg.
> Hawdd y gwrendy gyhudded,
> Hawdd arnaf, ni chaf ei ched.
> Heddwch a gawn, dawn a dysg,
> Heddiw gyda'm dyn hyddysg.
> Herwr glân heb alanas
> Heno wyf o'i phlwyf a'i phlas (GDG 102, 5–16).

*(She sowed within my breast—this shatters it—/ love's seed, a wild enchantment./ My punishment: the harvest of my care/ she will not let me have—this girl of day's bright hue./ Enchantress and lovely goddess,/ magic is her speech to me./ She listens readily to any charge/ against me, so that I obtain no boon./ I may win peace, instruction and reward/ today from my erudite love;/ tonight, an outlaw utterly without redress/ I am from out her parish and her home.)*

In one *cywydd* (42) Dafydd compares Morfudd in a sustained image to the sun in its varied aspects: it not only provides light and warmth

---

[34] GDG 79, 18. Cf. T. Parry, *Yorkshire Celtic Studies* v (1949–52), 24.

[35] THSC 1913–14, 149. For this popular medieval combination see Gervase Mathew, *The Court of Richard II* (London, 1968), 131–2.

but can also dazzle and burn; it waxes and wanes, appearing and disappearing behind clouds. Dafydd's *cywyddau* have resounded far and wide like the notes of an organ; the *clêr* have carried his praise of Morfudd to the uttermost bounds of Wales. He will die if he does not obtain her:

> Ni fynnwn innau, f'annwyl,
> Fyw oni chawn fun wych ŵyl.
> Am hyn darfu fy mhoeni,
> Morfudd fwyn, marw fyddaf fi (GDG 57, 23–5).

*(I would not wish to live, my darling/ if I may not obtain my lovely bashful girl./ This is the cause of my affliction:/ sweet Morfudd, I shall die.)*

There were no real rivals to Morfudd in the poet's passionate love. But there is another girl who is mentioned, though much less frequently. She is Dyddgu, daughter of a certain Ieuan ap Gruffudd ap Llywelyn, and she presents an obvious foil and contrast to Morfudd in almost every possible way. Where Morfudd was fair, Dyddgu was dark; an aristocratic and unattainable beauty, well-nurtured and well-educated, graceful and courteous, but for ever remote. Addressing her father Dafydd says:

> Dy ferch, gwn na ordderchai,
> Feinwen deg o feinin dai.
> Ni chysgais, ni weais wawd,
> Hun na'i dryll, heiniau drallawd.
> Duw lwyd, pwy a'm dilidia?
> Dim yn fy nghalon nid â,
> Eithr ei chariad taladwy;
> O rhoid ym oll, ai rhaid mwy?
> Ni'm câr hon, neu'm curia haint,
> Ni'm gad hun, o'm gad henaint (GDG 45, 13–22).

*(I know your daughter will accept no wooing:/ fair slender maid in mansion built of stone;/ I have not slept a wink, nor had a scrap of it,/ I have composed no song, but have felt grievous ill./ Holy God, who will make me calm?/ nothing finds entrance to my heart/ except the thought of her inestimable love:/ if that were given me, could I need aught else?/ But sickness wastes me, for she loves me not,/ allowing me no sleep, were old age to allow it me.)*

Dafydd recognizes that he has aspired too high in loving Dyddgu. When he describes her we are reminded of the noble ladies who are the subject of distant and respectful admiration in the *Rhieingerddi*[36] or 'Maiden songs' composed by the poets of the preceding two centuries. Both

[36] T. Gwynn Jones, *Rhieingerddi'r Gogynfeirdd* (Dinbych, 1915); J. E. Caerwyn Williams 'Cerddi'r Gogynfeirdd i Wragedd a Merched', LlC xiii, 1–112.

Morfudd and Dyddgu were clearly well-born; Dyddgu was even of the royal line of the princes of Deheubarth.[37] But she remained for ever beyond the poet's reach; she may in fact have died unmarried.

In one poem (GDG 98) the attractions of a third woman are described ironically: she is Elen, the wife of Robin Nordd,[38] an English wool-merchant, apparently a burgess of Aberystwyth. Clearly this Elen laid herself out to win the poet's attentions:

> *Elen chwannog i olud,*
> *Fy anrhaith â'r lediaith lud,*
> *Brenhines, arglwyddes gwlân,*
> *Brethyndai, bro eithindan,*
> *Dyn serchog oedd raid yno,*
> *Gwae fi nad fyfi fai fo!* (GDG 98, 17–22).

*(Elen avid for wealth:/ my darling with the persistent alien speech,/ queen and lady of wool,/ and ware-houses, ready land for gorse-firing;/ there was need there for a lover—/ woe to me if such one were not I!)*

In spite of the graspingness she evinced in her business transactions, Elen was nevertheless prepared to supply the poet with good woollen stockings—*hosanau da*—in payment for his tribute of poetry. But clearly Elen Nordd offered no serious rivalry to Morfudd and Dyddgu for Dafydd's affections.

Many years ago[39] Sir Ifor Williams propounded the theory that the names 'Morfudd' and 'Dyddgu' were no more than pseudonyms, used indiscriminately by Dafydd to conceal the identity of many different girls. When he wrote in 1914, this view seemed a plausible one, since it was a common custom among both continental and English poets in the Middle Ages to refer to their mistresses by such secret pseudonyms. Not only does Dafydd himself lay frequent stress on the necessity for secrecy in conducting his love-affairs, but there are poems in which he may even be himself using the names 'Efa' and 'Luned' as pseudonyms, either for Morfudd herself or for some other girl. But this view

---

[37] GDG[1] xliv (= GDG[2] xxv), *o Dewdwr lwyth* (95, 40). Bartrum lists, as witness to a charter in 1387, a certain 'Ieuan ap Gruffudd ap Llywelyn' (cf. GDG 45, 1–3) among the descendants of Tewdwr Mawr ap Cadell, *Welsh Genealogies*, 4, 847. This was a collateral line to that of Rhys ap Tewdwr (HW 767). No daughter of the name of Dyddgu is listed, though Ieuan (surprisingly) had a daughter Morfudd who in her turn had a daughter named Dyddgu (ibid. I, 206). Is it too fanciful to speculate that this later 'Dyddgu' may have been named in memory of an aunt who died unmarried, and for this reason was left unrecorded in the genealogies? (Nevertheless we must remember that 'Dyddgu' was one of the commonest names for women in the fourteenth century; THSC 1965, 40). D. J. Bowen notes the connection of the descendants of Rhys ap Tewdwr with Tywyn in south Ceredigion, LlC xiv, 192.

[38] GDG li (= GDG[2] xxix), and n. 40 below.

[39] 'Dafydd ap Gwilym a'r Glêr' THSC 1913–14, 147–9.

can no longer be held: research has shown that both Morfudd and
Elen Nordd appear to have been real women of flesh-and-blood, and
that they were the wives of two of Dafydd's local neighbours. In 1937
Mr David Jenkins cited the evidence of an Assize Roll for Cardigan,
relating to the month of July 1344, which states that a certain Howel
ap Gronow was fined forty pence for having two years previously stolen
a silver cup worth eight shillings from a man called 'Robert le Northern',
a burgess of Aberystwyth.[40] A number of men are named as having
stood surety for Howel's payment of his fine, and these include *Howel
ap Gwillym Seys* (= *Sais* 'English') and *Ebowa baghan* (*sic*). Here, surely
is Morfudd's husband *Y Bwa Bach*,[41] mentioned officially at a date
which fits admirably with the period when Dafydd may be conjectured
to have been in the early years of his career. The importance of this
evidence cannot be dismissed: in the face of it, it may be significant
that a farm named *Cwm Bwa* exists to this day within a mile of Dafydd's
early home at Brogynin. The conjunction of the names 'Robert le Northern' and *Ebowa baghan* within the same contemporary document remains
an extraordinary coincidence. Recent evidence has come to light, also,
which supports the belief that Dyddgu was a real person, since her
father 'Ieuan ap Gruffudd ap Llywelyn' may now be plausibly identified
in a genealogy of the descendants of Tewdwr Mawr ap Cadell, thus
placing Dyddgu's father in a collateral line to that of Rhys ap
Tewdwr[37]—the royal line of Deheubarth. Ieuan was a man who, according to Dafydd's account, offered generous hospitality to *y glêr*. A further
argument in favour of the real existence of Morfudd and Dyddgu is
that Gruffudd Gryg names both girls in the course of his poetic contention with Dafydd.

In a number of poems Dafydd gives expression to his grief and
exasperation at Morfudd's perversity, her fickleness and her failure

[40] B viii, 144–5. In 'Dafydd ap Gwilym a Cheredigion', LlC xiv, 186 D. J. Bowen
cites references from PRO records published in R. A. Griffiths, *Principality*, to this Hywel
ap Goronwy ap Meilyr (p. 438), to his father Goronwy ap Meilyr (pp. 442, 528), and
to two other of the sureties who stood for Hywel—Trahaiarn ap Maredudd (p. 443)
and Ieuan Llwyd ab Ieuan Fwyaf (p. 449), to the latter of whom Dafydd addressed
his *awdl* GDG no. 14. These are all named in the records as holding responsible positions
(beadles, reeves, and constables) in the commote of Genau'r Glyn in the 1330s, 40s,
and 50s: they were clearly all of *bonheddig* status. D. J. Bowen notes a further reference
to 'Robertus le Northern' as one of the bailiffs of Aberystwyth who swore allegiance
to the Black Prince in 1343 (B xxv, 26–7).

[41] D. J. Bowen (*loc. cit.*) has identified both 'Y Bwa Bychan' (*sic*) and his son Maredudd
(beadle of Genau'r Glyn) in the PRO records published in *Principality* pp. 438, 453.
'Y Bwa Bychan' acted for the reeve of Perfedd (a commote of Penweddig) in 1339–40.
These independent records therefore establish that Y Bwa Bach/Bychan was an individual, and that his name cannot be merely a nickname for his predecessor in the list
of sureties—a point which the lack of punctuation on the document had previously caused
to be ambiguous.

to reward him for his verses or to respond to his love:

> *Ba dal a'm bu o'i dilyn?*
> *Boed awr dda beidio â'r ddyn* (GDG 81, 7–8).

*(What reward have I had from following her?/ It were high time to have done with the girl.)*

In one poem (GDG 96, 1–4) he claims to have been afflicted by his love for Morfudd for the length of nine years; and he describes how he follows her to church on Sundays and at festivals, where he will clasp his hands together and weep; how no one but Morfudd has the power to comfort him, and without her he would not be able to live (GDG 102, 28). He beseeches St Dwynwen,[42] the patroness of disappointed lovers (her shrine in Anglesey was a much-frequented place for pilgrimage in Dafydd's day), to intercede for him with Morfudd, in lines whose evident grief is the more poignant from the audacious religious imagery which the poet employs throughout the poem:

> *Dwywen deigr arien degwch,*
> *Da y gŵyr o gôr fflamgwyr fflwch*
> *Dy ddelw aur diddoluriaw*
> *Digion druain ddynion draw.*
> *Dyn a wylio, gloywdro glân,*
> *Yn dy gôr, Indeg*[43] *eirian,*
> *Nid oes glefyd na bryd brwyn*
> *A êl ynddo o Landdwyn* (GDG 94, 1–8).

*(Dwynwen, your beauty like the hoar-frost's tears:/ from your chancel with its blazing waxen candles/ well does your golden image know/ how to assuage the griefs of wretched men./ What man soever would keep vigil in your choir/ (a holy, shining pilgrimage),/ you with Indeg's*[43] *radiance,/ there is no sickness nor heart's sorrow/ which he would carry with him thence from Llanddwyn.)*

Dafydd's bitterness increases in the poems which relate to Morfudd's marriage to *Y Bwa Bach* (what may perhaps be an alternative name for him is given on one occasion (GDG 73, 27) as 'Cynfrig Cynin'):

> *Ni chefais, eithr nych ofal,*
> *Nid amod ym, dym o dâl,*
> *Eithr ei myned, gweithred gwall,*

---

[42] For the cult of St Dwynwen see LBS ii, 387–92; *Cy.* xxiii, 323; Hugh Owen, *Hanes Plwyf Niwbwrch* (Caernarfon, 1952), 62–3.

[43] A legendary heroine, whose story has not survived, but whose proverbial beauty is frequently alluded to by Dafydd ap Gwilym and his poetic contemporaries, see TYP 412–13.

*Deune'r eiry, dan ŵr arall,*
*I'w gwneuthur, nid llafur lles,*
*Yn feichiog, fy nyn faches* (GDG 85, 27–32).

*(I obtained no payment, but languishing care,/ I had no contract and no reward/ other than her going, snow-coloured, under another man, a wrongful act,/ and her being made pregnant—it was a labour which brought no profit—my little one.)*

In one of his most effective extended images (GDG 87),Dafydd devotes a whole poem to describing how he cherished the seeds of love, preparing winter-tilth in January, ploughing and sowing, and enclosing the young growing crop in May—until at last when all was ripe for harvest there came a disastrous storm which destroyed everything—an outcome which evidently symbolizes some painful event, possibly that of Morfudd's marriage. Another time he complains bitterly that after he has given her all, she has now cast him aside like an empty barrel (GDG 93, 43–4). All his attentions to her have been in vain. Though no names are given, it is not improbable that it is Morfudd's husband who is the *bygegyr* ('drone-bee') who is intended as the person whom Dafydd wishes to be drowned as he sets off with others by ship on a military expedition to France (GDG 75, 9). In order that he may force himself to relinquish her, he persuades himself that her beauty has become corrupted:

*Gorau gan Eiddig oeryn,*
*Gi du, na bai deg y dyn.*
*Llychwinodd llwch o'i enau*
*Lliw'r dynyn mireinwyn mau.*
*Rho Duw a Chadfan, rhaid oedd*
*Rhad a geidw; rhydeg ydoedd* (GDG 81, 41–6).

*(The wretched Jealous One, the black dog, prefers that she should not be fair./ The dirt from his lips has corrupted the complexion of my brilliant darling./ By God and by St Cadfan, there were need for protecting grace: she was too fair.)*

In a savage mock *llatai* or 'love-messenger' poem (113), Dafydd sends a messenger in fancy to the nuns at the Cistercian convent of Llanllugan in Montgomeryshire, inviting any one of them to meet him—even the abbess herself (the *sieler* or 'gaoler' as he calls her) who imprisons all those beautiful girls. They are swallows, they are like gossamer and as pure as snow; each one is a sister to Morfudd. In reality, Dafydd is here giving voice to his angry frustration: the lovely young nuns in the convent are for him as unattainable as is Morfudd herself, and so he pretends that any one of them, including the abbess, would suit him just as well as she.

Nevertheless, Dafydd maintains that the liaison continued even after

Morfudd's marriage: although Morfudd has sworn to give him up, he speaks of having 'deputized' for her husband, and

> Cyd bai brid ein newid ni,
> Prid oedd i'r priod eiddi (GDG 98, 7–8).

*(Though our exchange was costly,/ it was costly too for her husband.)*

and again, he reports Morfudd as having said that she cares more for the track of Dafydd's feet in the forest than for her wretched sombre husband and all that belongs to him (GDG 77, 15–18). In one of his greatest poems, Dafydd dispatches the Wind itself, a symbol of the free forces of the elements, to go as his messenger to Morfudd's home (and Dafydd's own early home) in Uwch Aéron, where he himself may no longer go because of the tragic complications of his love:

> Uthr yw mor aruthr y'th roed
> O bantri wybr heb untroed,
> A buaned y rhedy
> Yr awron dros y fron fry ...
> Nythod ddwyn, cyd nithud ddail,
> Ni'th dditia neb, ni'th etail
> Na llu rhugl, na llaw rhaglaw,
> Na llafn glas na llif na glaw.
> Ni'th ddeil swyddog na theulu
> I'th ddydd, nithydd blaenwydd blu.
> Ni'th ladd mab mam, gam gymwyll,
> Ni'th lysg tân, ni'th lesga twyll.
> Ni'th wŷl drem, noethwal dramawr,
> Neu'th glyw mil, nyth y glaw mawr;
> Noter wybr natur ebrwydd,
> Neitiwr gwiw dros nawtir gŵydd.
> ... Hydoedd y byd a hedy,
> Hin y fron, bydd heno fry,
> Och ŵr, a dos Uwch Aeron
> Yn glaer deg, yn eglur dôn.
> Nac aro di, nac eiriach,
> Nac ofna er Bwa Bach
> Cyhuddgwyn wenwyn weini;
> Caeth yw'r wlad a'i maeth i mi. (GDG 117, 5ff.)

*(It is strange how marvellously you were sent/ lacking a foot, from out the store-house of the sky,/ and how swiftly it is you run/ this moment now across the slope above .../ Though you might winnow leaves, seizing the nests,/ none will indict you, neither swift troop/ nor hand of magistrate will hold you back,/ nor blue blade nor flood nor rain,/ neither officer nor retinue can hold you/ in you life-time, scatterer of the tree-tops' feathers;/ no mother's son can strike you—it were a wrong to mention it,/ no fire burns you, nor treachery restrains you./ No eye can see you with your great barren wall,/ but*

*a thousand hear you, nest of the great rain,/ swift-natured annotator of the clouds,/ fair leaper across nine fallow lands .../ You fly the full length of the world,/ the hill's limit: be above tonight,/ ah, man, go to Uwch Aeron,/ be gentle and kind, with voice easily heard./ Do not stop, do not hold back/ nor fear, inspite of the Bwa Bach/ —that whining accuser, serving jealousy./ That land is closed to me, with its nourishment (*or which nourished her*).

Reading these poems together, it is difficult to doubt but that a genuine, intense, and ultimately bitter experience underlies Dafydd's poems about Morfudd. That in the last resort, the husband won his legal rights and the relationship ended in bitter renunciation is also indicated,

> *Chwarëus fuam, gam gae;*
> *Chwerw fu ddiwedd ein chwarae* (GDG 82, 25–6).[44]

*(We were playful; a false obstruction (?)/ bitter was the end of our game.)*

When winter comes and summer is gone, everything favours *Yr Eiddig*, the 'Jealous Husband', and the identification between *Yr Eiddig* and winter is everywhere implicit, even when it is not directly expressed. There is something deeply mournful in Dafydd's lines:

> *Nithiodd y gaeaf noethfawr,*
> *Dyli las, y dail i lawr* (GDG 145, 61–2).

*(Winter's great bareness has winnowed the green web of the leaves to the ground.)*

---

[44] Morfudd is not actually named in this poem, but cf. Eurys Rowlands, LlC vi, 106.

# VII

For Dafydd ap Gwilym is above all the poet of Summer:

> Gweled mor hardd, mi chwarddaf,
> Gwallt ar ben hoyw fedwen haf.
> Paradwys, iddo prydaf,
> Pwy ni chwardd pan fo hardd haf? (GDG 24, 13–16).

*(I laugh when I see how fine/ is the hair on Summer's sprightly birch-tree's head./ I sing to Paradise: who does not laugh when Summer is so fair?)*

The constant impulse towards personification which caused Dafydd to see the green birch-leaves as 'hair' on the tree, is extended to the months and to the season itself. May is a *cadarn farchog* (GDG 69, 3) 'a strong horseman' and a *hylaw ŵr mawr hael* (GDG 23, 10) 'a free and generous nobleman', and Summer a *teg wdwart* (GDG 27, 3) 'a fair wood-ward' (forester), who departs when August comes. Dafydd personifies Summer when he greets the coming of the months of May, June and July:

> Gwasgod praff, gwisgiad priffyrdd,
> Gwisgodd bob lle â'i we wyrdd.
> Pan ddêl ar ôl rhyfel rhew,
> Pill doldir, y pall deildew—
> Gleison fydd, mau grefydd grill,
> Llwybrau Mai yn lle Ebrill—
> Y daw ar uchaf blaen dâr
> Caniadau cywion adar;
> A chog ar fan pob rhandir,
> A chethlydd, a hoywddydd hir;
> A niwl gwyn yn ôl y gwynt
> Yn diffryd canol dyffrynt;
> Ac wybren loyw hoyw brynhawn
> Fydd, a glwyswydd a glaswawn;
> Ac adar aml ar goedydd,
> Ac irddail ar wiail wŷdd;
> A chof fydd Forfudd f'eurferch,
> A chyffro saith nawtro serch (GDG 69, 13–30).

*(In a dense screen, the clothing of the high-roads,/ he has dressed all places in his web of green./ When there comes, after battle with the frost,/ the tent of thick leaves to invigorate the fields,/ green will be the paths of May/ succeeding April—birds' chirping is my faith—/ on topmost branches of the oak will come/ the singing of the new-fledged*

*birds,/ and the cuckoo high over each land,/ and a songster;/ with a long and joyful day,/ and white mist-haze after the wind/ protects the middle of the valley,/ and sky at afternoon is clear and glad/ with green trees and fresh gossamer,/ and crowds of birds upon the trees,/ and fresh leaves on forest saplings,/ and Morfudd my golden girl, will come to [my] mind/ with all love's seven-times-nine tumultuous turns.)*

When August follows the three perfect months, the poet bids farewell to Summer:

> *Aed bendithion beirddion byd*
> *A'u can hawddamor cennyd.*
> *Yn iach, frenin yr hinon,*
> *Yn iach, ein llywiawdr a'n iôn,*
> *Yn iach, y cogau ieuainc,*
> *Yn iach, hin Fehefin fainc,*
> *Yn iach, yr haul yn uchel*
> *A'r wybren dew, bolwen bêl.*
> *Deyrn byddin, dioer ni byddy*
> *Yn gyfuwch, fryn wybrluwch fry,*
> *Oni ddêl, digel degardd,*
> *Eilwaith yr haf a'i lethr hardd* (GDG 27, 41–50).

*(Let the blessings of the world's poets go with you,/ and their hundred greetings./ Farewell, king of splendid weather,/ farewell, our ruler and our lord,/ farewell, the young cuckoos,/ farewell, June's fair-weather slopes,/ farewell, the Sun on high/ and the plump cloud, a white-bellied ball./ Lord of an army, in truth you will not be/ so high, with hill of drifting snow above/ until there comes—the fair garden unveiled—/ once more the Summer with his splendid slopes.)*

These poems reflect a mood of serene tranquillity, and—if indeed we may speculate so far—they belong with the bird-poems quoted earlier to the period of Dafydd's as yet untroubled love and of his real or imagined forest-idyll, in which he escaped with Morfudd to the woodland *deildy*, where the pair plighted their troth and wove for each other garlands of leaves and twigs. Here in the forest the poet could enjoy the same irresponsible immunity from the cares of society as was enjoyed by the birds—nature's own poets—who paralleled his activities in their own, and in the same idyllic surroundings.

# VIII

Realism and fantasy go hand-in-hand in much of Dafydd's love-poetry: realism in the sense of startlingly minute factual observation together with the record (obscurely outlined) of what was evidently a deeply emotional experience. This personal experience is implied as lying behind such poems as the invocation to St Dwynwen and *Y Gwynt* ('The Wind'): its poignancy gives to them a depth and intensity which place them among Dafydd's supreme achievements. But the accompanying fantasy is no less essential to the distinctive quality of such poems. Both belong to the group of *llatai* or 'love-messenger' poems (the word has been explained as derived from *llad* 'a gift' with an old noun termination in—(*h*)*ai*), in which the poet sends in imagination some bird or creature with a message to his sweetheart—the Lark, the Seagull and the Cock-Thrush are all employed in this way. Similarly, the poet sends the Stag (a 'tall baron') as the bearer of a love-letter to Dyddgu at her home, accompanied by minute directions as to his journey:

> Grugwal goruwch y greigwen,
> Gweirwellt a bawr gorwyllt ben.
> Talofyn gwych teuluaidd,
> Llammwr allt, llym yw ei raidd.
> Llama megis bonllymoen
> I'r rhiw, teg ei ffriw a'i ffroen.
> Fy ngwas gwych, ni'th fradychir,
> Ni'th ladd cŵn, hardd farwn hir.
> Nod fawlgamp, n'ad i filgi
> Yn ôl tes d'oddiwes di.
> Nac ofna di saeth lifaid,
> Na chi yn ôl o chai naid.
> Gochel Bali, ci coesgoch,
> Ac Iolydd, ci celfydd coch,
> Adlais hued a gredir,
> O dôn yn d'ôl Dywyn dir.
> Ymochel rhag dy weled,
> Dros fryn i lwyn rhedyn rhed.
> Neidia goris hen adwy
> I'r maes ac nac aro mwy.
> Fy llatai wyd anwydael,
> A'm bardd at Ddyddgu hardd hael (GDG 116, 9–30).

*(He grazes the tough grass of his heathery lair/ above the crag, this wild-headed one,/ asking a fair payment for a poet(?),/ sharp-antlered, leaper of the height/ —as a bare-*

*rumped lamb he leaps—to the hill-slope, fair his nose and face.*/ *My fine lad, you will
not be betrayed,*/ *no hounds will slay you, tall and handsome baron.*/ *A worthy feat
must be your aim: allow no hound*/ *after the heat to overtake you,*/ *have no fear of
sharpened arrow*/ *nor hound pursuing you, if you can jump.*/ *Look out for Pali, a brown-
legged hound*/ *and Iolydd, brown and skilful one.*/ *The baying of the hunt is to be given
heed*/ *should they pursue you to the land of Tywyn.*/ *Give good care lest you be seen—*/
*run to the bracken-thicket across the hill.*/ *Jump underneath the ancient gap*/ *into the
field, and make no more delay.*/ *You are my generous-natured messenger*/ *and my poet
to handsome, generous Dyddgu.)*

The Stag is directed to return at night, and to meet the poet 'by the
dyke at the edge of the forest', and to bring him Dyddgu's kiss. May
God and St Cynfelyn bless him, and may his glossy coat be never
used to cover up an old Saxon.

The *llatai* poems recall the starling which Branwen dispatched across
the Irish sea with a letter to her brother; but numerous parallels to
the employment of bird-messengers may indeed be found in other literatures, as for instance in French and in Provençal. Significantly, it is
birds alone whom Dafydd endows with the power of speech,[45] so that
he imagines them as holding dialogues with him. On occasion, indeed,
they may address him somewhat tartly, as in *Cyngor y Biogen* (GDG
63) ('The Magpie's Counsel'), in which the busy, nest-building bird turns
on the poet and rebukes him roundly for his impotent and un-productive
love-longing; or the Woodcock, who refuses the embassy which Dafydd
proposes to him, both on account of the bad weather and because,
according to him, the girl has already chosen another mate (GDG 115).
But no convincing parallels have as yet been found in any other literature
to the conventional pattern of the *llatai* poems as practised in the fourteenth century by Dafydd and by certain of his contemporaries. Each
contains most or all of the following elements: an initial greeting, followed by a full description of the messenger; a request to carry a message, to give an assurance of love, or to ask for a kiss; an account
of the proposed journey and a warning to avoid its hazards; a brief
mention of the girl and of the journey's object. The description of the
messenger, which is often very elaborate, offered Dafydd the opportunity
to exercise the technical device of *dyfalu*, one much favoured by him.
*Dyfalu* ('likening' or 'comparison') means a minute description by means
of fanciful comparisons and extravagant images ('riddling' has been
suggested as the nearest English equivalent for it). The most outstanding
examples draw upon the full range of the poet's resources in vocabulary
and in imaginative expression. His description of the Wind, part of
which has been quoted above, has overt echoes of a much older riddling
poem on the Wind in the Book of Taliesin.[46] He describes the Wind,

[45] See ch. 2, n. 86, pp. 78–9.
[46] J. G. Evans, facsimile edn. of the *Book of Taliesin* (Llanbedrog, 1910), 36–8, trans.
J. P. Clancy, *The Earliest Welsh Poetry* (London, 1970), 105–7.

among other things, as *Saethydd ar froydd eiry fry/ Seithug eisingrug songry* ('shooter upon the snow-fields up above, of futile noisy piles of chaff'). In another poem, the Star which guides him is:

> Cannaid o'r uchel Geli,
> Cannwyll ehwybrbwyll yw hi.
> Ni ddiflan pryd y gannwyll,
> A'i dwyn ni ellir o dwyll.
> Nis diffydd gwynt hynt hydref,
> Afrlladen o nen y nef.
> Nis bawdd dwfr llwfr llifeiriant,
> Disgwylwraig, dysgl saig y saint.
> Nis cyrraidd lleidr o'i ddwylaw,
> Gwaelod cawg y Drindod draw.
> Nid gwiw i ddyn o'i gyfair
> Ymlid maen mererid Mair.
> Golau fydd ymhob ardal,
> Goldyn o aur melyn mâl.
> Gwir fwcled y goleuni,
> Gwalabr haul gloyw wybr yw hi (GDG 67, 23–38).

*(A radiant beacon from the Lord on high,/ a candle of a clear nature is she,/ a candle whose beauty will not fade,/ and which cannot be stolen by deceit./ No wind on its autumnal course can quench her,/ she is the consecrated wafer from the roof of Heaven./ The water of cowardly torrents will not extinguish her,/ waiting-woman with the communal platter of the saints./ No thief's hand can reach towards her,/ the bottom yonder of the Trinity's bowl./ It is useless from his dwelling [here below]/ for any man to covet Mary's pearl./ She will shed brightness over every region,/ a refined coin of yellow gold,/ a true buckler of the light,/ she is the image of the sky's brilliant Sun.)*

The Fox is:

> Lluman brain gerllaw min bryn,
> Llamwr erw, lliw marworyn.
> Drych nod brain a phiod ffair,
> Draig unwedd daroganair.
> Cynnwr fryn, cnöwr iâr fras,
> Cnu dihaereb, cnawd eirias.
> Taradr daeargadr dorgau,
> Tanllestr ar gwr ffenestr gau.
> Bwa latwm di-drwm draed,
> Gefel unwedd gylfinwaed (GDG 22, 31–40).

*(A scare-crow, near to the hill's edge,/ leaping the furrows, ember-hued./ Image of raven-target (?) and magpies at a fair,/ like to the Dragon of the prophecies,/ the summit of commotion (?), one who gnaws fat hens,/ proverbial pelt, bloodthirsty flesh,/ a piercing auger of the earth's hollow belly,/ a lantern in the corner of a window that is closed,/ a copper-coloured bow, with lissom tread—/ like pincers is his bloody snout.)*

The art of *dyfalu* seems to be closely bound up with the development of the *cywydd*: the earliest recorded example of a *cywydd* (in the Bardic Grammar) is in fact a *cerdd dyfalu* describing a horse;[47] it may well belong to the genre of the *cywydd gofyn*, or 'asking poem' which subsequently grew in popularity, and to which the convention of the *llatai* poem appears to have borne an oblique relation. *Dyfalu* was itself an adaptation of an old and indigenous tradition of imaginative riddling poetry developed to conform with the emphasis which the medieval rhetoricians placed upon *descriptio* in its various forms. *Dyfalu* belongs characteristically to praise-poetry, and may be used for either praise or for satire; but Dafydd ap Gwilym does in fact employ it far more frequently for satire than for praise, so that although it is sometimes suggested that *dyfalu* had its origin in riddle-making, such as is found in Latin and Anglo-Saxon poetry, it seems nevertheless more probable that it is to be related to the richly figurative, vituperative, and elaborately-compounded language of bardic satire, as this is exemplified both in Welsh and in Irish, and hence is likely to have sprung from an ancient tradition common to the two branches of the Celtic peoples.[48] Dafydd employs *dyfalu* most frequently of all when he abuses some object or force which has prevented or obstructed his love-making. Ice is described as *Plats cron gledr dwyfron dyfredd* ('thick plate-armour of the breast of the valleys'); the Mist is

> Cnu tewlwyd gwynllwyd gwanllaes
> Cyfliw â mwg, cwfl y maes.
> Coetgae glaw er lluddiaw lles,
> Codarmur cawad ormes (GDG 68, 25–8).

*(A thick, pale-grey, weakly-trailing fleece,/ like smoke, hooded cowl of the plain./ A hedge of rain, impeding progress:/ coat-armour of the oppressive shower.)*

The Hare (whose hunt is but a symbol of the poet's own love-pursuit) is described with rich invective:

> Gwrwraig a wnâi ar glai glan
> Gyhyrwayw i gi hwyrwan.
> Genfer, gwta, eginfwyd,
> Gwn dynghedfen lawdrwen lwyd (GDG 46, 9–12).

*(Hermaphrodite who on the clean loam/ would give a muscular pain to a slow feeble hound./ Short-of-jaw, bob-tailed, fed on young shoots,/ I know the fate of the grey, white-trousered one.)*

[47] GP 12, 31, 52. See ch. 4 p. 152.
[48] On the nature and range of *dyfalu* see P. Sims-Williams 'Dafydd ap Gwilym', p. 305 in B. Ford (ed.) *Medieval Literature: The European Inheritance* (Harmondsworth, 1983).

In *Y Don ar Afon Dyfi* (GDG 71) ('The Wave on the River Dovey') Dafydd pleads with the river in flood to allow him to cross to Llanbadarn so that he may visit Morfudd: the *dyfalu* here is skilfully inverted, so that the poet becomes the butt of his own imaginatively extravagant comparisons:

> *A ganodd neb â genau*
> *O fawl i'r twrf meistrawl tau,*
> *Gymar hwyl, gem yr heli,*
> *Gamen môr, gymain' â mi?*
> *Ni bu brifwynt planetsygn,*
> *Na rhuthr blawdd rhwng deuglawdd dygn,*
> *Nac esgud frwydr, nac ysgwr,*
> *Nac ysgwydd gorwydd na gŵr,*
> *Nas cyfflybwn, gwn gyni,*
> *Grefdaer don, i'th gryfder di.*
> *Ni bu organ na thelyn,*
> *Na thafawd difeiwawd dyn,*
> *Nas barnwn yn un gyfref,*
> *Fordwy glas, â'th fawrdeg lef* (GDG 71, 9–22).

*(Did anyone's lips ever sing so much praise as I of your masterly tummult,/ sail's companion, gem of the waves, loop of the sea?/ There is no wind sent by the planets' signs,/ nor vehement swift attack between two banks,/ nor swift battle, nor strong branch,/ nor shoulder of a horse nor yet of man,/ that I have not compared (well do I know the anguish),/ strong forceful wave, to your strength./ There was never organ nor harp,/ nor man's tongue with faultless praise,/ that I have not adjudged as strong,/ grey flood, as is your splendid voice.)*

This poem implies that for Dafydd the art of *dyfalu*—a sequence of imaginatively inspired comparisons—represented the very essence of the craft of poetry.

# IX

Mainly fantasy also, one may suppose, are those poems of situation and incident, mildly ironical and self-mocking in tone, in which the poet recounts his failures and frustrations in the pursuit of love. Humour invoked at the narrator's own expense is not an exceptional stance among medieval poets: Chaucer (or rather, perhaps, 'the Chaucerian narrator') commonly presents himself in his poems as an incompetent or slightly bewildered actor-observer; and there is yet another analogy to be found in Ovid's characteristic portrayal of himself. Dafydd surveys 'his parish' while attending service on Sunday:

> *Ni bu Sul yn Llanbadarn*
> *Na bewn, ac eraill a'i barn,*
> *A'm wyneb at y ferch goeth*
> *A'm gwegil at Dduw gwiwgoeth* (GDG 48, 19–22).

*(There was no Sunday in Llanbadarn/ that I would not be (and others will condemn it) facing the lovely girl,/ with my nape to God's true loveliness.)*

But the girl (is it Morfudd?) although she 'would not be ashamed to see me in a leafy hide-out' whispers disparaging remarks about him to her companion, and will have none of him:

> '*Y mab llwyd wyneb mursen*
> *A gwallt ei chwaer ar ei ben,*
> *Godinabus fydd golwg*
> *Gŵyr ei ddrem; da y gŵyr ddrwg* (GDG 48, 27–30).'

*('That grey-faced flirt of a boy/ wearing on his head his sister's hair,/ lascivious is the look he has,/ he has a side-long glance; he must know mischief well.')*

The transposition of lively colloquial exchanges into his difficult chosen metre, with the exacting requirements of *cynghanedd*, was a wholly novel achievement, which is exemplified in a number of poems, such as the poet's dialogue with the Magpie in *Cyngor y Biogen* (GDG 63), his dialogue with his own shadow in *Ei Gysgod* (GDG 141), or his dawn-parting from a girl in *Y Wawr* ('The Dawn'). There are suggestions in this last poem that he is intentionally parodying the continental *alba*: the poet disputes his lady's assertion that the dawn has come:

> '*Gair honnaid, pei gwir hynny,*
> *Paham y cân y frân fry?*'
> '*Pryfed y sydd yn profi,*
> *Lluddio ei hun, ei lladd hi.*'
> '*Mae cŵn dan lef ny dref draw*
> *Ag eraill yn ymguraw.*'
> '*Coelia fy nag yn aros,*
> *Cyni a wna cŵn·y nos* (GDG 129, 25–32).'

(*'Assuredly, if that were true/ why is the raven croaking up above?'/ 'Vermin are attempting there/ to kill her—keeping her from sleep.'/ 'Hounds are baying in the hamlet yonder,/ and others too are fighting with each other.'/ 'Believe me, my denial comes near the mark,/ it is the Hounds of Night cause this distress.'*)[49]

In a night of sleet and torrential rain, the poet begs for admittance to Morfudd's home, and complains of her cruelty because she will not admit him: *Dan y Bargawd* (GDG 89) ('Under the Eaves') transposes the typical situation of the southern *serenade* to conform with foreseeable weather conditions in west Wales. On another occasion it is the icicles, hanging sharp as a harrow from the eaves of her house, which torment the serenading poet, and which he abuses in elaborate *dyfalu* (GDG 91). Or he calls to the girl through the oak-shutter which covers her window; but she refuses his request for so much as a kiss, and Dafydd concludes with violet abuse both of the frustrating window, and of the carpenter who made it (GDG 64). In *Y Rhugl Groen* (GDG 125) his love-meeting is interrupted by the raucous noise made by a countryman with a 'rattle-skin' (apparently a skin bag filled with stones) with which to scare birds, and this too is anathematized with powerful *dyfalu*. In rich invective, drawing upon forgotten folk-lore and belief, he abuses the bog-hole into which he fell with his horse on a dark night, having neither moon nor stars to guide him:

> *Pysgodlyn i Wyn yw ef*
> *Fab Nudd, wb ynn ei oddef!*
> *Pydew rhwng gwaun a cheunant,*
> *Plas yr ellyllon a'u plant.*
> *Y dwfr o'm bodd nid yfwn,*
> *Eu braint a'u hennaint yw hwn.*
> *Llyn gwin egr, llanw gwineugoch,*
> *Lloches lle'r ymolches moch.*
> *Llygrais achlân f'hosanau*
> *Cersi o Gaer mewn cors gau* (GDG 127, 29–38).

[49] The 'Hounds of Night' were the ghostly companions of Gwynn ap Nudd, the mythical huntsman of Welsh tradition. On him see ch. 5 pp. 146–7 and Eurys Rowlands, 'Cyfeiriadau Dafydd ap Gwilym at Annwn', LlC v (1958–59), 122–4.

*(It is Gwyn ap Nudd's fish-pond, alas that we suffer it!/ a pit between moor and ravine,/ home of sprites and their children./ Not willingly would I drink its water/ for that is their ointment and their prerogative./ A lake of vinegar, a red-brown flood,/ lair where pigs wash themselves./ I completely spoiled my kersey hose/ (Chester-made) in the false quagmire.)*

*Trafferth mewn Tafarn* (GDG 124) ('Trouble at a Tavern'), the most vivid of the poems of incident, recounts the poet's chance encounter at an inn with a girl whom he entertains lavishly with food and wine; in attempting later at night to reach her room, he encounters a series of impediments, and noisily arouses the three sleeping English tinkers, Hickyn and Jenkins and Jack, who fear for the safety of their packs, and immediately raise the hue-and-cry after the supposed Welsh thief: in the resultant confusion the poet escapes safely into the outer darkness. The excited, jerky movement of the verse, with its interjections and inverted *sangiadau*, reflects admirably the anecdotal character of the poem: one can well imagine that the adventure (real or imaginary) would have lost nothing in the telling, as the poet recited it to a chosen circle of friends:

> Cefais, pan soniais yna,
> Gwymp dig, nid oedd gampau da;
> Haws codi, drygioni drud,
> Yn drwsgl nog yn dra esgud.
> Trewais, ni neidiais yn iach,
> Y grimog, a gwae'r omach,
> Wrth ystlys, ar waith ostler,
> Ystôl groch ffôl, goruwch ffêr.
> Dyfod, bu chwedl edifar,
> I fyny, Cymry a'm câr,
> Trewais, drwg fydd tra awydd,
> Lle y'm rhoed, heb un llam rhwydd,
> Mynych dwyll amwyll ymwrdd,
> Fy nhalcen wrth ben y bwrdd,
> Lle'dd oedd gawg yrhawg yn rhydd
> A llafar badell efydd.
> Syrthio o'r bwrdd, dragwrdd drefn,
> A'r ddeudrestl a'r holl ddodrefn,
> Rhoi diasbad o'r badell
> I'm hôl, fo'i clywid ymhell;
> Gweiddi, gwr gorwag oeddwn,
> O'r cawg, a'm cyfarth o'r cŵn (GDG 124, 25–46).

*(I made a noise and got a wretched fall—/ nought prospered for me [there]:/ easier it was—foolhardy mischief—/ to get up clumsily than expeditiously./ Not jumping without hurt, I struck/ my shin—woe to my leg—above my ankle/ against the side—some ostler's negligence—of a stupid noisy stool./ Getting up, it was a sorry tale,/ Welshmen love me!/ I struck—for too much eagerness is bad—my brow against the table's edge/ where*

*there was placed for me—I could not jump safe—/ a frequent snare—stupidity to hit it—a basin standing loose/ and a clattering brass bowl./ The table fell—it was a mighty piece of gear—/ with two trestles and all the furniture,/ the brass bowl cried out after me/ —it could be heard far off—/ I was an idiot, with the basin screaming,/ and the dogs barking after me.)*

In *Athrodi ei Was* (GDG 128) ('Defaming His Servant') (which is located in the Anglesey borough of Rhosyr, later Newborough) the poet sends a present of wine to a girl who rejects his advances out of hand, throwing the wine at his messenger's head. *Y Cwt Gwyddau* (GDG 126) ('The Goose-Shed') tells how he took refuge from the fury of the 'Jealous Husband' in a goose-shed where he was set upon by an irate and startled mother-goose, defending her young. This poem comes closer even than *Trafferth mewn Tafarn* to the stock pattern of the medieval *fabliaux*, belonging as they do to the timeless literature of jest and anecdote, which typically present the triangle situation of old husband (*Yr Eiddig* or *Le Jaloux*), young wife and clerk-lover. It is as the latter that Dafydd consistently presents himself, for ever unsuccessful in his frustrated attempts to outwit *Yr Eiddig*.[50] He chooses for himself the clerk's role in another poem which echoes the popular medieval 'Clerk *versus* Knight' controversy,[51] in that he replies to a girl who reproaches him for his cowardice by pointing out to her the advantages which his affectionate care for her could provide over the behaviour of a soldier-lover, who at the first rumour of war would make off for France or Scotland, and come back all covered with scars—if indeed he came back at all.

Poems such as these are the ones whose themes most obviously reflect the poet's awareness of corresponding European literary *genres*. But it would be fruitless to search for exact prototypes for them in such continental models as the *alba* or the *serenade*, the *fabliaux* or the poems of debate. They merely echo poems or songs that Dafydd had at some time heard recited, sung, or read; perhaps in the cultured homes of his aristocratic friends, perhaps in the less exalted company of the taverns he frequented in the boroughs which had been established on the Anglo-Norman pattern. Such poems and songs would have acted as catalysts in his mind, suggesting wholly new and original variants of his own making, in which native and foreign traditions were triumphantly blended. Nor can we ever be certain to what extent such themes had not already become acclimatized in the popular unrecorded verse of the humbler *clêr ofer*, or popular poets,[52] so that Dafydd may even

[50] See ch. 2, pp. 66, 73–4.

[51] Ch. 2, pp. 75–6.

[52] On the *clêr* see GDG 439–41; Morris-Jones, *Cerdd Dafod*, 310 n., and 352, where *clêr* are identified with *oferfeirdd*. The word *clêr* is not attested before the fourteenth century, when both Casnodyn and Gruffudd ap Dafydd ap Tudur both allude to *y glêr ofer*. For *oferfeirdd* see TYP 21–2; TYP[2] 532, and cf. ch. 4 below.

have come to know of them through the medium of Welsh. Some years ago Mr Saunders Lewis memorably epitomized the fusion of cultural traditions which must have existed in parts of western and north-western Britain in the thirteenth and fourteenth centuries, when he said, 'We shall not get a proper idea of the cultural climate of the late Middle Ages in Britain unless we recognize that Anglo-French and Middle English and Welsh were all cheek by jowl in the Welsh Marches and Crown Lordships'.[53] The integration and synthesizing in his poetry of multiple streams of tradition of disparate origin was Dafydd ap Gwilym's supreme achievement.

---

[53] Saunders Lewis (in review of GDG) *Blackfriars* xxxiv (1953), 133; reprinted in A. R. Jones and Gwyn Thomas, *Presenting Saunders Lewis* (UWP 1973), 161.

# X

The question as to whether it was either legitimate or desirable to introduce into Welsh poetry such alien themes as these—bringing with them as they did the unfamiliar imagery of love's sickness and warfare, and of the spears and arrows by which it was inflicted or waged—is the matter at issue in Dafydd's *ymryson* or poetic contest with the Anglesey poet Gruffudd Gryg.[54] There is no need to look for any foreign model for the actual poetic form of this debate, such as the comparable Provencal *tenso*, since bardic contests had long been traditional, alike in Wales and in Ireland; though both the length and the serious implications of this contest were unprecedented. Each poet contributed four *cywyddau* to the debate, and in it real issues are undoubtedly at stake, and issues which are of fundamental importance in the literary history of fourteenth-century Wales. Much, unfortunately, remains extremely obscure in the controversy: not least obscure is the fact that Gruffudd appears to be upholding a conservative view as to poetic standards which gains no support whatever from his own practice of poetry, if we are to judge from the poems which have survived in his name. All of these are in the new *cywydd* metre, and include poems to girls as well as praise-poems addressed to friends and patrons: it is Dafydd, not Gruffudd, whom we know to have composed *awdlau* in praise of patrons in the older traditional metres of *toddaid* and *englyn*.[55] But there can be no mistaking the import of Gruffudd Gryg's initial attack upon Dafydd's verse: he accuses him of monotony of theme and of obvious and blatant 'untruth' by his exaggeration of the plight to which the spears and arrows of his love for Morfudd have reduced him over the past ten years (GDG 147). Such exaggeration would have outraged the conventional standards of truth as recognized hitherto in bardic praise-poetry, and Gruffudd claims that missiles of this kind would have been quite sufficient to kill any other man, even the great Arthur himself. Implicit in this charge is an even deeper one: that of departing from the formal restraints imposed by the *rhieingerdd* convention, in order to introduce improper and irrelevant personal feelings into his poetry.

Dafydd retorts with a much-discussed couplet in which he defends his own practice of the new kind of poetry, defending it as of no less

---

[54] GDG nos. 147–154. On the matters at issue in the *ymryson* see ch. 2, pp. 68–70.
[55] GDG nos. 5, 11–15.

value that that which characterized poetry in the old familiar tradition:

> *Nid llai urddas, heb ras rydd,*
> *No gwawd, geuwawd o gywydd* (GDG 148, 5–6).

*(No less the honour (though) without free favour/ Than a praise-poem, a cywydd of false praise.)*

A '*cywydd* of false praise' means Dafydd's own love-poetry. He asserts that Gruffudd is merely *cynnydd cerdd bun unflwydd* 'the product of the maiden-song of a single year'—which is as much as to say that he is a new-comer to the practice of love-poetry, compared with Dafydd himself. In obscure and even cryptic language, but with striking imagery, Dafydd then asserts that the mature technical accomplishment of his own *cywyddau* is such that it would give distinction even to the meanest of antiquated, worn-out harps, if such a one were to accompany it, or to the tattered pages of the most ragged song-book in which such verses as his own might be written: without the harp's accompaniment of song, or the barely-legible love-poetry inscribed in the book, both of these would by themselves be valueless and even despicable.

> *Telyn ni roddid dwylaw*
> *Ar ei llorf, glaeargorf glaw,*
> *Ni warafun bun o bydd*
> *Ei chyfedd gyda chywydd.*
> *Traethawl yw o cheir trithant,*
> *Traethawr cerdd, truthiwr a'i cant.*
> *Yn nhafarn cwrw anhyful*
> *Tincr a'i cân wrth foly tancr cul.*
> *Hwn a'i teifl, hyn neud diflas*
> *Hen faw ci, hwnnw fo cas.*
>
> *Cwrrach memrwn, wefldwn waith,*
> *I'r dom a fwrid ymaith,*
> *Diddestl wrth ei fedyddiaw*
> *Ei bennill ef, bin a llaw,*
> *A geisir â'i ddyir ddail*
> *A'i bensiwn serch heb unsail* (GDG 148, 11–26).

*(A harp on whose column no hands would be placed, its sounding-board rain-sodden/ —no girl will begrudge it if it is her companion with a cywydd./ It can be played even if it has only three strings,/ proclaiming song, (even) a ministrel (?) has played it./ In a disorderly ale-tavern/ a tinker plays it by his tankard's slender bowl./ He casts it aside—dog's dirt—a loathsome thing, that may (indeed) be hateful.*

*A tattered manuscript (or 'scroll'), of dog-eared form/ that would be cast into the rubbish-heap,/ its verse mis-shapen from its (watery) baptism/ will yet be sought out, pen and hand (i.e. its handwriting) with its withered leaves: with no other basis love will be its reward.)*

Adopting attack as the most satisfactory form of defence, Dafydd
then introduces another issue into the *ymryson*: he claims that Gruffudd
lacks originality, that he takes his subject-matter from the verse of
others, including Dafydd's own poetry, and that in doing so he debases
it—*gwyrodd â'i ben gerdd y byd* (GDG 148, 34) 'his mouth has distorted
everyone's song'. Gruffudd replies by hotly denying the charge that
Dafydd is his *athro*, his teacher in respect to the content of his verse,
and he asserts confidently that his own high attainments are fully recognized in his own country: *Cyd boed cryg ... fy nhafod i ... Nid cryg, myn
Mair, gair o'r gerdd* (GDG 149, 25–8) 'Though my tongue may stammer,
by Mary, there is no stammering in any word of my verse.' And it
is only fair to Gruffudd's defence against the charge of imitating Dafydd,
to recall that his poetic predecessors in Gwynedd included both Hywel
ab Owain Gwynedd and Gruffudd ap Dafydd ap Tudur—two poets
who significantly anticipated Dafydd ap Gwilym in the introduction
of elements of the foreign tradition of *amour courtois* into their poetry.
Gruffudd nevertheless concedes that in the past Dafydd's poetry had
introduced a major novelty into Gwynedd:

> *Hoff oedd yng Ngwynedd, meddynt,*
> *Yn newydd ei gywydd gynt* (GDG 149, 43).

*(A favoured novelty in Gwynedd, they say,/ his cywydd was when new.)*

—it was a short-lived wonder which caused as much stir at the time
as did two other similar marvels: the wooden hobby-horse (an adjunct
of the morris dance) and the new organ in Bangor cathedral—but these
too have long since become familiar and are no longer novelties. In
his second *cywydd*, Dafydd refuses to withdraw his charge of plagiarism
and issues a challenge: since both contestants are *prifeirdd* or established
and qualified poets, let them grapple together in a word-contest in
the manner of their craft—a fitting test, indeed, as to the high degree
of technical accomplishment to which each laid claim. The last two
*cywyddau* by both poets consist of a series of charges and counter-charges
with richly vituperative invective. Gruffudd offers a contest with swords
as an alternative to a word-contest, but claims confidence in his ability
to win in either kind; he is a lion and Dafydd a calf, an eagle-chick
and Dafydd a hen-chick; moreover, he is not a 'Rhys Meigen' to be
slain, as the latter was said to have been, by the weapon of Dafydd's
satire (GDG 151, 70). Dafydd compares Gruffudd to an *arblastr* or
cross-bow, shooting at every target at random (even the Pope receives
no protection) and of being *eithinen iaith Wynedd* (GDG 152, 24) 'gorse-
bush of the speech of Gwynedd'—who can do nothing but hurl abuse.
He claims to have many friends in the north who would welcome him
if he were to visit there, but that if Gruffudd should be so rash as

to come to Dyfed he will be treated (in recollection of an incident in *Mabinogi Pwyll*) as a 'badger in a bag' (GDG 152, 46). There is much obscure allusion and innuendo in the argument which inevitably escapes us, but the scurrilous claim made by both contestants to be the 'father' who has begotten the other is perhaps no more than a crude metaphor reverting to their basic difference: the argument as to the real parentage of the *cywydd bun* or new love-poetry in whose composition Dafydd was plainly regarded by his opponent as the pre-eminent and unassailed master in his own day. The controversy breaks off—if indeed there were not 'missing links' in the shape of poems which have not survived[56]—without any clear decision having been reached either as to Gruffudd's charge of exaggeration or Dafydd's of imitation.

Clearly there was a serious and important issue underlying the *ymryson*, in so far as it concerned the clash between the older established poetic modes and Dafydd's thematic innovations—though the other major poetic innovation of the fourteenth century, the development of the *cywydd* metre, is not an issue at all in their argument: it was the medium accepted by both poets, without comment or justification, as the appropriate medium for their discussion, as indeed it was for them for all kinds of personal and 'untraditional' poetry. It is a great deal more difficult to assess the temperature and the emotional climate of the controversy: how far can the mutual accusations on a personal level be described as 'shadow boxing' (to adopt an apt term from Glanmor Williams),[57] how far do they reflect a tone of genuine anger and bitterness? It is easy to believe that the mood of Gruffudd's opening *cywydd* was urbane enough, but that nevertheless Dafydd could have been genuinely offended by his opponent's charge of insincerity, as well as by the belittling of the reality of his passionate love for Morfudd, with what had perhaps already become for him its tragic consequences. But we do not know that this was so, and probably we can never know.

Some further light on the mutual relationship between the two poets is to be gleaned from the *marwnadau* which each composed upon the other. Both cannot be genuine elegies: probably both are 'fictitious', and were composed during the life-time of the other. It is at least certain that Dafydd's *Marwnad Gruffudd Gryg*[58] was composed during its subject's life-time, and prior to the *ymryson*, to which it makes no allusion at all. It is first and foremost as a love-poet that Dafydd eulogizes his later rival—he is *eos gwŷr Môn* 'the nightingale of Anglesey's men'— and Dafydd allots only two lines to his prowess in praise-poetry: *Gweddw y barnaf gerdd dafawd/ Ac weithian gwan ydyw gwawd* (GDG 20, 55–6)

[56] According to David Jones, Llanfair, there were 22 poems in the *ymryson* (BDG xviii, n.), but these have not survived; see D. J. Bowen, LlC viii, 11n., and ch. 2, p. 70, n. 53 below.
[57] Glanmor Williams, *The Welsh Church from Conquest to Reformation* (UWP 1962) 192.
[58] GDG p. 427.

'Widowed I adjudge the craft of song,/ and now weak is praise'. But Gruffudd Gryg's *marwnad*[58] to Dafydd refers explicitly to the *ymryson*, and in words which suggest that serious feelings were involved in it; he recognizes there to have been error on both sides, and forgives Dafydd for his words. In spite of his earlier denial, he acknowledges Dafydd to have been his teacher and he his pupil, and places Dafydd in the long line of poets from Aneirin, Taliesin, and Myrddin, to Cynddelw Brydydd Mawr and the poets of the Welsh princes. That is to say, he puts all the emphasis of his praise on Dafydd as an upholder of the classical tradition of praise-poetry, going back to the earliest times, and—strangely enough—makes no allusion whatever to his love-poetry.

The essentials of Dafydd's defence of his poetry in the *ymryson* are set forth in plainer and more unambiguous terms, though transposed into a somewhat different context, in his dialogue poem with the Grey Friar. He imagines the Friar as rebuking him in the confessional for his way of life, and urging him, in what must have been the familiar tones of an itinerant Franciscan preacher,[59] to consider the needs of his soul and to abandon love's pursuit and its celebration in song. Dafydd's reply is that there is room in the world for people of all kinds, and that there is a time for everything, and that to compose verse in praise of girls is commendable, since God himself has not disdained the tribute of praise-poetry:

> Pand englynion ac odlau
> Yw'r hymnau a'r segwensiau?
> A chywyddau i Dduw lwyd
> Yw sallwyr Dafydd Broffwyd (GDG 137, 57–60).

*(What else are hymns and sequences but englynion and odes?/ The psalms of the prophet David are themselves 'cywyddau' to holy God.)*

Dr Gwenallt Jones has called this poem 'the most important of Dafydd's poems from the point of view of literary criticism'[60] but the defence which Dafydd makes is one which he amplifies more fully, though in less simple language, in the *ymryson*. The *traethodl* which Dafydd chooses as his medium for the imagined dialogue with the Friar is a looser and humbler verse-form than the *cywydd*, in that the strict rules of *cynghanedd* are not dominant in it; and this choice of a popular measure, it has been suggested, may itself reflect the custom of friars in other lands of composing carols and popular songs as a medium for elementary religious instruction.

[59] Cf. D. J. Bowen, LlC x, 115–18.
[60] D. Gwenallt Jones 'Rhethreg yng Nghyfundrefn y Beirdd', *Y Llenor* xii (1933).

# XI

As yet there is no final agreement among scholars as to the authentic canon of Dafydd ap Gwilym's poetry. Many would like to see restored to this canon several very fine poems, previously accepted, which Dr Parry has excluded from his critical edition of the poet's work—in particular the *cywyddau Yr Sêr* and *Yr Eira* ('The Stars' and 'The Snow'), *I'r Llwyn Banadl* ('To the Grove of Broom') and *Claddu'r Bardd o Gariad* ('The Poet's Burial for Love') and a couple of poems urging a nun to forsake her calling in the interests of love—all of them poems which have since received honourable inclusion in Dr Parry's OXFORD BOOK OF WELSH VERSE, under the caption 'Anonymous'. The difficulty in establishing the true canon has increased and grown over the years, owing to the fact that from the fifteenth century onwards scribes engaged in copying the *cywyddau* in manuscripts have been tempted to append the name 'Dafydd ap Gwilym' to an increasingly large number of poems, which cannot by any means all have been his work—hence the attribution to Dafydd of nearly two hundred and fifty poems in the 1789 BARDDON-IAETH DAFYDD AP GWILYM. These false attributions have led to an amount of confusion in determining the poet's genuine work which was not helped by Iolo Morganwg's inclusion, as an 'Appendix' to the same volume, of sixteen additional poems of his own composition. These were accepted by everyone as authentic for a century afterwards, until in 1926 G. J. Williams in a brilliant analysis[61] proved them to be skilful imitations of Dafydd's characteristic manner.

Nevertheless, Dr Parry's authoritative edition has laid down the main lines which help to distinguish poems composed in the fourteenth century from those of the fifteenth; though within the fourteenth century itself we still lack secure criteria by which to distinguish Dafydd's own work from that of some gifted contemporary. But a clearer understanding of the poet's identity emerges as a whole from a study of the poems assembled together and edited by Dr Parry; though the publication of the greatly improved texts of the poems which he has made available has meant that a great deal of earlier critical work, particularly in relation to external influences, has needed to be severely modified in their light.

Even allowing for marginal uncertainty as to the authentic canon, the hundred and fifty poems which Dr Parry has published in Dafydd's name represent a larger *corpus* of verse than has been preserved of the work of any other medieval Welsh poet (not excepting Tudur Aled). The survey which I have given above has indicated the range of Dafydd's

---

[61] G. J. Williams, *Iolo Morganwg a Chywyddau'r Ychwanegiad* (1926).

poetry both in themes and in variety of styles, and the excerpts given
from his work will (I hope) have indicated something of his confident
mastery of his chosen medium, and of the linguistic and metrical
resources which enabled Dafydd to extend and to develop the *cywydd*
to suit the widely varied purposes to which he adapted the metre of
his choice. The 'new dimension' which Dafydd gave to Welsh poetry
is epitomized above all in his manipulation of the language: his demand
for a constant awareness on the part of his hearers to all the potential
nuances held by any given word is underlined by his use of imaginative
imagery, as expressed both in his *dyfalu*, and in his more elaborately
developed metaphors—these may, indeed, be occasionally developed
throughout the length of a whole poem, as in *Morfudd fel yr Haul*
(GDG 42) ('Morfudd like the Sun'), *Yr Ysgyfarnog* (GDG 116) ('The
Hare') and *Hwsmonaeth Cariad* (GDG 87) ('Love's Husbandry'). This
special *expertise* is evinced also in the superimposition of one layer of
meaning upon another—at times such a meaning may even seem to
be opposed to it—both in ambiguous words and couplets, and in whole
poems which may be interpreted upon more than one level.

Such an imaginative demand upon his hearers, whatever may have
been the degree to which it was fulfilled by the original listeners to
Dafydd's *cywyddau*, must inevitably go beyond the capacity of modern
readers to fulfil in every detail. We are ignorant of the circumstances
which led to the composition of any given poem, and the attrition of
the intervening six centuries has placed us at too great a disadvantage
with respect to background knowledge. Too frequently, indeed, we feel
at a loss by reason of our inability to adjust ourselves to such strange
conventions as that of the fictitious *marwnad*, to the undercurrents
obviously present in the debate between Dafydd and Gruffudd Gryg:
or, above all, perhaps, to Dafydd's audacious use of religious imagery
(which he shares with other medieval poets), by which religious formulas are borrowed in order to give poignancy to secular matter. *Offeren
y Llwyn* (GDG 122) ('The Woodland Mass') and *Galw ar Ddwynwen*
(GDG 94) ('Invoking St Dwynwen') certainly demand a response on contrasting if not on opposing levels: the level of genuine devotion is as
assured in these poems as is that of supremely daring and provocative
fantasy.

This difficulty, which recurs not infrequently, as to the precise manner
in which we ought properly to respond to individual poems, has led
to a degree of uncertainty and disagreement as to what *kind* of a poet
Dafydd ap Gwilym may be. As far back as the eighteenth century,
when Goronwy Owen meted out to him the disparagement of faint
praise by saying that he 'often wished that he (Dafydd) had raised
his thoughts to something more grave and sublime'[62] we can trace

[62] *Poetical Works of the Rev. Goronwy Owen*, ed. Robert Jones (London, 1876), II, 26.

the nucleus of the idea that Dafydd was a 'gifted amateur' who composed light verse for the delectation of an intimate circle; a supremely sensitive craftsman in language and in metrical *finesse*, no doubt, but nevertheless a poet who has left behind no testimony to any profundity of thought beyond these qualities—that he lacked, in fact, the quality of 'high poetic seriousness' which Matthew Arnold denied to his very different, but no less great contemporary, Geoffrey Chaucer.

This view seems to me to be wholly untenable. Indeed, the evidence which is to be adduced from the poems as now presented to us in Dr Parry's edition renders it difficult, one would think, to maintain it further. The spectrum of changing moods which this poetry reflects includes both subtle indications and, more rarely, overt expression of deep and sombre reflection on the fleetingness of all that makes life lovely. Morfudd's beauty, though it has caused the poet a life-time of sleeplessness and sorrow, is in the end, after all, only a dream:

*Breuddwyd yw: ebrwydded oes* (GDG 139, 36).

*(It is a dream: how swiftly life passes.)*

*Yr Adfail* ('The Ruin') is a poignant presentation of a theme which hauntingly pervades both medieval Welsh and also medieval Irish poetry—the lament for a ruined and desolated homestead. The poet addresses the fallen masonry:

> *Ai'r gwynt a wnaeth helynt hwyr?*
> *Da y nithiodd dy do neithiwyr.*
> *Hagr y torres dy esyth;*
> *Hudol enbyd yw'r byd byth.*
> *Dy gongl, man ddeongl ddwyoch,*
> *Gwely ym oedd, nid gwâl moch,*
> *Doe'r oeddud mewn gradd addwyn*
> *Yn glyd uwchben fy myd mwyn;*
> *Hawdd o ddadl, heddiw'dd ydwyd,*
> *Myn Pedr, heb na chledr na chlwyd.*
> *Amryw bwnc ymwnc amwyll,*
> *Ai hwn yw'r bwth twn bath twyll?* (GDG 144, 29–42)

*('Was it the Wind which caused of late this havoc?/ Last night it swept right through your roof;/ ugly the way in which it tore your spars:/ A dangerous deception is the world always./ Your corner—mine to interpret with two sighs—was my bed: it was no lair for pigs./ You were yesterday in happy state/ being a shelter overhead for my sweet love;/ today, by Peter—a matter of ease—/ no rafter and no cover has been left to you./ So many, so diverse the causes of delusion:/ can some such deception be this ruined shack?')*

The Ruin then answers the poet:

> *Aeth talm o waith y teulu,*
> *Dafydd, â chroes; da foes fu.*

*(Dafydd, the household's span of work is done,/ beneath the cross: it was a decent way of life.)*

Reflection on the universal human predicament gives rise, very occasionally, to the expression of a pessimism more characteristic of Dafydd's fifteenth-century successor Siôn Cent:

> *Rhidyll hudolaidd rhydwn,*
> *Rhyw fyd ar ei hyd yw hwn.*
> *Y macwy llawen heno*
> *Hyfryd ei fywyd a fo,*
> *Breuddwyd aruthr ebrwyddarw,*
> *A dry yfory yn farw* (GDG 19, 1–6).

*(This world throughout is like a broken sieve;/ a lad who may be joyous tonight, however happy his life may be/ —a terrible swift harsh dream/ will strike him dead tomorrow.)*

These lines certainly admit of interpretation in either a general or in a particular sense, with reference to the contemporary situation in newly-conquered Wales: life is at best uncertain, and death may at any time violently supervene. Dafydd makes oblique, but never direct, references to contemporary conditions: for instance, in the frequent figurative use of borrowed technical terms relating to legal administration and to the new officialdom—the Cock Thrush is consecutively a *siryf* 'sheriff', *ustus* 'justice' and *ystiwart llys* 'steward of the court'. Pleading with Morfudd for admittance beneath the dripping eaves outside her home, he comments with weighty significance:

> *Ni bu'n y Gaer yn Arfon*
> *Geol waeth no'r heol hon* (GDG 89, 27–8).

*(There was never in Caernarfon castle a worse jail than is this road.)*

Characteristically, it is in relation to his idealized bird-life that Dafydd lets fall what is perhaps his saddest allusion to his country's predicament—there are inescapable overtones in the lines in which he alludes to the care-free existence of birds as that of:

> *Cenedl â dychwedl dichwerw*
> *Cywion cerddorion caer dderw* (GDG 121, 21–2).

The second line means 'the fledgeling minstrels of the oak-tree fortress', and the first line is in apposition to it: it can be interpreted either as 'a people of sweet discourse' or as 'a nation whose history is not bitter'—as good an example as any of Dafydd's ambivalence. *Y Mwdwl Gwair* ('The Haycock') gives a remarkable extended image which compares the abrupt scything of the meadow-grass with the fate of *arglwyddi*—the lords who may in like manner be removed at any moment and be hung without warning:

> *Erfai o un y'th luniwyd,*
> *Un fath, llydan dwynpath llwyd,*
> *Un dramgwydd ag arglwyddi*
> *Teg, ac un artaith wyd di.*
> *Ef a'th las â dur glas glew,*
> *Bwrdais y weirglodd byrdew.*
> *Yfory, sydd yty sir,*
> *O'th lasgae, wair, y'th lusgir.*
> *Drennydd, uwch y llanw manwair,*
> *Dy grogi, a gwae fi, Fair!* (GDG 62, 19–28)

*(Faultlessly you were shaped by someone,/ in a like manner, broad grey mound,/ and of like destiny to that of noble lords,/ and you are like them too in agony./ By a blue blade you have been boldly slain,/ the burgess of the hay-field, short and thick./ Tomorrow— joy that is awaiting you—/ from your green field, hay, you will be dragged./ Next day, above the tide of stubble/ you will be hanged, woe's to me, Mary!)*

Imagery of this kind springs from an attitude in the poet's mind which transcends any conventional use of personification, for it emanates from an impulse to reach out and encounter sentient life in all created things, both animate and inanimate, in the wind, in mist and snow and rain, and in the very seasons themselves. The birds who are the poet's most congenial companions are the small musicians and poets of the woodland, the Stag is a 'tall baron'; but equally the Haycock is a 'burgess' and has a soul which the poet commends to heaven, and the Ruin is credited implicitly with a personal capacity to mourn the warm human life which has departed from it. Summer is 'a fair woodward', the month of May 'a strong horseman' and 'a generous nobleman'. Above all, the Wind is a *gŵr eres* 'a marvellous being', whose essential nature is most fully described by reference to the human restrictions from which its cosmic freedom renders it exempt. Dafydd looks up and around, and can express his awed reverence before the major forces of the universe no less than before the small miracles of the surrounding woodland: the Wind, the depths of the high firmament to which the Skylark ascends, and the Stars which pattern the night sky. Yet the Wind, like the Skylark, is in imagination tamed to do the poet's bidding, and to act as his love-messenger.

These are ways in which Dafydd's poetic personality emerges more distinctively than had ever been found attainable, or even conceivable, by any Welsh poet.

In common with some other medieval poets,[63] Dafydd has left us his Retraction, or poem of recantation, *Edifeirwch* ('Repentance') in which he recalls his life's pressing pre-occupation, and pleads for divine forgiveness:

> *Prydydd i Forfudd wyf fi,*
> *Prid o swydd, prydais iddi.*
> *Myn y Gŵr a fedd heddiw*
> *Mae gwayw i'm pen am wen wiw,*
> *Ac i'm tâl mae gofalglwyf;*
> *Am aur o ddyn marw ydd wyf.*
> *Pan ddêl, osgel i esgyrn,*
> *Angau a'i chwarelau chwyrn,*
> *Dirfawr fydd hoedl ar derfyn,*
> *Darfod a wna tafod dyn.*
> *Y Drindod, rhag cydfod cwyn,*
> *A mawr ferw, a Mair Forwyn*
> *A faddeuo 'ngham dramwy,*
> *Amen, ac ni chanaf mwy* (GDG 106, 1–14).

*(I am Morfudd's poet:/ I sang to her, it was a costly task./ By Him who rules today/ my head aches for the fair girl,/ and sickening sorrow wears my brow;/ for my golden girl I die./ When death comes, cramping the bones,/ with its sharp arrows,/ life's end will be stupendous,/ man's tongue will become silent./ Lest there come lamentation with great misery/ may the Trinity and the Virgin Mary/ forgive me for my great offences,/ Amen, and I shall sing no more.)*

After a life-time in which he gave expression to so great a capacity both for joy and for suffering, it is to be hoped that the poet may have finally closed his eyes in peace.

---

[63] Exx: Llywelyn Goch ap Meurig Hen (RP 1301); Gruffudd ap Maredudd (RP 1332–4) Siôn Cent (IGE² lxxxiv). These may be compared with the *marwysgafnau* or death-bed poems of earlier poets; see Glanmor Williams, *Welsh Church*, 111. Chaucer's 'Retraction' at the end of his Parson's Tale may also be compared.

# 2. TRADITION AND INNOVATION IN THE POETRY OF DAFYDD AP GWILYM

THE Honourable Society of Cymmrodorion has had a long and close association with the study of Dafydd ap Gwilym. This association started as far back as the year 1789, when Owain Myfyr (a former secretary of the Society) financed and organized the publication of the first edition of Dafydd ap Gwilym's poems, a work which was published under the editorship of William Owen Pughe.[1] What we may call the international aspects of Dafydd ap Gwilym's poetry have claimed the attention of scholars for nearly a century,[2] and important pioneer articles on this subject appeared in *Y Cymmrodor* for the year 1878 by Professor E. B. Cowell, and in the Society's *Transactions* for the years 1906–8 by the Rev. G. Hartwell Jones, the Rev. J. Machreth Rees

---

[1] Owen Jones and William Owen Pughe: *Barddoniaeth Dafydd ap Gwilym* (London, 1789). This work was based primarily on the manuscript collections made by the Morris brothers, and the publication was officially sponsored by the Gwyneddigion. See T. Parry, 'Barddoniaeth Dafydd ap Gwilym, 1789', *Journal of the Welsh Bibliographical Society*, VIII (1954–7), 189 ff.; GDG¹ lxxvi, clxv–ix; *History of the Cymmrodorion*, 97.

[2] 'Nearly two centuries' would be more correct, had Iolo Morganwg published his speculations concerning Rhys Goch ap Rhiccert and Troubadour influences in Wales, which remained unpublished during his life-time. The following passage appears in his *History of the Bards* (Llanover MS. C 21) 134–5: 'About 1130 flourished Rhys Goch ap Rhiccert ap Collwyn in Glamorgan ... In this poet's sentiments and manner we find something of the manner of the Provençal Troubadours. The Norman barons who had settled in Glamorgan were those who opened the way for this new cast in poetry, their castles and courts were the Gates through which it entered Wales ... In the works of Rhys Goch ap Rhiccert the clear dawn of this new manner appears, which in a century and a half afterwards brightened into the bright summer of Dafydd ap Gwilym'. Brief extracts from this work were published by Cadrawd, *Gwaith Iolo Morganwg* (*Cyfres y Fil*, 1913). On Rhys Goch ap Rhiccert see further G. J. Williams, *Iolo Morganwg a Chywyddau'r Ychwanegiad* (London, 1926); *Iolo Morganwg* (UWP 1956) 297. The poems attributed by Iolo to Rhys Goch were printed by Taliesin ab Iolo in the *Iolo MSS.* (1848) 228–251, and have been recently re-edited by P. J. Donovan, *Cerddi Rhydd Iolo Morganwg* (UWP 1980).

and Professor W. Lewis Jones.[3] All these essays were directed towards
setting Dafydd's poetry in a European context: they examined external
parallels and suggested the possibility of foreign literary influences.
Then, in the *Transactions* for 1913–14, Sir Ifor Williams's long discussion[4]
inaugurated a new era in the study of this aspect of the poet's
work.

All these, and certain other early studies,[5] came to be synthesized
and developed further in a monumental book by a Dutch scholar, the
late Theodor Chotzen, whose *Recherches sur la Poésie de Dafydd ap Gwilym*
was published at Amsterdam in 1927. This has remained until the
present day the standard work on the subject of Dafydd's indebtedness
to foreign literature and ideas—a mine of information for all investiga-
tors. Nevertheless, it would be difficult to name any one of the contributory studies drawn upon by Chotzen which has not seen very great
advances in the forty years which have now elapsed since the publication
of his book. First and foremost, we now have an inestimable advantage
in Dr Thomas Parry's critical edition, *Gwaith Dafydd ap Gwilym*
(1952)—a major work of scholarship which has made substantial progress towards determining the linguistic and metrical criteria by which
we may distinguish the *cywyddau* of the fourteenth century from those
which are of later date. We now have a working basis which Chotzen
did not have, and it is inevitable that it should make necessary the
modification of some of his conclusions.

In one sense, of course, it is true that the output of a major poet
can stand above the quest for sources. This view is indeed frequently
taken by the literary critic, who would claim that the investigation
of sources can have no relevant bearing on our appreciation of a poet's
work, and is of interest purely as a matter of literary history. I do
not believe, however, that questions of literary sources and influences
can ultimately be separated from questions of literary value: all such
studies may contribute to the appreciation of a poet's response to his
intellectual surroundings, and so to the comprehension of his achievement.[6] The investigation of such literary influences as may have

---

[3] E. B. Cowell, 'Dafydd ap Gwilym', *Cy.* II (1878) 101 ff.; G. Hartwell Jones, 'Italian
Influence on Celtic Literature' THSC 1905–6, 84 ff.; J. Machreth Rees, 'Dafydd ap
Gwilym a'i Gyfnod', *ibid.* 31 ff.; W. Lewis Jones 'The Literary Relationships of Dafydd
ap Gwilym' THSC 1907–8, 118 ff.

[4] 'Dafydd ap Gwilym a'r Glêr', THSC, 1913–14, 83–204.

[5] The most important of these was L. C. Stern, 'Davydd ab Gwilym, ein walisischer
Minnesänger', *Zeitschrift für celtische Philologie*, VII, 1–251.

[6] 'Considered in its full implication, the problem of literary influence is an integral
part of the problem of literary creation, and this can never be differentiated—not to
say solved—until what a writer of genius does with his material becomes the object
of a more intuitive type of scholarship than is common today.'—P. Mansell-Jones, *Background of Modern French Poetry* (Cambridge, 1951) vii. These words have been quoted
by Professor E. Vinaver as a preliminary to his study of the use made by Sir Thomas

reached Dafydd from outside Wales, and the manner in which he responded to them, is one which I do not think can properly be neglected from any full study of his versatile genius: it is also one to which scholarship in recent years has paid the least attention, and which certainly needs re-examination now that we have the new edition. In the case of Dafydd ap Gwilym, I suggest also that such studies may even have their part to play in determining what individual qualities of style and treatment can be recognized as distinguishing his authentic work from that of his contemporaries and successors. And this is, after all, the major problem which confronts the present generation with respect to Dafydd ap Gwilym: for, in a manner comparable to his remote predecessors Aneirin and Taliesin, the distinction recognized both by his contemporaries and by succeeding generations has caused the accumulation round his name of a mass of spurious verse. Thus Dr Parry's intensive study of fourteenth-century language and metrics has reduced the canon of the poems which he regards as authentic to rather over half the number which are attributed to Dafydd in the 1789 edition, and less than half of those which are attributed to him in the manuscripts. Even if it should turn out that this estimate requires further extension or modification in the future, it can safely be presumed that much dead wood has now been cleared away, and, as a result, it is already apparent that contemporary scholarship is beginning to turn to the problem of what may constitute personal characteristics in the poet's work, in a way which was hardly possible before.

In the last forty years, also, much fresh work has been done upon the literary works in other languages which have most bearing on the study of Dafydd ap Gwilym: on Troubadour poetry, on the medieval lyric in Latin, French and English, and on the influence of Ovid on the Middle Ages—particularly in respect to a very relevant and influential French poem of the thirteenth century, that is, the *Roman de la Rose*.[7] Again, on the purely Welsh side, much progress has taken place in the last forty years in the study of the poets who were Dafydd's

---

Malory of his antecedent French sources, *The Arthurian Legend in the Middle Ages*, ed. R. S. Loomis (Oxford, 1959), 546. They are no less appropriate to the study of Dafydd ap Gwilym's poetry, even though the external influences upon his work are far less easily traced than is the case with Malory.

[7] A few outstanding titles must suffice: F. J. E. Raby, *Secular Latin Poetry in the Middle Ages* (1934: second ed. 1957); A. Jeanroy, *La Poésie Lyrique des Troubadours* (1934); C. S. Lewis, *The Allegory of Love* (1936); G. Paré, *Les ideés et les lettres au XIIIe siècle: Le Roman de la Rose*, (Montreal, 1947); Carleton Brown, *English Lyrics of the Thirteenth Century* (1932); G. L. Brook, *The Harley Lyrics* (1948). The Welsh affinities of the Harley Lyrics have become even clearer in the years which have elapsed since Sir Ifor Williams in THSC 1913–14 first drew attention to their importance in relation to Dafydd's literary background. To this list should now be added P. Dronke, *Medieval Latin and the Rise of European Love Lyric* (Oxford, 1965); L. T. Topsfield, *Troubadours and Love* (Cambridge, 1975).

predecessors, contemporaries and immediate successors, upon the early
Bardic Grammar,[8] upon the development of *cynghanedd* and of the
*cywydd* metre—and here again I must refer to the important contributions published in the *Transactions* of this Society in the 1930's by Professor W. J. Gruffydd[9] and by Dr Thomas Parry,[10] and to the volume
devoted to Sir Idris Bell's study of the poet in 1942.[11] Progress has
also been made in the editing and evaluation of the *canu rhydd*,[12] and
this too has its importance in relation to Dafydd ap Gwilym. All
branches of these studies have seen such rapid progress in the last
years, and are continuing to progress in such a way that my remarks
now can only be regarded as of an interim nature. I should like, then,
to try to re-define a few of the many outstanding problems concerning
Dafydd ap Gwilym—problems which, in any case, it is easier to set
forth than to provide with satisfactory answers. And, incidentally, I
should like to stress the importance for this study of work which has
been proceeding in other fields and has, for the most part, been quite
differently orientated. For instance, much of the research that has gone
into the social and literary background of Chaucer's poetry has its
relevance to the study of his near-contemporary Dafydd ap Gwilym.
Then, if we look at the literature of the country which is Wales's other
neighbour, across the sea, we find that in Ireland during the life-time
of Dafydd ap Gwilym, the third Earl of Desmond was engaged in composing love-poetry on the French model, but in the strict metres of
Irish bardic verse—a parallel fusing of the Celtic with the continental
tradition to that which was taking place in Wales at the same time.[13]
In Ireland also, the thesis has been recently advanced that many of
the themes of medieval French courtly verse were introduced in the
wake of the Norman Conquest, to survive by a long sub-literary tradition

[8] G. J. Williams and E. J. Jones, *Gramadegau'r Penceirddiaid*, see ch. 4 below.

[9] 'Rhagarweiniad i Farddoniaeth Cymru cyn Dafydd ap Gwilym', THSC, 1937, 257 ff.

[10] 'Twf y Gynghanedd', THSC, 1936, pp. 143 ff.; 'Datblygiad y Cywydd', THSC, 1939, 209 ff.

[11] *Dafydd ap Gwilym: Fifty Poems*; with Introductory Essays by Idris Bell and David Bell (Hon. Soc. Cymmrodorion, 1942).

[12] T. H. Parry-Williams, *Canu Rhydd Cynnar* (UWP, 1932); Brinley Rees, *Dulliau'r Canu Rhydd* (UWP, 1952); D. Gwenallt Jones, *Y Ficer Prichard* a '*Canwyll y Cymry*' (Caernarfon, 1946).

[13] On Gerald third Earl of Desmond (1359–98), see T. F. O'Rahilly, *Dánta Grádha* (Cork, 1926), no. 4, and introduction by R. Flower; R. Flower, *The Irish Tradition* (Oxford, 1947), 143–4 (here 'fourth' should read 'third earl'; see G. Murphy, *Eigse* ii, p. 64). The *duanaire* or poem-book of Gerald the Earl from the fifteenth-century Book of Fermoy has recently been edited (in Irish) for the first time by Gearóid mac Niocaill, *Studia Hibernica*, 3 (1963), 7 ff. Cf. J. E.Caerwyn Williams, *Traddodiad Llenyddol Iwerddon*, 153–4; Frank O'Connor, *Kings, Lords, and Commons* (London, 1961), x. (Since writing this, a similar comparison has been made independently by Gwyn ap Gwilym 'Dafydd ap Gwilym a Gearoid Iarla', *Taliesin* 28, 43–51).

which eventually came to the surface in the popular free-metre poetry of the seventeenth and eighteenth centuries.[14] There is here the possibility of an analogy which could have considerable importance for the relation subsisting between Dafydd's poetry and certain of the themes in the Welsh *canu rhydd*, a subject about which we know all too little as yet.

I have taken 'Tradition and Innovation' as my title, because in order to form any estimate of the new influences which came into Welsh poetry with Dafydd ap Gwilym and his contemporaries, it is of course necessary to examine both sides of the question, and to try to understand as much as we can about the literary inheritance which Dafydd received from his predecessors. Here I should like to quote the words in which, after the lapse of a quarter of a century, Sir Ifor Williams alluded retrospectively to the conviction which inspired his own study of this subject:

> *(Ni) fedrwn i ddeall canu Dafydd ap Gwilym heb fynd y tu allan i Gymru. Fedrwn i mo'i ddeall ef chwaith heb gofio ei ddyled i feirdd ei wlad ei hun yn y canrifoedd o'i flaen ef. Mewn llenyddiaeth fyw ceir dwy duedd sy'n mantoli ei gilydd, sef cadw'r hen, a chroesawu'r newydd. Bob tro y cawn fudiad llenyddol newydd ym mywyd Cymru, dyna sy'n digwydd, ieuo'n gymharus elfennau Cymreig ag elfennau estron, a ffrwyth y briodas honno fydd genedigaeth a chreadigaeth newydd, arbennig i'n gwlad a'n cenedl ni.[15]*

Dr Parry's edition begins with a series of twenty-one poems composed partly, but not wholly, in the older metres of *englyn* and *awdl*, and in the conventional style. They deal with the traditional themes of twelfth- and thirteenth-century bardic poetry: eulogy and elegy addressed to patrons, an interesting example of satire, and a handful of religious poems.[16] This group includes the important praise-poems to Dafydd's patron, Ifor Hael, whose authenticity Dr Parry has indeed questioned, but on external rather than on internal evidence, and this evidence has subsequently received a different interpretation by other scholars.[17] These bardic poems as a group express all the old *ethos* of the Gogynfeirdd: the praise of noble descent and the virtues of courage and generosity,

---

[14] Seán Ó Tuama, *An Grá in Amhráin na nDaoine* (Dublin, 1960).

[15] *('I was not able to understand Dafydd ap Gwilym's poetry without going outside Wales. Nor was I able to understand it without remembering Dafydd's debt to the poets of his own land in the centuries which preceded him. In a living literature there are two tendencies which balance each other: to preserve what is old, and to welcome what is new. Each time that we encounter a new Welsh literary movement, this is what happens, Welsh elements become mated with foreign elements, and the fruit of this conjunction is the birth of a new creation which is unique to our country and to our nation.')* THSC, 1938, 52–3.

[16] To those included in GDG should now be added the *englynion* 'I'r Grog o Gaer', *Llawysgrif Hendregadredd*, 312–13; see GDG[2] (1963), xix, 556.

[17] Saunders Lewis, LlC ii, 201–2; Dafydd Bowen, 'Dafydd ap Gwilym a Morgannwg', LlC v, 164–73. For a discussion of the evidence, and a further suggestion, see now GDG[2], xix–xxii; Gwyn Thomas, LlC vii, 249–251, Eurys Rowlands, LlC viii, 109.

with the repeated assertion that the bard's patron has no peer,[18] the interdependence of bard and patron, and the idea of the intimate relation subsisting between a ruler and his territory, which commemorates his death by storms and swollen rivers. The *marwnadau* re-iterate the persistent Celtic elegiac theme of the lament for the deserted home, and the manner in which the poet addresses the dead man directly, calling on him to rise up and answer, is another feature typical of laments both in Welsh and in Irish.[19] The imagery characteristic of the praise-poetry of preceding centuries is recurrent: Llywelyn and Ifor are, in turn, referred to metaphorically as a stag, a hawk, a lion, an eagle. The full range of reference to the characters of early heroic tradition is employed for the purpose of eulogy: Ifor Hael derives the epithet which has clung to him from a comparison of his generosity with that of Nudd, Rhydderch and Mordaf, in the ancient triad of the *Tri Hael* or Three Generous Men[20] (GDG 7, 10), and Dafydd compares Ifor's home to *neuadd Reged*—the hall of Taliesin's patron, Urien—and speaks of himself as another Taliesin, for the rewards which he has received from Ifor (GDG 9, 33–35; 10, 27–34). Again, the *marwnad* to Llywelyn describes him as *Deifr helgud* (GDG 13, 13), 'pursuer of the men of Deira'—by now an epithet which must have lost much of its meaning, but one which leads directly back to the cradle of Welsh poetic tradition in the old British North, and implies a familiarity on the part of Dafydd's audience with all the old concepts of praise-poetry. The antithesis of all this encomiastic imagery was traditionally expressed by the Court Poets in satire and abuse—and we have as an example Dafydd's satire on a rival poet, Rhys Meigen (GDG 21), whose personal characteristics and wretched verse are attacked in a string of *englynion* so involved and obscure in their range of abuse that it is not too difficult to credit the later story that the unfortunate victim fell down dead as the result of hearing them.[21] Whether true or false, the tradition is a forcible reminder of the supernatural power which was always attributed to the words of the poet in early Celtic society; and there are many comparable examples in Irish of the devastating effects brought about by a poet's satire, as well as of the extortionate demands the poets were enabled to make by reason of the fear of being satirized. As late as the fifteenth century, a parallel instance is recorded of an Irish poet's

[18] The figure corresponds with Curtius's *topoi* of 'inexpressibility' and 'outdoing'; *European Literature and the Latin Middle Ages* (English edn. trans. W. R. Trask, 1962), 159, 162.

[19] In YB i, 131, R. G. Gruffydd cites parallels to this feature in *Marwnad Lleucu Llwyd*. Cf. also CLlH, I, 17–21.

[20] On the outstanding popularity of this triad among the bards at all periods, see TYP, 5–6, and introduction lxxv–vi.

[21] GDG[1] lxix–lxx (=GDG[2] xl–xli).

satire causing death.[22] Satire and eulogy were in both countries the two complementary facets of the bardic tradition, and the deadly effects attributed to the one emphasize by implication the great social significance attached to the other. All professional poets must indeed be able to show their paces in both, as is recognized by Dafydd in his contention with Gruffudd Gryg, when he offers his opponent a contest in words, as an alternative to one with swords, and Gruffudd then refers back to the earlier incident by asserting that he is not a Rhys Meigen to be slain by satire (GDG 150, 39–44; 151, 70). In all these bardic poems, Dafydd shows himself to be an adept in the earlier metrical techniques, and with all the resources of the traditional learning at his command. This is apparent in the richness of his vocabulary, imagery, and allusion to historical and legendary matter, including the knowledge he shows of old legal terminology. We can observe the apparatus of praise-poetry being transferred into the new *cywydd* metre, and these poems give evidence that Dafydd could excel in the *cywydd mawl* no less than in the *cywydd serch*. But I think it is noticeable that the older modes of expression are used for what is most deeply felt, and thus it is the *englyn* or a combination of *englyn* and *toddaid* which is used in the personal laments composed on the death of his uncle, of Ifor Hael and of Angharad,[23] while the *cywydd* is employed for the less formal lament for Rhydderch (composed on behalf of another person) and for the fictitious *marwnadau* to fellow-poets still living.

Dr Parry has shown that the adaptation of the *cywydd* to praise-poetry was a metrical innovation of the fourteenth century, for which it is questionable whether Dafydd can be held as personally responsible.[24] In a great number of ways, the themes and techniques of the older poetry were carried over into the new metre; and it is in the first place, as an example of this continuity of the accepted moulds of bardic expression that I would like to refer to Dafydd's *Ymryson* with Gruffudd Gryg. For contentions in verse between rival poets were a feature of the common Celtic bardic tradition, and go back to an early date both in Wales and in Ireland. Although there was a general and widespread fondness throughout the Middle Ages for debates of all kinds, the form given to this contest can be fully accounted for as arising out of native poetic

[22] Sir John Stanley, Lord Lieutenant of Ireland, was satirized by Niall Ó'hUiginn, and 'lived after this satire but five weeks, for he died of the virulence of the lampoons'. The event is said to have taken place in 1414 (*Annals of the Four Masters*, ed. John O'Donovan (Dublin, 1848), ii, 819). See also J. E. Caerwyn Williams, *Traddodiad Llenyddol Iwerddon*, 147.

[23] GDG nos. 11, 13, 16. The last poem is striking in its conformity with the older tradition; as an elegy on a woman, it invites comparison with Gruffudd ap Maredudd's *awdl* to Gwenhwyfar o Fôn, *Oxford Book of Welsh Verse*, no. 38, rather than with any of Dafydd ap Gwilym's other work.

[24] THSC, 1939, 215. See ch. 4 below.

conventions, whatever may be said as to the deeper issues which may be involved in it. I think, therefore, that there is no need to attach much weight to the comparison which has been made at various times between the form of the *Ymryson* and the poetic debates which occur in Provençal poetry[25] as a framework for discussing a wide range of abstract problems—for the Celtic precedents are much older than these. Their existence, indeed, is indicated among the earliest poetic traditions in both countries,[26] and the form continued to be used long after the Middle Ages. Thus it is interesting to find that the opposition between north and south Wales, which is played upon by Dafydd ap Gwilym and Gruffudd Gryg, is paralleled on a far larger scale in Irish as late as the seventeenth century, in a long bardic contention between poets representing the north and south of Ireland.[27] One suspects that there could have been earlier precedents which have not come down for this aspect of the controversy, since in both countries certain recognized literary tendencies have always distinguished the north from the south. In Wales, the *Ymryson* between Dafydd and Gruffudd Gryg may be regarded as a reflection of the recurrent opposition between the conservative tenacity of the north, and the south's more ready receptivity to new literary modes.[28] The earliest contests in both languages represent a kind of jockeying for position between rival poets, sometimes with a definite appointment as *pencerdd* to a certain patron as their reward, as in the contest for supremacy between Cynddelw Brydydd Mawr and Seisyll Bryffwrch at the court of Madog ap Maredudd,[29] and probably in Phylip Brydydd's contest with the *gofeirdd* or inferior

[25] The types known as the *tenso* and the *joc parti* have been somewhat tentatively compared with the form of the *Ymryson*, though any connexion between the two was rejected by Ifor Williams, THSC, 1913–14, 121. For references to the opinions expressed on this matter, see Chotzen, *op. cit.*, 17. The greater antiquity of the Welsh contests is pointed out by T. Gwynn Jones, 'Bardism and Romance', THSC, 1913–14, 296; but he does not cite the supporting evidence for their antiquity which comes from Ireland.

[26] The evidence for *stories* about bardic contests goes back in both countries to the ninth or tenth century, and is of such a kind as to imply that the custom itself is far older. In Wales, it consists of the traditions about Taliesin's contest with the bards of Maelgwn Gwynedd (on the date of which see Ifor Williams, *Chwedl Taliesin*, UWP, 1957), and of Nennius's account of the contest between Ambrosius and the *magi* of Vortigern. With these, cf. the Irish tale *Immacallam in dá Thuarad*, the 'Colloquy of the Two Sages' (ed. Whitley Stokes, *Revue Celtique*,xxvi, 4–64), for which a ninth-century date is proposed by K. Jackson, *Man*, xxxiv (May, 1934), 67. Further evidence as to the existence of such contests may be adduced from the Welsh Laws and manuscripts of the early poetry.

[27] *Iomarbháigh na bhFileadh*. 'The Contention of the Poets', ed. and trans. Lambert McKenna, *Irish Texts Society*, vols. xx, xxi. See E. Knott, *Irish Classical Poetry*, pp. 74 ff.; Caerwyn Williams, *op. cit.*, 173.

[28] W. J. Gruffydd, *Llenyddiaeth Cymru*, 1450–1600, 67–8: 'Y Gogledd sy'n cadw, y Dê sy'n cychwyn' ('The North preserves, the South initiates'). For Ireland cf. Alwyn and Brinley Rees, *Celtic Heritage* (London, 1961), 101.

[29] *Llawysgrif Hendregadredd*, 180–181.

poets at the court of Rhys Ieuanc.[30] But in Dafydd's contest with Gruffudd Gryg, as again in the most interesting of the later Welsh contests of which we have record,[31] the matter at issue is some fundamental difference between the participants as to the theory and practice of poetry—one might say, therefore, that these bardic controversies represent the earliest examples of literary criticism in Welsh. They tend also to take the form of a debate between a poetic innovator on the one hand, and the 'Establishment' upon the other. But Gruffudd Gryg, who came from the commote of Llifon in Anglesey,[32] and who may or may not have been Dafydd's junior in age, is a poet whose own surviving compositions hardly qualify him as a satisfactory exponent of the conservative bardic standpoint, since they are all *cywyddau*, and *cywyddau* which show at times a *finesse* and versatility in theme and treatment which rival Dafydd's own.[33] It may be said of some of these poems, however, that the weightier character of the subject-matter dealt with throws a possible light on Gruffudd's criticism of Dafydd; moreover, they include no *fabliaux* or poems of love-escapades, and Gruffudd's *cywyddau* to girls are recognizably in the older tradition of the *rhieingerddi* composed by the court poets. It would be interesting to know whether these *cywyddau* are in fact all poems of Gruffudd Gryg's later career, and whether or not they were composed after the *Ymryson* was concluded. I shall return later to the substance of Gruffudd Gryg's attack upon Dafydd's poetry.

These, then, are the poems for whose framework Dafydd ap Gwilym is in one way or another indebted to earlier bardic models. They represent only a small part of his total output, and it is not, of course, on these, but on his far more numerous *cywyddau serch* that his distinctive reputation in succeeding generations has been based. For the greater part of his work, as it has come down to us, comprises those poems of personal situation which introduce a whole range of new themes, barely—if at all—touched upon in Welsh poetry of the previous generations, in so far as the extant evidence can tell us. These are the poems of love and nature, centred on the attendant circumstances of the woodland *oed*, the meeting-place to which he invites Morfudd or Dyddgu or some un-named girl: tales of broken appointments and frustrations

[30] *ibid.*, 226–229. See T. Gwynn Jones, 'Bardism and Romance'. THSC, 1913–14, pp. 240–1, 290–294.

[31] i.e. those of Rhys Goch Eryri with Siôn Cent and Llywelyn ap y Moel on the nature of poetic inspiration, and the seventeenth-century contest between Edmund Prys and William Cynwal, on which see Gruffydd Aled Williams, YB viii (1974), 70–109.

[32] On the Anglesey connexions and date of Gruffudd Gryg, see E. D. Jones, *National Library of Wales Journal*, x, 230–1 and note p. 159 below. His poem *I'r Lleuad* (*Oxford Book*, no. 56), with its reference to *tir Harri*, proves that he was alive at the end of the century. See Ifor Williams's note, DGG², 228, and ibid. introduction, xcviii–xcix.

[33] Cf. pp. 155–6 below.

of various kinds, such as losing his way in the dark or the mist, the interference of 'Yr Eiddig' (the 'Jealous Husband') or the competition of other lovers, and the poems more specifically concerned with love-escapades, such as *Trafferth mewn Tafarn* (GDG 124), and *Y Cwt Gwyddau* (GDG 126). The last has the three stock figures of the Wife, the Jealous Husband and the Clerk-lover (that is, Dafydd himself), like the international *fabliaux* to which these poems as a class bear some relation. Then there are the poems in which Dafydd champions the advantages of the natural life against the austerity advocated to him by the friars. In all these poems, the detailed and sensitive nature descriptions which we associate particularly with Dafydd ap Gwilym are, for the most part, very loosely and indirectly linked with the main theme, and this is particularly apparent in the group of *llatai*[34] or love-messenger poems, where the poet's chief interest is in elaborating the *dyfalu* or descriptive address to a bird or an animal.

Yet even here, where we might least expect to find them, in the poems whose subject-matter has almost no real precedent in earlier Welsh poetry, many facets of the older tradition of praise-poetry can be traced. There are the stock comparisons for a girl's beauty, taken over from the Gogynfeirdd.[35] Among the most popular of these in the older poetry were comparisons with the beauty of moving water, both of sea-foam and the rough water of rivers—in such recurrent phrases as *deuliw y don* and *hoen geirw afonydd*; with all forms of light, especially of the dawn—*gorne gwawr fore*–and of the sun, moon and stars, candles and lamps;[36] with gossamer—*gwawn wedd*; and the very popular comparisons with snow—*gorlliw eiry mân* (GDG 42, 2), *hoen eiry di-frisg* (GDG 33, 18), and the like. All these and others,[37] recur constantly with

---

[34] The question of the literary antecedents of this type of poem is complicated, and their style suggests a connexion with the *cywyddau gofyn*. Another view has linked the *llatai* poems with the *gorhoffedd* poems of the Gogynfeirdd, some of which contain an address to the poet's horse; see T. Gwynn Jones, *Rhieingerddi'r Gogynfeirdd*, (Dinbych, 1915), 17–26, 41–2; T. Parry, *Hanes Llenyddiaeth Gymraeg*, 87; Saunders Lewis, *Braslun o Hanes Llenyddiaeth Gymraeg*, (UWP 1932), 90–91.

[35] For the earlier instances see T. Gwynn Jones, *Rhieingerddi*, 27–31; for some additional examples from Dafydd ap Gwilym and his contemporaries, see Chotzen, *op. cit.*, 204 ff.

[36] Exx: *cannwyll Gwynedd* (GDG 111, 22); *Fy nghariad oleuad lamp* (GDG 37, 2); *bryd wyth wiwlamp* (GDG 35, 54); *llugorn llon* (GDG 81, 28).

[37] Chotzen (*op. cit.*, 203) makes the important point that some of the more unusual of these stock comparisons appear also in Irish poetry, but that they appear to be restricted to Irish and Welsh. These include the comparisons with gossamer (*loyne gwawn*, GDG 54, 26; *gwawn ei gwedd*, (GDG 85, 48); with lime (*dyn galch*, GDG 42, 19); and of the hair and eyebrows with the colour of the blackbird (*ail blu mwyalch*, GDG 30, 39; *Duach yw'r gwallt/ no mwyalch*, GDG 45, 30–1). They point both to the antiquity and to the independence of the Celtic *formulaé* for ideal beauty. The whole subject needs further investigation.

minor verbal changes[38] in Dafydd's poetry, though the manner in which he uses them may be sometimes lightly ironical,[39] so that the reader is led to expect that more subtle nuances of implication may at any time be present than when these same phrases are used by Dafydd's more conservative contemporaries, Iolo Goch and Gruffudd ap Maredudd. He frequently introduces the names of the traditional heroines, *Indeg, Tegau, Luned,* and others. Again, Dafydd pays his tribute of admiration by composing poetry, *gwawd y tafawd,* in honour of the girl he is addressing (GDG 84, 2); he tells us that he makes public her praise, singing it in the presence of lords at feasts or else causing others— the *clêr ofer* or lesser poets—to do so (GDG 85, 11, 23), and by this means spreading her fame through all Gwynedd (GDG 34, 14), throughout Wales (GDG 137, 15), or as far as the English border (GDG 85, 23).[40] Just as in the conventional praise-poetry, a generous material payment was counted on by the bard from his patron, so Dafydd plainly considered himself as equally entitled to a definite reward for his labours in the form of favours from the girl, and, of course, his frequently reiterated complaint is that he does not receive this reward.[41] Similarly, he can threaten a girl who has cast him off with the powerful weapon of satire (GDG 7, 17–20). There are suggestions in the earlier *rhieingerddi* of Cynddelw and Hywel ab Owain Gwynedd[42] that due payment is expected for praise-poetry addressed to women, no less than such rewards were expected from men. And indeed Hywel ab Owain Gwynedd provides another kind of precedent for Dafydd, since he appears to complain of his failure[43] as often as to exult in his success in his love-affairs. These *rhieingerddi* of the Gogynfeirdd were addressed sometimes to girls, sometimes to married women[44] in the manner of the Provençal troubadours, and Dafydd ap Gwilym also has both kinds. It has been remarked[45] that his delineation of Dyddgu comes close to the outlines set in the earlier bardic tradition: the unmarried girls of the *rhieingerddi,*

---

[38] Exx: *unne dydd* (GDG 85, 6); *goleudon lafarfron liw* (42, 5); *Hoen geirw tes* (39, 40); *dyn eiry peilliw* (37, 37); *od gawad* (52, 20).

[39] Obvious examples are *haul Wynedd* in *Athrodi ei was* (128, 5); *lliw haul dwyrain* in *Trafferth mewn Tafarn* (124, 9); but in many instances the irony is more subtle; cf. for instance the series of epithets addressed to Morfudd in *Gofyn Cymod* (GDG 52)—or, in a different way, the epithets applied to the nuns (GDG 113, 17–22).

[40] This seems to be the implication of the phrase *hyd eithaf Ceri,* if *Ceri* here means the commote in Powys adjacent to the border; see editor's note.

[41] Exx: GDG nos. 54, 84, 85, 88, 101, 137.

[42] See OBWV, nos. 22 and 28. Similarly Gruffudd ap Dafydd ap Tudur records the gift of *aur a main* in payment for his poem to a girl, MA, 318 a; T. Gwynn Jones, *Rhieingerddi,* 32.

[43] Cf. T. Gwynn Jones, *Rhieingerddi,* 13–14.

[44] The women named in Hywel ab Owain's *gorhoffedd* (OBWV, no. 22) are described as *gwragedd*: compare his two poems to girls (*ibid.,* nos. 23 and 24), and Cynddelw's *rhieingerdd* (*ibid.,* no. 28).

[45] T. Parry, 'Dafydd ap Gwilym', *Yorkshire Celtic Studies* v, 26.

who possess, in addition to beauty of form and feature, the stock qualities of gentleness, courtesy, kindness and unaffected demeanour—qualities which are named in the Bardic Grammar[46] as the standard virtues for which nobly-born girls should be praised.

These are some of the ways in which the idiom and concepts of the older praise-poetry were carried over into the new medium. The metrical aspects of this transition have been the subject of particular examination by Dr Parry, and I omit all reference to them here. Yet, ever since the content of Dafydd ap Gwilym's poetry has been the subject of comparative study, themes have been discovered in it which seem to correspond with elements in a very different poetic tradition— the conventions of *amour courtois* which originated in Provence in the eleventh century, and which were afterwards developed further in France, from whence they spread to England and to the other countries of Europe. The ultimate source for many elements in this poetic convention were the poems of Ovid—for the idea of Love as an art or science, which could be taught by precepts, and practised according to rules, for love as a sickness, and as a form of warfare. The Troubadours gave further development to these ideas: they exalted Love as an idealized form of service (there may have been here an implicit comparison with the feudal relation which bound a man to his lord), and a service which enjoined secrecy on its followers, so that they referred to their ladies under fictitious names. Even when unreciprocated, love must constitute its own reward. They developed the idea of Love's warfare by frequent references to the spears and arrows with which it was waged. It was the references to these things in Dafydd's *cywyddau* which Gruffudd Gryg regarded as artificial and alien to the whole tradition of Welsh poetry, as indeed they were. It was not that Dafydd exaggerated the perfections of Morfudd, for idealism of this kind would have been a recognized and accepted feature of bardic technique, but rather that he exaggerated their effect upon himself: what Gruffudd jeered at were the repeated references to the spears and arrows of love and to their disastrous effect upon Dafydd, bringing him near to death.[47] The charge made against him can indeed be substantiated from Dafydd's *cywyddau*, with their frequent allusions to the spears and arrows[48] and to the

---

[46] G. J. Williams and E. J. Jones, GP, 16, 35, 56; Saunders Lewis, *Braslun*, 87. Cf. GDG nos. 56; 79.

[47] For an important discussion of the significance of the *Ymryson* in Dafydd's poetry, see Eurys Rowlands, *Y Traethodydd* cxxii (Ionawr, 1967), 15–35 especially 26–27. See also Glanmor Williams, *op. cit.* 192.

[48] *Gwayw, gwewyr* occur far more frequently in Dafydd's poetry than *saeth(au)*, but the figurative usage of these words seems to be in every respect equivalent, except that the first may have the secondary meaning of 'pangs', Exx: GDG 56, 11–14; 78, 45–46; 84, 17; 88, 13–14; 95, 43; 100; 111. Cf. Ifor Williams, THSC, 1913–14, 160.

sickness and sleeplessness[49] caused by love, while the accompanying criticism of monotonously harping on a single theme is also admitted by Dafydd in the *cywydd* (GDG 34) in which he says that, like the cuckoo, he has only a single tune to sing, and this is the theme of Morfudd's praise: *Unllais wyf ... / â'r gog, morwyn gyflog Mai* (GDG 34, 31–2). But it is worth remembering that Gruffudd's attack may well have derived additional force from the evidence of poems which have not survived. And the particular type of exaggeration of which he accuses Dafydd is to be found neither in Gruffudd Gryg's own *cywyddau* to girls nor in the few which have come down of the work of Dafydd's other contemporaries, Madog Benfras and Iolo Goch. It is, however, a charge which any poet who took it upon himself to represent the accepted standards of the Welsh poetic tradition would feel justified in bringing against one who made use in his verse of the exotic elements in the continental convention of Courtly Love—elements which are only slightly and sporadically discernible in the work of any Welsh poet before Dafydd ap Gwilym.[50] It makes no difference to this charge of insincerity in his work that Dafydd's use of the foreign convention appears to be ironical more often than it is serious: he is accused of a type of innovation which led to a departure from the standards of truthfulness recognized in praise-poetry. Whereas the *cywyddau* to girls by Dafydd's contemporaries are a recognizable development from the earlier *rhieingerddi* of Hywel ab Owain Gwynedd and the other Gogynfeirdd poets, the continental attitude of extreme abasement in love which Dafydd chooses to affect at times is essentially alien to the *rhieingerdd*, and it is one which Gruffudd Gryg evidently considered that he demeaned his bardic status by adopting. In his reply to this onslaught, Dafydd does not, in fact, deny the substance of the accusation, for in calling his love-poetry *geuwawd o gywydd*, 'a *cywydd* of false praise' (GDG 148, 6), he virtually admits that it is not defensible by the older standards of the bards. Nevertheless, he asserts that such a *cywydd* is, in a different way, as honourable as a praise-poem, for the things which some people have no use for can still be of value to others—and he backs up this claim with his striking metaphors of the rejected worn-out harp and the parchment scroll[51] or book which has become brown-edged and illegible: a use can be found for both of these in different

---

[49] Exx: GDG 36, 17–28; 45, 15; 46, 43; 56, 4; 63, 1; 84, 5; 94, 108. Note also the emphasis which is placed on secrecy, and the many references to the necessity for it: GDG 30, 20; 40, 31–2; 74; 78; 98, 41 ff.

[50] The most significant of Dafydd's predecessors as regards his subject-matter is Gruffudd ap Dafydd ap Tudur (*cira* 1300; MA², pp. 318–20), and it is interesting that Dafydd actually repeats a couplet of his work (GDG 13, 23–24; see note). See T. Parry, HLl 49; T. Gwynn Jones, *Rhieingerddi*, 31–40; *Aberystwyth Studies*, iv, 85–96.

[51] On *cwrrach*, see J. Lloyd-Jones, *Ériu*, xvi, 125.

strata of society from those which responded to aristocratic praise-poetry. And he counter-attacks by accusing Gruffudd of continuing to uphold an obsolete and exhausted tradition, because of the poverty of his own inspiration, and of carping criticism of the work of others— Gruffudd, he says, is *craig lefair beirdd*, the 'sounding-stone' or echo of the poets. The debate is continued throughout eight *cywyddau* which become increasingly abusive, as both poets resort increasingly to the traditional bardic armoury of satire. At the end, neither can be said to have won, and neither has fully answered the charge brought by his opponent. This lack of any final decision has been noted as a feature characteristic of medieval debates,[52] so that it is quite probable that the concluding *cywyddau* represents the end of the series, yet there is some evidence that there may have been a number of additional poems in the *Ymryson* which have not survived.[53]

The charge which Gruffudd brings against Dafydd, virtually that of undermining the tradition by introducing into Welsh poetry alien concepts and conceits, is, therefore, corroborated by Dafydd's own *cywyddau* in such a way as to distinguish them from the poems addressed to girls by his contemporaries. Since the origin of these conceits is clearly traceable among the stock conventions of the continental code of Courtly Love, I shall limit my discussion of foreign influences in this paper to a consideration of the sources from which Dafydd could have derived these elements in his poetry. In the course of trying to discover these, it has seemed to me that Dafydd's rejections, if we could know more about them, might prove as interesting and as significant as what he chose to accept from foreign models, and that characteristics which throw light on his individual genius are, perhaps, to be traced in the very nature of his response to such external influences as reached him. But in commenting on this response, I shall, of course, only be tackling a small part of the subject of innovation in the style and matter of Dafydd's poetry.

First of all, then, the references which Dafydd makes to Ovid, who is the only foreign poet to whom he ever refers by name. Many of the basic conceits of Courtly Love are ultimately derived from Ovid's poetry, and he is constantly cited by the poets of this convention (as, for instance, by Chrétien de Troyes) and, indeed, by medieval writers in general, as the paramount authority on all matters relating to love. For Dafydd, *llyfr Ofydd*, 'the book of Ovid', has practically come to mean 'the affairs of love', and he refers to himself as *dyn Ofydd*, 'Ovid's man', and to love-songs as *ofyddiaeth*. Evidence for the actual knowledge

---

[52] See J. W. H. Atkins, *The Owl and the Nightingale* (1922), lvii.

[53] A note in *Llanstephan MS.*, 133 by David Jones of Llanfair (reproduced by J. H. Davies, THSC, 1905–6, 72), claims that there were twenty-two *cywyddau* in the *Ymryson*. The substance of this passage is quoted in the introduction to the 1789 *Barddoniaeth Dafydd ap Gwilym*, xviii–xix, n.

of Ovid's work in Wales goes back to much earlier times, and to the oldest sources of written Welsh, for among the ninth-century glosses in Bodleian MS. *Auctor. F.4.32*—Zeuss's *Oxoniensis Prior*—are Welsh glosses on the first book of the *Ars Amatoria*.[54] One or two possible references to Ovid occur in Welsh poetry before the time of Dafydd, including one in a love-poem by Hywel ab Owain Gwynedd, but all apparent references now need to be carefully scrutinized in the light of J. Lloyd-Jones's study of a number of bardic compounds which contain the second element *ofydd*, and which he has shown may arise from a modified or a lenited form of one or other of two separate words, *dofydd* and *gofydd*, meaning 'ruler', 'afflictor' or the like.[55]

Dafydd ap Gwilym's poetry, then, provides the earliest incontrovertible allusions to the poet Ovid in Welsh, and the chief point of interest raised by these allusions is, of course, the question of whether or not Dafydd can have had any direct knowledge of the poet's work at all, or whether his citations merely reflect hearsay knowledge of Ovid's reputation, combined with the medieval fondness for an appeal to authority. The question is complicated by the fact that so many of the stock Ovidian ideas—Love as a form of warfare, as an art, and as a sickness—as well as the Ovidian characters of the old hag, the churlish doorkeeper, and the possessive 'husband'—became taken up into the courtly and bourgeois traditions[56] in French poetry at an early stage, and could have reached Dafydd by any one of a number of indirect channels, among others, the *Roman de la Rose*. The *Ars Amatoria* was the first of Ovid's works to become widely known in the vernacular:[57] more than one translation into Old French was made in the course of the twelfth and thirteenth centuries, and it has, at various times, been suggested[58] that Dafydd could have known the *Ars Amatoria* through the medium of one of these. It is interesting, therefore, to find that in the earliest extant French translation of this work, Ovid is brought up to date for twelfth-century France by making the church take the place of the Roman theatre, and clerical mystery plays that of the race-course, as suitable meeting-places at which to encounter girls[59]—although, of course, it is hardly necessary to suggest any authority other than actual custom for the various passages in which Dafydd

---

[54] Zeuss, *Grammatica Celtica*, 1054–1059; B v, 1–8; vi, 112–15.

[55] B xv, 198–200.

[56] That is, into both romance and *fabliau*. See. C. Muscatine, *Chaucer and the French Tradition* (California, 1960), chapters II and III.

[57] For French versions of Ovid, see Gaston Paris, *La Poésie du Moyen Age* (Paris, 1885), 192–208; *Histoire Littéraire de la France*, vol. xxix, 455–525.

[58] W. Lewis Jones, THSC, 1907–8; W. J. Gruffydd, *Trans. of the Guild of Graduates*, 1908, 32.

[59] Kuhne and Stengel, *Maistre Elie'e Ueberarbeitung der ältesten franz. Uebertragung von Ovid's Ars Amatoria* (Marburg, 1886), 37 ff. Cf. G. Paris, *La Poésie du Moyen Age*, 192–3; L. P. Wilkinson, *Ovid Recalled* (Cambridge, 1955), 387.

ap Gwilym refers to such meetings in church, as in the two well-known poems in which he alludes to the suitability of Llanbadarn church and Bangor cathedral for this purpose (GDG nos. 48, 111).

This point of contact with the French adaptations of the *Ars Amatoria* may, therefore, be entirely fortuitous, and if we discount it, I can see no incontrovertible evidence in Dafydd's work for any direct knowledge of the *Ars Amatoria*. But there is another work of Ovid which offers a series of far more striking resemblances to poems by Dafydd. In the *cywydd* (GDG 71) in which he apostrophizes the river Dyfi in spate, he beseeches it not to prevent him from crossing to Llanbadarn to visit Morfudd. In Ovid's work the *Amores*[60] there is an address to one of the Italian rivers, swollen with melted snow, which prevents the poet, in a similar way, from crossing to visit his lady. Each poet, in apostrophizing the river, claims that it ought to sympathize with him as a lover: Ovid points out that rivers too have been in love, and gives a long list of the loves of various rivers for nymphs, while Dafydd claims that no one has praised the wave of the Dyfi so much, or compared it to so many different things—its strength to the shoulder of a horse or man, its voice to a harp or an organ, and so on. I am not aware that any close parallel,[61] other than Ovid, can be found for Dafydd's *cywydd*, and I think that this by itself offers at any rate a presumption that Dafydd knew of the *Amores* in some form. In addition, it gives significance to other passages in the *Amores*, not paralleled elsewhere in Ovid, which are highly suggestive in comparison with certain of Dafydd's poems. These are the symbolic dream,[62] for which Ovid seeks an interpreter, in which his lady is personified as a white heifer; the discussion as to whether a soldier or a poet makes a more desirable lover;[63] and the figure of the slave who acts as a churlish doorkeeper,[64] keeping the girl shut away behind a creaking door. Each of these incidents has its separate parallel in one or other of Dafydd's *cywyddau*, and, taken as a group, they do seem to be highly suggestive. However, I shall presently point out that there exist other parallels which are much closer in treatment to Dafydd's rendering of these themes, in certain Old French poems which have come down. The Ovidian parallel to the address to the river Dyfi is the only one of these themes of which I do not know of any other vernacular version, but, of course, this does not mean that none such existed in the past. What the evidence

---

[60] *Amores*, iii, 6.

[61] There is a partial parallel in an Irish tale in which the legendary poet Athirne is said to have satirized the river Mourne for refusing to provide him with a salmon. This is quoted in an apologue by the thirteenth-century bard Giolla Brighde Mac Con Midhe (*Poems*, ed. N. Williams, Irish Texts Soc. vol. LI, 1980, no. xi, pp. 122–3).

[62] *Amores*, iii, 5.

[63] *Amores*, iii, 8.

[64] *Amores*, i, 6; ii, 12.

seems to amount to, then, is merely this, that if Dafydd ap Gwilym had any knowledge *at all* of Ovid's poetry in the original, it is more likely to have been of the *Amores* than of any other of his works. This is the more interesting because the *Amores*, unlike the *Ars Amatoria*, was, apparently, among the less well-known of Ovid's works in the Middle Ages, for no early vernacular translations of it appear to have come down.[65] He gives no indication anywhere of having had any knowledge of Ovid's *Metamorphoses*, and this, generally speaking, was the most widely quoted and influential of all Ovid's works in the four-teenth century; but then, Dafydd had his own inheritance of native mythology and legend on which to draw for those purposes of illustration and comparison for which the poets of other nations made an extensive use of the *Metamorphoses*.

The most important of the original works through which Ovid's legacy was transmitted to the later Middle Ages was, undoubtedly, the thirteenth-century French poem the *Roman de la Rose*.[66] This is an immensely long allegorical love-story, set within the framework of a dream, and it formed the pattern for many later medieval poems. The first part was composed about 1230 by Guillaume de Lorris, but this poet died before completing his work. Much of Ovid's teaching on the art of love is unfolded in Guillaume's presentation of his various allegorical and type-figures—Idleness, Fair Welcome and Danger, and his conventional characters of the Friend, the Slanderer, and the ancient hag who has charge of the girl. But he left his long and involved narrative unfinished, to be taken up some forty years later by a very different poet, one Jean de Meun, whose continuation of the poem could hardly present a greater antithesis. Just as the work of Guillaume de Lorris is essentially courtly, idealistic and youthful, and written from an aris-tocratic standpoint, so Jean de Meun is cynical, middle-aged and expres-sive of middle-class opinion. He was, however, a widely-read and well-informed man, who used the framework of his predecessor's unfinished poem as a means of popularizing for a lay-audience his teaching and opinions on a great diversity of subjects, such as the hypocrisy of the mendicant orders, the faithlessness and unreliability of women (and he gives a poignant account of the trials of the Jealous Husband), together with his views on the nature of man and the universe—his opinions about almost everything, in fact, except for his predecessor's exposition of the doctrine of Courtly Love.

When we come to consider the evidence for Dafydd ap Gwilym's knowledge of this poem, it is worth remembering first that actual docu-mentary evidence has come down for the existence of a manuscript

---

[65] Cf. G. Paris, *Histoire Littŕaire*, 488.
[66] ed. E. Langlois, *Société des Anciens Textes Francaises* (Paris, 1914–1924) For subsequent studies, see n. 7 above, also C. Muscatine, *op. cit.*, chs. II and III.

of the *Roman de la Rose* in Glamorgan, and in the early years of the fourteenth century. Its significance has been noticed both by Chotzen and by Professor G. J. Williams.[67] The work is listed by name, together with three un-named manuscripts written in Welsh, among the confiscated possessions of a certain Llywelyn Bren (the steward of Gilbert de Clare), who was executed in 1317. This chance reference, so fortuitously preserved, is curiously suggestive in relation to Dafydd's literary background, both as regards time and also place. For scattered through Dafydd's work are a number of things for which the most likely source seems to be the poem by Guillaume de Lorris. Some of these, indeed, are among the commonplaces of Courtly Love: the spears and arrows, the sleeplessness, and the obligation of secrecy. The old woman who is, for Dafydd, one of the *Tri Phorthor Eiddig*, the Jealous Husband's Three Gate-keepers (GDG 80), could well have been suggested to him by the similar figure who appears in the *Roman de la Rose*. There is also the association of May with youth and love and generosity, together with the opposite view, that the old and miserly must have an antipathy to the spring-time, and an affinity only with winter. The custom which Dafydd refers to so frequently, of bestowing the *cae bedw* or garland of birch-twigs by one lover on another, whatever be its origin, certainly suggests the French custom of bestowing garlands of flowers and leaves, which appears in the *Roman* and is, indeed, a commonplace in Old French poetry, being apparently connected with May-Day observances.[68] There are a number of other suggestions in Dafydd's work pointing to influences from the *Roman de la Rose*: it could have been from the *Roman* that Dafydd derived the idea for the allegorical presentation of his breast as a fortress given to him to defend (GDG 140), while his simile of the Bird-Catcher (GDG 30), in which he presents himself as caught by a girl's eyes like a bird trapped in bird-lime beside a pool, has a striking parallel in the image of the fountain of Narcissus, also representing the girl's eyes, by which the lover is entrapped at the beginning of the *Roman*.[69] Taken by themselves, perhaps none of these resemblances would appear conclusive, but Dafydd has one image which is so closely paralleled in the work of Guillaume de Lorris that I find it impressive as evidence for his actual knowledge of the French poem. This is the husbandry simile,[70] of the lover who has sown his grain and watched it grow, only to find it destroyed by a storm just before it is harvested. Guillaume's lover applies this rather unusual simile to himself at the point when the girl has been taken away from him and shut up so that he cannot reach her. Dafydd elaborates the

---

[67] Chotzen, *op cit.*, 110; G. J. Williams, *Traddodiad Llenyddol Morgannwg*, 146.

[68] See G. L. Marsh, 'Chaplets of Leaves and Flowers', *Modern Philology*, iv (1906–7), 153 ff; D. A. Pearsall (ed.) *The Floure and the Leafe* (Nelson, 1962), 27–8.

[69] Cf. C. S. Lewis, *Allegory of Love*, 128–9. *Roman*, ll. 1537–1614.

[70] *Roman*, ll. 3960–70. Cf. Chotzen, *op. cit.*, 331–2.

same image throughout a whole poem (GDG 87), and with a wealth of technical terminology: he has nourished his love like winter-tilth, it has been ploughed and harrowed, and in the early summer enclosed against the time of reaping, but suddenly the wind changed (by some such disaster, perhaps, as Morfudd's marriage) and the poet's tempestuous tears caused the crop to be lost. This poem seems to me to be as persuasive evidence for Dafydd's direct knowledge of the work of Guillaume de Lorris as is his poem to the Dyfi for his knowledge of Ovid's *Amores*.

The *Roman de la Rose* was not an isolated work. It was, rather, the culminating expression of a whole trend or tradition in thirteenth-century French poetry, from which it sprang, and which continued to exist alongside it. In examining other works which belong to this tradition,[71] I came upon a number of features which seem to me to be relevant to the consideration of French influences upon Dafydd ap Gwilym, although these features have not been retained in the *Roman* itself. From about 1200, a type of dream-vision was popular in French and Anglo-Norman literature, which had a framework consisting in a forest or garden scene on a May morning, in which a paean of bird-song heralds the appearance of the god or goddess of Love, who comes to arbitrate between disputants upon a question of love, which either may or may not be personal to them in its application. In some of the earliest of these poems, it is the birds themselves who represent the jury, so to speak, since it is they who debate the problem at issue. And one of the most popular subjects of this bird-debate is the question as to whether, in human society, the clerk or the knight is the most desirable lover for a woman—or as a variant, whether any but clerks and knights are in fact entitled to love at all. It has been pointed out above that this theme occurs already in Ovid's *Amores*,[72] and it has certain medieval Latin intermediaries before it re-appears in French and Anglo-Norman, set within the framework of the bird-debate.[73] In every version that has come down, with a single exception,[74] judgement is given consistently in favour of the clerk against the knight—an indication, of course, as to the presumed authorship of the poems. Another theme of the dream-visions, also attested previously in the *Amores*, is the pursuit and

[71] I am here above all indebted to E. Langlois, *Origines et Sources du Roman de la Rose* (Paris, 1891), and to C. Oulmont, *Les Débats du Clerc et du Chevalier* (Paris, 1911). See also E. Faral, 'Les Débats du Clerc et du Chevalier' in his *Sources Latines des Contes et Romans Courtois du Moyen Age* (Paris, 1913); W. A. Neilson, *The Origins and Sources of the Court of Love* (*Studies and Notes in Philology*, vi, Harvard, 1899).

[72] *Amores*, iii, 8.

[73] The relevant poems are *Concilium Romarici Montis, Altercatio Phyllidis et Florae; Blanchfleur et Florence; Florence et Blanchfleur; Melior et Idoine; Li Fablel dou Dieu d'Amors; De Venus la Déesse d'Amor*. On the Latin poems, see Raby, *Secular Latin Poetry* (Oxford, 1934), ii, 290–296.

[74] The Anglo-Norman *Blanchefleur et Florence* (Oulmont, *op. cit.*, 40).

capture of a magic animal,[75] who is interpreted as representing the girl sought after by the dreaming poet. In one poem,[76] the judgement given by Venus on a question of love is preceded by a service of the Mass at which all the birds assist in their different capacities. Again, a sequel to some of the bird-debates consists in the death of the lover whose cause has lost, and his or her burial within the precincts of the garden of Love, in a tomb surrounded by birds who sing incessantly for the lover's soul.[77]

These four themes present striking parallels with certain of the *cywydd-au*. Dafydd ap Gwilym gives a personal application to his discussion of the comparative merits of the clerk and the knight, for he puts forth the clerk's point-of-view in his own person (GDG 58). He adduces arguments in his own favour, and against the merits of the soldier, which are closely similar to those employed in the French poems; and significantly enough, the version which comes nearest to Dafydd's treatment of the theme is one of the Anglo-Norman versions written in England.[78] Dafydd has two poems recounting dream-experiences: one is the poem in which he abuses a striking clock which disturbs his sleep, (GDG 66), with its echo of earlier Celtic dream-belief, such as we meet in *Breuddwyd Maxen*, to the effect that the spirit actually leaves the body while dreaming. The other (GDG 39) is the poem in which Dafydd dreams at day-break that he is in a forest, that he releases his hounds after a white doe, and that after a long pursuit she turns and comes to him for protection. This allegorical dream is interpreted for him by an old woman: the white doe represents the girl he is seeking, and the hounds are his *llateion* or love-messengers. This type of enigmatic or symbolic dream, which could only be understood by means of a skilled interpreter, belonged to one of the recognized medieval divisions of the *somnium*, according to the popular commentary on dreams by Macrobius.[79] Both Dafydd's dream poems bear witness to the intense

[75] *La Panthère d'Amors* by Nicole de Margival, *circa* 1300 (ed. H. Todd, SATF Paris, 1883); cf. *Amores*, iii, 5.
[76] *La Messe des Oiseaux* by Jean de Condé (ed. A. Scheler, *Dits et Contes de Baudouin de condé et de son fils Jehan de Condé*, Brussels, 1866–7), vol. iii, 1 ff.; J. Ribard, *La Messe des Oiseaux et le dit des Jacobins et des Fremeneurs* (Geneva: Paris, 1970).
[77] *Blanchefleur et Florence; Li Fablel dou Dieu d'Amors; De Venus la Déesse d'Amors.* Mr Peter Dronke has suggested to me that in the poems of bird-mass and bird-requiem we have yet another theme which is ultimately derived from Ovid's *Amores* (ii, 6), and from Statius' *Silvae* (ii, 4).
[78] *Melior et Idoine.* Some parallels are quoted by Chotzen, *op. cit.*, 229.
[79] *Macrobius: Commentary on the Dream of Scipio.* Translated by W. H. Stahl (Columbia, 1952), Bk. I, ch. 3; see also W. C. Curry, *Chaucer and the Mediæval Sciences* (revised edition, 1960), 199, 207–8. The *cywydd* GDG 39 is of great interest in several ways; firstly, because of what we may call the literary history of the White Doe in Celtic and Romance sources (on this see my paper 'Celtic Dynastic Themes and the Breton Lays', *Études Celtiques*, ix, pp. 117–152); and, secondly, because the setting given to it links Dafydd's poem with the special treatment given to this theme in the continental poems, in which the

interest which was commonly felt in the Middle Ages in the significance and interpretation of dreams. As for the Bird-Mass, Chotzen has already drawn attention to the resemblance between the early fourteenth-century poem by Jean de Condé, *La Messe des Oiseaux*,[80] and Dafydd's *cywydd, Offeren y Llwyn*, 'The Woodland Mass' (GDG 122). But he did not point out that the French poem is inset in the typical dream-framework, that it takes place in a woodland setting, and is presided over by Venus, the love-goddess, and that it precedes a bird-debate on a question of love. In the French poem, the nightingale officiates, and definite parts of the service are assigned in every detail to the blackbird, the lark, the thrush, the linnet, the chaffinch, and others. The nightingale and the thrush are the only birds specifically mentioned by Dafydd. There is, however, a striking resemblance in the handling of the theme of the Mass in the two poems; and in both, the audacious parallel with divine service goes so far as to include the elevation of the Host, which, for Dafydd, is a leaf, for Jean de Condé, a red rose. Even so, I feel very doubtful as to whether Jean de Condé's poem can properly be regarded as a source for Dafydd's treatment of the same theme. The case here for a direct source is very different from that which I have advocated in respect to the two *cywyddau*—*Hwsmonaeth Cariad* and *Y Don ar Afon Dyfi*—since in each of these poems the imagery presents a striking and virtually isolated[81] parallel with an external source. On the other hand, the recurrence of imagery in which birds and bird-song are described in terms of the service of the Mass, and its ministers and accessories, is so frequent in Dafydd's *cywyddau*, and indeed so fundamental to his poetic thought, that the manner in which he envisaged birds as poets and preachers can hardly be considered as conscious imagery at all. To him, birds were natural poets in their own right, singing in the court of the woods as he did in human courts, and indeed, praising God in the service of their song. Moreover, the implicit parallel which was felt to exist between bird-song and church-services is expressed widely in medieval literature.[82] The significance of Jean de Condé's poem would be much less, I think, if it were not that the French poem belongs also to the complex of dream-visions and bird-debates. Nevertheless, it seems to me more likely that in this case the

---

hunt for a heroine who is transformed into a doe or other animal is one of the various possible elements of which the dream-vision is composed, just as the bird-debate is another. For the dream-belief reflected in GDG 66, see LlC ii, 206; v, 119.

[80] Cf. Chotzen, *op cit.*, 187–8, and note 76 above.

[81] There is one other instance of the metaphor of sowing the seed of love in Dafydd's work: *Heodd i'm bron .../ had a gariad .../ heiniar cur* (GDG 102, 5–7). Metaphors concerned with sowing the seed of praise-poetry also occur, but these are not exactly parallel (GDG 7, 36; 34, 16; 133, 38).

[82] Cf. Chaucer's *Book of the Duchess*, ll. 301–305. Some of the numerous French examples are cited in the references to birds' 'Latin', n. 86 below.

influence was contributory and indirect rather than literary and direct, for it sometimes happens that external models may give a vigorous stimulus to tendencies already manifest or latent in a national literature.[83] This is a point to which I must return later in connexion with the *Ymddiddanion* between men and birds which are prominent in the *canu rhydd*.

Finally, the French bird-debates on the Clerk *versus* Knight controversy in at least three instances combine this theme with that of the burial of a victim of love, in a tomb surrounded by birds who sing in perpetual chorus about it. The *cywydd*[84] describing the poet's burial for love has been rejected by Dr Parry from the canon of Dafydd's authentic work, but it is too important in this connexion to be omitted from the discussion on that account, since if not contemporary, it can hardly have been composed much later than his day. In this poem, the poet says that if he dies for love he will be buried in the forest, the church will be one of summer leaves with an altar of branches, seagulls will carry his bier, a chorus of birds will sing the service and the cuckoo will chant paternosters and psalms. A curious point is that one[85] of the French poems which provides a parallel for this theme describes the language in which the birds sing as *son Latin*—their Latin. This phrase for bird-song is found in the *Roman de la Rose* and elsewhere in Old French poetry, most frequently in the typical May-morning context.[86] The Welsh poem refers to the *lladin iaith*, in which the birds sing the poet's obsequies. I have so far failed to discover, or to hear of, any other occurrence of this expression for bird-song in Welsh poetry of the period: its occurrence here, even if the poem is not by Dafydd, seems unmistakably to corroborate the evidence for the underlying influence of the French poems of bird-debate.[87]

In view of the importance of these bird-debate poems among the foreign literary influences which by some undetermined channel appear to have reached Dafydd ap Gwilym, I think it is significant that of all the creatures who are individually delineated in his work, it is birds

---

[83] Since writing this, a similar observation has been made by P. Mac Cana in 'Conservation and Innovation in Early Celtic Literature', *Études Celtiques* xiii (1972), 106–7. He compares the Old Irish *nua litride*—poets who composed the early hermit and nature lyrics—as having drawn together 'the indigenous sub-learned tradition with the classical-ecclesiastical culture of the monasteries'. He then alludes to the parallel of Dafydd ap Gwilym's poetic achievement. Cf. pp. 80–81 below.

[84] OBWV, no. 61; DGG², 28–30.

[85] *Li Fablel dou Dieu d'Amors* (ed. Oulmont, *op. cit.*), st. XXV: *Puis apiela cantant en son latin/ Tous les oysiaus ki a lui sont aclin.*

[86] *Roman de la Rose*, I. 8408. For further references, see Tobler-Lommatzch, *Alt-französische Wörterbuch*, s.v. *latin*. In the parallel English examples there is confusion between *laeden* (<*Latinum*) and the native *leden, loeden*, 'language'; see NED, s.v. *leden*.

[87] The *lladin* of the Owls in R. Williams-Parry's lyric (*Cerddi'r Gaeaf*, 6) is but one of the many echoes of Dafydd ap Gwilym which occur in this poet's work.

alone whom he endows with the power of speech–and indeed, with the ability to use this power on occasion somewhat caustically. The Cock-Thrush, certainly, gives the poet advice entirely to his own mind about the enjoyment of the birch-woods in May (GDG 36), but the other two birds who address him adopt an aloof and even critical attitude. The Woodcock is the only one of the *llateion* or love-messengers commissioned by Dafydd who roundly refuses the embassy suggested to him, on the grounds that it is too late in the year and too cold for such a journey, and that because of his delay the girl has chosen another companion (GDG 115). The Magpie, busily occupied with her mate in building their nest of leaves and mud, offers Dafydd the gratuitous advice that he would be better sitting at home by the fire than getting wet out in the wood pining for love, and that in any case he had better give up his unrewarded suit and become a hermit (GDG 63). The contrast here indicated between the Magpie's productive, nest-building activity and the fruitless unproductive love of the poet is paralleled in Old French lyrics of the type known as the *reverdie*[88]—poems of greeting to spring, which also sometimes make this contrast between the poet's thwarted love and the mating of birds. Dafydd's ironic use of the convention is apparent: *Cyngor y Biogen* is, in its way, as forcible an indictment of his affected subservience to the code of Courtly Love as is Gruffudd Gryg's attack, or that of the Grey Friar; only that here, Dafydd ironically imagines the indictment as coming from the words and actions of a *bird*.

In portraying his admonitory birds in this way, Dafydd seems to be drawing on antecedent popular tradition; there are indications that this had already taken shape in earlier Welsh poetry.[89] There are, of course, a number of precedents in Welsh, as elsewhere, for talking birds; whether prophetic, or didactic,[90] or endowed with the wisdom which comes with great age, like the Eagle, the Owl and the Blackbird, who are classed among the Oldest Animals in *Culhwch ac Olwen*. The wisdom of birds is proverbial in folk poetry. The rather numerous

---

[88] Cf. G. L. Brook, *The Harley Lyrics* 8 and no. 11; Theo Stemmler, *Die englischen Liebesgedichte des MS. Harley* 2253 (Bonn, 1962), pp. 129 ff. I am indebted to Peter Dronke for referring me to the following poems which represent early examples of the theme: *Levis exsurgit zephirus* in the eleventh-century 'Cambridge Songs' (*Oxford Book of Medieval Latin Verse*, ed. Raby, 1959, 173, *Penguin Book of Latin Verse*, ed. F. Brittain, 166); and William of Poitier's *Ab la dolchor del temps novel* (C. Appel, *Provenzalische Chrestomathie*, Leipzig, 1895, 51). Further instances, with some parallels from later Gaelic popular love-poetry, are cited by Ó Tuama, *Ar Grá in Amhráin na nDaoine* 108–9.

[89] Cf. ch. 3, p. 92 below.

[90] The *Ymddiddan Arthur a'r Eryr* (B ii, 272 ff) provides an earlier Welsh precedent, and one which, if we accept the editor's dating (*circa* 1150), must antedate the French bird-debates. So also must the englyn *Chwerdit mwyalch mewn celli* (GP 9), which Dafydd ap Gwilym knew and quoted (GDG 76, 23–28), and which reflects the same popular attitude to birds as *exempla*. On the *englyn* see p. 108 below.

*areithiau* and *ymddiddanion* which have come down in the *canu rhydd*—
dialogues between a bird and a man who has come to ask the bird's
advice[91]—are significant in this respect. Although they go back only
to the sixteenth century in their extant form, the general and, at times,
the close resemblance in points of detail which they present with certain
of Dafydd's *cywyddau* cannot, I think, be entirely accounted for as due
to the influence of the *cywyddau* upon them.[92] There are, indeed, certain
marked differences in treatment between the *cywyddau* and the free-metre
poems, which indicate that direct influence of the one upon the other
can only be superficial, and that two separate poetic traditions are
here involved. There is nothing in the later Welsh poems at all like
the elaborate *dyfalu* of the bird or animal addressed, or the directions
for its journey, which characterize this class of Dafydd's *cywyddau*.[93]
One of the ultimate models for these dialogues in the *canu rhydd* must
lie in the French bird-debate poems to which I have referred: if these
were already established in Welsh popular poetry by the fourteenth
century, then Dafydd ap Gwilym is as likely to have imbibed these
influences through the popular poems which were the prototypes of
those which have come down,[94] as he is to have derived them from
a direct knowledge of the originals.

The differences between the *cywyddau* and the *canu rhydd* are indeed
in themselves a measure of those very qualities in which Dafydd's poetry
strikes us as most remarkable when set against the background of medieval poetry in other languages: that is, in his inspired observation of
wild life, and in the imaginative command of language which enabled
him to impart some of his own heightened vision. In his expression
of this sense of fellowship with wild nature, combined with wonder
at nature's infinite variety, Dafydd ap Gwilym's poetry looks back in
a significant manner to an earlier Celtic precedent: that is, to the early
Irish hermit verse, which offers a similar vision of community with
nature, and one which is expressed with a comparable clarity and direct-
ness.[95] Here, then, it seems to me that Dafydd, with his unique gifts,

---

[91] CRCy, nos, 33–36, *et passim*; ibid. lxxxiii, *n.* 2. As with Dafydd ap Gwilym, these
poems overlap with the *llatai* poems, but also exist independently of this theme.

[92] Brinley Rees, *Dulliau'r Canu Rhydd* (UWP, 1952), 65–6; D. Gwenallt Jones, *Y Ficer
Prichard a 'Canwyll Cymry'* (Caernarfon, 1946), 44.

[93] Brinley Rees, *op. cit.*, 69.

[94] For opinions and inferences as to the antiquity of the tradition underlying the sixteenth-century *canu rhydd*, see CRCy, xvi, xx; and cf. Ifor Williams, THSC, 1913–14,
115–16.

[95] Apparently Alfred Nutt was the first person to observe this affinity; see his edn.
of *Arnold's Celtic Literature* (1910), Appendix, 138. On this aspect of the hermit poetry,
cf. K. Jackson, *Early Celtic Nature Poetry*, 108–9: '... The ultimate significance of the
hermit's relationship with nature is something that transcends both nature and hermit
alike. ... Through it all, rarely expressed, always implicit, is the understanding that
bird and hermit are joining together in an act of worship; to him the very existence

is but giving individual expression to an attitude towards nature which is itself deeply rooted in the Celtic tradition, and one which has found recurrent expression in its literature at different periods. But it is an attitude which implies as strong a contrast as possible between Dafydd's portrayal of bird-life and that which we find in the French poems and in the Welsh *canu rhydd*, whose bird-protagonists are, in both cases, only thinly-disguised human beings. Only in his presentation of the nightingale as essentially the bird of love,[96] do we seem to find in Dafydd's poetry any kind of echo of the characteristics attributed to birds in the French bird-debates. A parallel to this rejection of the common medieval view-point is seen in Dafydd's treatment of animals, as in the *cywydd* (GDG 22), in which he describes his sudden vision of the Fox, sitting unaware and unconcerned outside his lair. The emphasis at the same time on the animal's total unconcern, independence and self-absorption, and on the vivid spectacle he presents is as far removed as possible from the wily Reynard of the French beast-epic, of which it seems unlikely that Dafydd would not have known,[97] and in terms of which his contemporary, Geoffrey Chaucer, delineated *his* Fox. But the subjective exploitation of the natural world was as alien to Dafydd as were the allegorical abstractions and psychological analysis of the poets who composed the dream-visions and the *Roman de la Rose*. For he appears to have had no sympathy for, or interest in, the fundamental ideas which inspired these works, so that he rejected both the high idealism of Courtly Love and the contrasting cynicism to which it gave rise, and which is forcibly expressed in the work of Jean de Meun. But we can see that while rejecting the spirit which informed them, and the greater part of their substance as well, the things in these foreign sources which acted as touchstones for his imagination were, in fact, most characteristic: that is, he found in them

---

of nature was a song of praise in which he himself took part by entering into harmony with nature.' The personification of the blackbird in one quatrain as a 'hermit who does not clang a bell' (K. Meyer, *Bruchstücke der älteren Lyrik Irlands* (Berlin, 1919), 66), deserves comparison with Dafydd ap Gwilym. For text and translation of this quatrain, see J. Carney (ed.), *Early Irish Poetry* (The Mercier Press, Cork, 1965), 11–12, trans. K. Jackson, *op. cit.* 11, no. x. On the whole subject, see now Mac Cana's article, cited n. 83 above.

[96] Cf. J. Glyn Davies, THSC, 1912–13, 114–15, 'Whatever nucleus of fact there may have been, there can be no doubt that it was the European convention that kept the nightingale so much to the fore in Dafydd's love-poetry.' Distribution of the nightingale does not, according to modern records, extend much further west than the Welsh border—except in isolated instances. It remains possible that climatic conditions may have favoured a wider distribution in the fourteenth century.

[97] It seems to have been after Dafydd's life-time that the fables of Odo of Cheriton were translated into Welsh, late in the fourteenth century (Ifor Williams, *Chwedlau Odo*, Wrexham, 1926). The Welsh version contains a tale (no. XVI) in which the fox outwits Chantecleer in typical fashion. Cf. Chaucer's 'Nonnes Priestes Tale'.

suggestions for imagery, out of which he developed and extended images of his own.

Any discussion of the content and style of Dafydd ap Gwilym's poetry must indeed resolve itself in the end into a discussion of his imagery, since this really implies an examination of his whole use of language, and of all but the purely metrical aspects of his work. The most immediately arresting of these images are, perhaps, the extended ones (in his day a new thing in Welsh poetry), in which a metaphor or a simile is elaborated throughout a whole poem. One need but refer to such poems as *Morfudd fel yr Haul* (GDG 42) or *Serch fel Ysgyfarnog* (GDG 46), in addition to those I have already mentioned, or to the metaphor of the man shooting at a nightingale, in terms of which he refers to the death of the poet Gruffudd ab Adda (GDG 18). But there is also the imagery which is implicit in his use of vocabulary, and here one must take count on the one hand of his recurrent use of the traditional and archaic phraseology of bardic poetry, loaded with evocative associations of a literary kind; and on the other hand, of his contrasting use of a vocabulary apparently simple and direct, but which may, in fact, be highly evocative in a different way. Dr Parry and Mr Eurys Rowlands, each by analysing a single poem,[98] have illustrated some of the nuances in meaning which Dafydd achieves in this way, whether or not by conscious intention. Alternative meanings may be suggested, either because of ambiguity in the meaning of a word itself, or in its pronunciation, or because of the association of ideas which it sets in train. Individual characteristics in Dafydd's practice of the art of *dyfalu* ('comparison') closely bound up, as is this device, with the evolution of the *cywydd* metre,[99] also need full investigation. In this connexion, Dafydd's frequent use of personification has been pointed out. Nature is interpreted in human terms—the summer is *teg wdwart* 'a fair woodward' (GDG 27, 3), the holly *gwas tabarwyrdd*, 'lad with the green tabard' (GDG 29, 28), the stag *hardd farwn hir*, 'a fair tall baron' (GDG 116, 16), and Dafydd refers more than once to the 'hair' of the birchtree in summer, *gwallt ar ben hoyw fedwen haf* (GDG 24, 14). Just as birds are described as preachers and priests, so, conversely, Dafydd compares his fellow-poets to birds in his *marwnadau* for them, and just as the sea-gull is a nun, *lleian ym mrig llanw môr* (GDG 118, 10), so in another poem nuns are seen as swallows, *gwenoliaid* (GDG 113, 20). Very new and modern images may be used to gain immediacy of impact and surprise effects, as in the poem on Envy with its series of metaphors drawn from the organized defence of contemporary fortifications (GDG

---

[98] Thomas Parry (on *Cywydd y Gwynt*), *Lleufer*, xii (1956), 119 ff. reprinted in YB ix (1976) 48–60. Eurys Rowlands, 'Cywydd Dafydd ap Gwilym i Fis Mai', LlC v, 1 ff.

[99] T. Parry, THSC, 1939, 216–217; *Hanes Llenyddiaeth*, 91; D. Myrddin Lloyd, LlC i, 164, *n.* 16. See ch. 1 and p. 152 below.

140).[100] In all these ways, Dafydd may be said to have flouted tradition by giving his audience the stimulus of what was new and unexpected, in place of what was customary and weighted with the *aura* of literary associations. Yet, after all, the technique by which forceful and vivid comparisons are attained by startling new associations of ideas was only the re-appearance in a new form of something which was itself very old in Welsh poetry, for it is the 'studied contrast' which Sir Ifor Williams has pointed out as a feature of the earliest poetry,[101] appearing again in a new setting.

Another aspect of Dafydd's fondness for gaining effects by using known words in unexpected contexts is to be seen in the particular ways in which he employs borrowed words of Romance origin. These borrowed words, whether they are taken directly from French, or indirectly through the medium of Middle English, consist, as is not surprising, almost entirely of nouns, and for the most part of nouns denoting concrete things. They are words for buildings and furnishings of all kinds (in terms of which he describes his woodland retreat in the *deildy* or *castell celli*); different kinds of weapons, especially the cross-bow, *arblastr*, and its adjuncts; and words for various types of currency—*coron*, *fflwring*, *copr*, *mwnai*, and so forth. There is also a less concrete series of words dealing with the law and official administration—*ustus*, *sieler*, *fforffed*, *ceisbwl*,[102] *corodyn*.[103] And when these borrowed words are used, they are employed far more often than not in a figurative sense, in that they are used right out of their normal prosaic context, to give the shock and stimulus of the unexpected.

The leaves of May are florins on the tops of the branches, they are *iawn fwnai*, 'true currency' (GDG 23, 11);[104] the stars are golden pieces of wrought metal, *goldyn o aur melyn mâl* (GDG 67, 36); ears are *ceiniogau cof* 'the pennies of memory' (GDG 26, 10); everyone is only a copper coin compared with Madog Benfras, *copr pawb wrthaw* (GDG 19, 44). Gruffudd Gryg is taunted with the epithet *arblastr*—he is a cross-bow for the number of words he hurls, shooting at every mark (GDG 154, 1). The mist is a parchment-roll, making a surface for the imprint of the rain—*rhol fawr a fu'n glawr i'r glaw* (GDG 68, 15), and in an elaborate sustained metaphor the cock-thrush is in turn sheriff, justice

---

[100] Cf. T. Parry, *Yorkshire Celtic Studies*, v, 29.

[101] *Lectures on Early Welsh Poetry* (Dublin, 1944), 33.

[102] 'Catchpoll'. *Ceis* in this word may, however, be ultimately of Welsh derivation: see J. Russell-Smith, *Medium Aevum*, xxii, 104–110. On *ceisiaid* 'sergeants' in the fourteenth century, see now R. A. Griffiths, *Principality of Wales in the later Middle Ages* (UWP 1972), 70–1.

[103] Idris Foster, *Medium Aevum*, xxiii, 43, compares Ml. Lat. *corrodium*, etc., Ml. Eng. *corrody*, 'supplies, maintenance', etc. The legal connotations of the word are apparent from the instances cited in NED and the *Middle English Dictionary* (Michigan).

[104] See D. Stephen Jones, B xix, 31, on this reference.

and steward of the court, reading a legal summons, again from a parchment-roll (GDG 123). The nightingale is indicted (*ditio*)—that is, legally charged and then banished from Coed Eutun (GDG 25, 52), and love is confirmed with the seal of a kiss (*inseilio*, GDG 133, 45).

Some of these types of imagery are exemplified in the work of Dafydd's contemporaries. Thus Gruffudd ab Adda speaks of the 'hair' of the birchtree,[105] and personifies its bare trunk, used as a May-pole, as *traetures llwyn*, 'traitress of the woodland'. It is interesting to find that Gruffudd Gryg describes the moon as *nobl* and *fflwring*,[106] since Dafydd also uses for the moon both *fflwring* and the disparaging word *polart* (GDG 70, 57)—meaning in this case that it is a base coin appearing in place of the sun, providing light where it is not desired, but no warmth—it is even capable of being reduced in size as though it were a clipped coin.

Nevertheless, it seems to me that there are here certain types of imagery as to which we should consider carefully whether they may not be personally characteristic of Dafydd ap Gwilym. Many years ago Saunders Lewis advocated as a significant personal trait of this kind the frequency of imagery which transfers all the conventional attributes of the *llys* to Dafydd's court in the woods;[107] a calculated reversal in his poetry of the conventional values of the bards, which Dafydd has summed up in the single line *Gwell yw ystafell, os tyf*, 'A room is better if it grows' (GDG 121, 8). This concept may indeed have originated with Dafydd ap Gwilym, to be elaborated further by other poets, since Dr Parry has detected late features in two of the *cywyddau* which best support the argument.[108] But there are other images which should be considered. These include the poet's frequent figurative use of two of the classes of borrowed words to which I have alluded—of words for coins and currency, and of imagery based upon legal words and concepts connected with official administration. In respect to the first, it has been pointed out by T. Jones Pierce,[109] that the use of coinage was spreading into Wales during the fourteenth century replacing the older custom of barter and payment in services. The figurative use of words for specific coins is extremely rare, and indeed exceptional, in the poetry

[105] DGG², lxv; OBWV, no. 54, l. 1.

[106] OBWV, no. 56, ll. 3, 14.

[107] *Braslun*, 82–84.

[108] 'Adeiliais dŷ fry ar fron' (BDG lxxxvii) and *Y Llwyn Banadl* (BDG xlvii, *Oxford Book*, no. 63). See GDG, clxxi ff., nos. 1 and 164.

[109] *Wales Through the Ages* (1959), i, 157. References to currency are to be found in the work of earlier poets, but these are literal and not figurative. Eg. Gruffudd ap Dafydd ap Tudur: *deugein swllt nod o ysterlingod* (RBP 1255, 8). The stock metaphor which describes a girl's hair as *aur mâl* is common at all periods, and is attested already in the Gogynfeirdd (see T. Gwynn Jones, *Rhieingerddi*, p. 29; IGE p. 3, l. 21; cf. Chotzen, *op. cit.*, 209). But it is, probably, gold as a substance, rather than gold coinage, which is here intended.

of the period outside Dafydd's own work: Gruffudd Gryg's use of coin-images for the moon could have been suggested to him by Dafydd's own poem, since on internal evidence his *cywydd* must have been composed at the very end of the fourteenth century,[110] later than the period which is generally assigned to Dafydd's life-span. The rejected *Cywydd y sêr*[111] refers to the stars as *dimeiau*, 'halfpennies', and here also the poet describes the darkness as surrounding him as though he were in a jail—*ynghanol geol gaead*. There is disagreement as to the authorship of this poem, and it has been argued by more than one writer that it should be restored to the canon of Dafydd's authentic work.[112] I think these images in it may, perhaps, provide some supporting evidence for doing so. Dafydd uses the same metaphor of the jail in his poem *Dan y Bargod* (GDG 89), when he is waiting under the dripping eaves: *Ni bu'n y Gaer yn Arfon/ Geol waeth no'r heol hon.* And there can hardly be a more forceful instance of this rather ominous type of imagery drawn from the world of official administration than his description of the Wind as endowed with freedom to move everywhere unrestricted: *Ni'th dditia neb, ni'th etail/ Na llu rhugl, na llaw rhaglaw*, 'No one accuses you, neither hand of governor nor swift host restrains you' (GDG 117, 14).

Another feature which may well turn out to be distinctive concerns the arrangement of some of Dafydd's more elaborate images: in a number of the *cywyddau* these occur in triple groups. For instance, in aspiring after Dyddgu, the poet compares his temerity firstly to some small climbing creature, a marten, pole-cat or squirrel, who ascends from branch to branch, but on reaching the top of the tree does not find it so easy to come down again; next, to the audacity of sailors who venture on the sea with only a thin plank between them and the deep (he, like them, cannot easily turn back); and, finally, to the marksman who, after many random shots, finally scores a bull's eye: may not Dafydd also aim successfully and win the girl in the end with his poems of praise (GDG 37)? In another *cywydd* (GDG 131) he cites a very different set of images in alluding to his persistency in the pursuit of Morfudd—he is like the flexible branch of an apple-tree which bends easily and yet does not break; like a starved old cat, long accustomed to being kicked and knocked about, who, in spite of all ill-treatment, nevertheless survives; and, finally, like one who reaches his destination

---

[110] See n. 32 above.

[111] DGG², xl; OBWV, no. 64.

[112] S. Lewis, LlC, ii, 201; D. J. Bowen, *ibid.*, vi, 44–5; vii, 193–205. Iolo Goch uses *geol* figuratively of a ship (IGE², p. 74, l. 29), and there are instances of this type of metaphor in the work of Dafydd's possibly younger contemporaries; e.g. Llywelyn Goch describes the snow-covered landscape as *cuchiog gwaeth na swyddog sir* (DGG² lxxxv, 11). The comparative prominence of these images in Dafydd ap Gwilym's poetry remains striking.

by walking while others run. His protest against girls putting on ornaments to go to the fair (GDG 49) is elaborated by reference first to
the sun, which can have no need of additional brightness; then to an
old broken bow, which is not to be mended merely by gilding it exter-
nally; and lastly, to a lime-washed wall which serves its function as
a wall as well as one which is painted with coats-of-arms. Again (GDG
60) he compares his fruitless endeavours to please a heedless young
girl to the efforts of those who try to tame wild animals, and describes
in turn a hare, a squirrel and a roebuck; in each case, in spite of their
fostering, their wild natures will cause them to make off to the wilds
at the first opportunity. More cynically, he compares his position in
relation to Morfudd's husband to that of one of the two oxen in a
yoke, to a ball which is tossed from one hand to the other, and to
a rejected empty barrel (GDG 93). Morfudd's beauty, polluted as a
result of her marriage, is compared to a splendid varnished carving
in negligent keeping, to a valuable English fur destroyed by peat-smoke,
and to an oaken palisade warped by the salt water of the sea (GDG
81).[113] A variant of this triple arrangement is found in the *Ymryson*,
when Dafydd backs his argument in favour of the despised *cywydd* by
his vivid illustrations of the worn-out harp and the discarded poetry-
book; to be answered by a similar triple arrangement in Gruffudd's
rejoinder, when he compares Dafydd's poetry with the two other short-
lived wonders recently seen in Gwynedd—the hobby-horse at the fair,
and the new organ in Bangor cathedral. And there are, of course, the
poems in which certain of the traditional triads are cited for comparison
with the subject of his praise: *Tair gwragedd â'u gwedd fal gwawn* (GDG
51), in which the girl is added as a fourth to the triad of the three
women who inherited the beauty of Eve,[114] and the *cywydd* (GDG 84)
in which Morfudd's powerful fascination is compared with the enchantment of the Three Famous Magicians.[115] In *Tri Phorthor Eiddig* (GDG
80), the gatekeepers of the Jealous Husband are the hound, the creaking
door, and the sleepless old hag—a triad which is actually quoted in
a slightly variant form in one of the early *canu rhydd*.[116]

This fondness for triple groupings brings us back again to the importance in Dafydd's literary inheritance of the store of oral learning on

---

[113] There are in fact four images in this poem, as is pointed out by Dr Parry in
*Poetry Wales:* Special Dafydd ap Gwilym Number (vol. 8, Spring 1973), 41—the 4th being
the Sun which, like the girl's beauty is obscured by fog.

[114] TYP, no. 50.

[115] For variants, see TYP, nos. 27, 28, Appendix IV, 4. It is significant to find that
Dafydd's comparison of a girls' attraction to the magic of Math is anticipated in the
third of the *englynion* quoted as examples in all texts of the early version of the Bardic
Grammar, GP, pp. 7, 26, 46; B ii, 191. See below p. 115.

[116] OBWV, no. 108. A similar popular provenance may be suggested for the triad
quoted GDG 137, 41–2: *Tri pheth a gerir drwy'r byd/ Gwraig a hinon ac iechyd.*

all levels; not only the tradition of the bards, but also the humbler and much-less-well documented tradition which has, in part, come down in the *canu rhydd*. It is now recognized that the new poets of the *cywydd* in the fourteenth century took over from the *clêr ofer* the popular measure of the *traethodl*, developing it and giving it *cynghanedd*.[117] The evidence of the *canu rhydd* indicates that the same class of poets continued to use this and others of the oldest Welsh metres in an unbroken succession which comes to light for the first time in sixteenth-century manuscripts. It seems unlikely that Dafydd and his contemporaries, in following certain of the poetic devices of the *clêr*, and taking from them one of their metres, should at the same time have wholly neglected the kinds of subject-matter treated of by these humbler poets. And thus it is that perhaps the greatest of all the problems concerning the manner in which foreign literary influences reached Dafydd ap Gwilym (and one to which we can hardly hope ever to know the full answer) is that of determining how far this subject-matter included themes of ultimate French origin, and to what extent these themes were already established in Welsh poetry in the fourteenth century. As an instance, I have suggested that the influence of the French bird-debates, which we find well-attested in the *canu rhydd* at a later date, could as well have reached Dafydd through popular channels as from specific French literary models. Again, a few of Dafydd's *cywyddau* show certain not-very-close affinities with some of the well-marked types of the medieval French lyric. I have suggested a parallel between *Cyngor y Biogen* and one of the recurrent themes of the *reverdie*; parallels have also been pointed out to the themes of the *pastourelle*; the *malmariée*, in which a young girl is married to an old husband; the *serenade*; and the *aube*, or dawn-parting of lovers[118]—and some at least of these types recur also in the *canu rhydd*.[119] I think, then, that it is important to make a clear distinction between influences on Dafydd's poetry from

[117] T. Parry, 'Datblygiad y Cywydd'. THSC 1939, 209–31.

[118] Direct influence seems extremely doubtful in all cases. The parallels are discussed by Ifor Williams, THSC, 1913–14, 118–21 = DGG², xl–xli. He compares GDG 41 with the *pastourelle* (cf. Brinley Rees, *op. cit.*, 49–50); GDG 89 with the *serenade*; GDG 129 with the *aube* (cf. W. Lewis Jones, THSC, 1907–8, 146–7). This last poem deserves comparison with *Cyngor y Biogen* in that it virtually approaches a parody of the foreign model. The authenticity of the second *aube*, BDG xcvii, discussed by Chotzen, *op. cit.*, 290–2, is now rejected; see GDG clxxxiii, no. 117. This poem and GDG 129 have been discussed again recently (with translation) by Prof. Melville Richards in *Eos: An Enquiry into the Theme of Lovers' Meetings and Partings at Dawn in Poetry*, ed. by A. H. Hatto (The Hague, 1965), 568–574. Dr Geraint Gruffydd has made the interesting suggestion that the form of Dafydd ap Gwilym's elegy on his uncle (GDG 13) has been influenced by the form of the *serenade*; YB i, ed. J. E. Caerwyn Williams (Gee, 1965), 131–132. On these poems see below, ch. 3, pp. 96–7.

[119] Brinley Rees, *op. cit.*, chs. II and III. The poem *Crys y Mab*, OBWV no. 102, is a clear example of a *pastourelle*. The *reverdie* theme recurs again in the *ymddiddanion* with birds, see p. 80 above.

specific literary works whose circulation must at all times have been through written channels—and here I have advocated the supreme importance for Dafydd's literary background of two works in particular, Ovid's *Amores* and the *Roman de la Rose*—and those indeterminate influences which could have reached him orally through songs and poetry current in Latin, French, English, and even Welsh. All these tongues must have been the medium of popular entertainment in the Norman boroughs established in Wales in the wake of the Conquest. We know that Dafydd ap Gwilym had close contact with these, and Saunders Lewis, in a striking article,[120] has stressed the polygot character of the community in which he must have grown up.

When we speak of Innovation, then, in reference to Dafydd ap Gwilym's poetry, we tend to mean either changes which he himself initiated, or at least such as appear for the first time in the poets of his generation: we think of the major metrical innovation of the fourteenth century, the development of the *cywydd*; and as regards subject-matter, of the new themes which appeared then in Welsh poetry for the first time, the new attitudes to life and society, the response to literary influences from abroad. But it is important to recognize also that Innovation in this sense may include the appearance for the first time in Dafydd's *cywyddau* of themes imbibed from the sub-literary tradition of popular poetry: for although it may be common for aristocratic modes to travel downwards, the opposite process is also a recognized phenomenon, and there is a tendency for elements in the humbler, more spontaneous kinds of poetry to come upwards and revitalize the tradition. This last is what Professor W. J. Gruffydd once called 'the vital impetus in the ancient literatures of the Celtic peoples'.[121] It may well have been principally through the vitality of this impetus that the new literary influences from abroad came to be combined with many of the oldest elements in the Celtic literary tradition in the poetry of Dafydd ap Gwilym.

---

[120] *Blackfriars*, March 1953, 131–6. Reprinted in A. R. Jones and Gwyn Thomas, *Presenting Saunders Lewis* (UWP, 1973), 159–163.

[121] W. J. Gruffydd, *Dafydd ap Gwilym* (UWP, 1935), 33.

# 3. THE SUB-LITERARY TRADITION

THIS subject involves a discussion of virtually the whole of Dafydd ap Gwilym's literary inheritance: of all that was bequeathed to him from his predecessors, whether these be individually identifiable or not. For there is no need to emphasize that the most significant inheritances in Dafydd ap Gwilym's poetry were the non-literary ones, since it is of the essential nature of the Celtic tradition, both in Wales and in Ireland, that the important influences which came to a medieval poet were those which reached him through oral channels. How Dafydd treated his various inheritances from the past, the nature of his acceptances and—no less significantly—of his rejections, the ways in which he blended and developed different streams of tradition in his poetry, is clearly a question which is fundamental to our efforts to comprehend the character and attributes of his individual genius.

I take it, therefore, that with the exception of an early version of the Bardic Grammar,[1] of the Welsh version of Geoffrey of Monmouth's *Historia Regum*, and perhaps of the native tales and foreign romances which may have become available to him in the White Book of Rhydderch,[2] virtually everything which Dafydd inherited from within the indigenous Welsh tradition came to him through non-literary channels. It is questionable whether he had ever seen in writing any of the poetry of his predecessors. There is, however, a distinction here to be made between non-literary and sub-literary (to which I shall return presently), but it seems to me that one can best approach the second by way of the first—that is by saying something briefly about Dafydd's acceptances from this native poetic tradition. In the first place, Dafydd inherited in its entirety the classical tradition of *canu mawl* or bardic praise-poetry, stretching back to Taliesin and the other Cynfeirdd. He composed praise-poems and *marwnadau* or elegies which are wholly in

---

[1] See ch. 4 below.
[2] Ch. 5 below.

the style of his predecessors the Gogynfeirdd, also religious poetry and satire: all of these being in the traditional metres of *awdl* and *englyn* as used by the official poets of the previous two centuries. These poems are completely expressive of the ethos, the concepts, and the values of his predecessors—the praise of noble descent, of generosity and of courage, and they lay emphasis upon the mutual inter-dependence between poet and patron, between a ruler and his land. In all this Dafydd drew for his imagery upon the inherited formulas of bardic encomium: animal symbolism (the subjects of his eulogy are referred to in turn as a lion, a hawk, a stag or an eagle), recurrent references back to the *hengerdd* or oldest poetry, and to the names of the traditional heroes—Gwalchmai, Cai Hir, Peredur, and to the heroines—Indeg, Tegau, Luned, Creirwy.[2] He makes use of the old stock expressions for a girl's beauty—*gorlliw eiry mân, mwyalchliw, loywne gwawn*[3]—and shows his knowledge of the old legal terminology pertaining to the Law of Hywel: in fact, he demonstrates his familiarity with all those branches of the traditional native learning which would in Ireland have been known as *seanchas*. And there appears now to be some evidence that this knowledge may have come to him as part of a family inheritance, perhaps derived from his uncle Llywelyn, perhaps from a long line of poetic forebears stretching back to that Gwynfardd Dyfed whose name is among the earliest of his recorded ancestors.[4]

In his praise-poetry in the older metres we can, then, observe two things: Dafydd's complete acceptance of this traditional inheritance, and his transposition of it into the new, more flexible medium of the *cywydd deuair hirion*, with the licence which this new verse-form imparted to treat of a wider range of themes than had hitherto lain within the range of official poetry. This is most clearly delineated, perhaps, in the *cywyddau* addressed to his friend and patron Ifor Hael, as for instance when he compares Ifor's home to the hall of Rheged, and claims to be himself another Taliesin. (In fact, as Eurys Rowlands once pointed out,[5] nothing could in the event be more true, since Dafydd himself was no less obviously the founder of a new poetic tradition than was Taliesin.) Such influences from the classical tradition of bardic praise-poetry which lay behind him may therefore be described as *overt* influences, in that they seem to require little explanation beyond what we have in the extant poetry of the Gogynfeirdd. But I think that, with one possible exception, there is no direct continuity to be traced between him and any one individual predecessor whose work has come

---

[3] See pp. 13n, 15 above.

[4] R. Geraint Gruffydd has made the suggestion that Gwynfardd Dyfed may have been the *pencerdd* attached to the court of Rhys ap Tewdwr (d. 1083), SC XIV/XV (1979–80), 99. See also his discussion 'A Poem in Praise of Cuhelyn Fardd', SC X/XI (1975–6), 199, and ch. 1, p. 13 above.

[5] Eurys Rowlands, *Y Traethodydd* cxxii (1967), 31.

down (as there is for instance when in a *rhieingerdd* Iolo Goch echoes the actual words of Hywel ab Owain Gwynedd),[6] and that Dafydd's bardic inheritance may very probably have come to him in the main from the poetry of the official poets of Dyfed and Glamorgan, whose works have for the most part been lost.[7] One exception to this may however be noted, and it is an exception which is interesting enough in itself: it is the two lines which form the second half of an englyn in Dafydd's *marwnad* for his uncle Llywelyn, and which are to be found also in the Red Book of Hergest in an *englyn* by Gruffudd ap Dafydd ap Tudur:

> *Nid diboen na'm hatebud,*
> *Nid hawdd ymadrawdd a mud.*[8]

*(Not without pain is your not answering me,/ it is no easy thing to converse with a mute.)*

But it is impossible to know for certain whether this represents a genuine borrowing by Dafydd from his predecessor, or whether it owes its incorporation in the poem to subsequent oral or manuscript conflation betweeen the works of the two poets.

If this acceptance of the antecedent bardic tradition is to be described as an *overt* influence upon Dafydd ap Gwilym's poetry, its transposition into the *cywydd* metre, developed and elaborated as this was out of the humbler *traethodl*, is an outstanding instance of the bringing together of two very different streams of tradition (I am of course here by-passing the question as to how far Dafydd may have been personally responsible for the adaptation of the *cywydd* to formal bardic praise-poetry).[9] And this brings us to the problem of Dafydd's acceptances from the humbler tradition of popular Welsh poetry incorporated in the *traethodl* and other relatively uncomplicated metres, and it is this which is more particularly my subject today. From a metrical point-of-view it is now accepted that the debt of Dafydd and his contemporaries to those popular poets who for brevity and convenience we may group together under the title of *y glêr*, was in some ways even greater than it was to the *penceirddiaid* or official bards, since it was they who supplied the metre which formed the basis for the development of the *cywydd* in the fourteenth century.

[6] IGE² 4, 11.17–20. Cf. Saunders Lewis 'Iolo Goch', *Y Llenor* V (1926), 158. Both poets describe the girl with the unusual epithet *cegiden*, which Ifor Williams interprets as 'woodpecker' (IGE² 405); this seems a more likely metaphor for a girl than 'hemlock' as proposed in GPC (*cegiden*¹).
[7] The background is well set out by R. G. Gruffydd, 'Early Court Poetry of South-West Wales' SC XIV/ (1979–80), 99–104. See also G. J. Williams, *Traddodiad Llanyddol Morgannwg* (UWP 1948), ch. I.
[8] GDG 13, 23–4; RP 1264, 3–4; MA² 318a.
[9] See ch. 6 below.

But for lack of evidence it is not possible to define and de-limit the subject-matter of their verse in the same way that it is possible to define the content of classical bardic praise-poetry. No doubt there had been in Wales, as also in the British kingdoms of the 'Old North', from immemorial times a sub-stratum of popular poets of every kind and degree, whose verse was only very spasmodically recorded—as for instance we find it to have been in the *pais Dinogad* stanza in the Gododdin.

Dafydd's indebtedness to earlier Welsh nature-poetry is obvious: to poetry such as the *englynion* linked in sequences beginning *Eiry mynydd* 'Mountain snow', *Glaw allan* 'Rain outside', *Kalan Gaeaf* 'Winter's Day', *Llym Awel* 'Keen is the Wind' and so on[10]—conventional formulas which are employed to introduce a series of frequently quite unconnected statements about nature and humanity, of a gnomic and proverbial character. These are the work of generations of nameless poets, who had occupied themselves over the centuries in the patient perfecting of concise and epigrammatic descriptive phrases, which often show a close and delicate observation of natural phenomena: it is a kind of poetry whose origins are dateless, but which in some instances was still being composed down to the fifteenth century, and perhaps even afterwards. A frequent constituent of the *englynion* introduced by such phrases as these is proverbs, and Dafydd shows a frequent fondness for quoting proverbs.[11] Another constituent is lines which recur in *englynion* of the Llywarch Hen cycle, of which there is again some rather tenuous evidence that Dafydd may have known.[12] His quotation of the *englyn* on the Blackbird from the Bardic Grammar[13] is further proof, if such were needed, of his familiarity with verse of this kind.[14] The lines are a re-adaptation of the words in the Gospel of Matthew 6,26, as was pointed out by Chotzen,[15] and it is interesting to find that the same words are re-echoed at least twice in subsequent Welsh popular poetry.[16] *Kyt boet bychan, ys keluyd / yd adeil adar yg gorwyd coet* (RP 1031) 'Though it be small, ingenious is the building of the birds on the wooded slope' runs another of these *englynion*, and Dafydd's portrayal of birds reflects a response to their activities as running parallel to those of human beings which had thus already found literary expression in Welsh, as

---

[10] K. Jackson, *Early Celtic Nature Poetry; Early Welsh Gnomic Poems.*

[11] GDG 72, 17–18 and 25–6; 84, 67–8; 115, 53–4; 131, 27–8, 135, 44. These proverbs are all to be found in the collection of John Davies, *Dictionarum Duplex*, 1632. See further R. M. Jones, 'Diarhebion', *Y Traethodydd* 1976, 219.

[12] Ch. 5, p. 143 below.

[13] GDG 76, 23–30. See p. 109 below.

[14] Ch. 4. p. 108.

[15] *Respice volatilia caeli, quoniam non serunt neque metunt neque congregant in horreo: et Pater vester caelestis pascit illa.* Cf. Chotzen, *Recherches*, 86.

[16] 'Ymddiddan y Saint a Chybi' MA² 134, a *traethodl*; also T. H. Parry-Williams, *Hen Benillion* no. 293. Cf. Saunders Lewis, *Braslun*, 72.

indeed it had also in many other languages: humans have long accepted birds as *exempla* from whom there is much that can profitably be learned by the wise. The antecedent tradition thus provides sufficient evidence that Dafydd's nature-poetry welled up from an indigenous spring, and there is as yet no need to look outside Wales for the sources of his inspiration. It is indeed here, with Dafydd's bird-poetry, that we encounter the very core and centre of the problem of the influences which impinged upon his work—the point of contact between the non-literary and overt native poetic tradition, and the possibility of influences from outside. I would define those influences on Dafydd's poetry as 'sub-literary' whose ultimate place of origin we may be able to determine with varying degrees of assurance, though we can never know for certain by what channels they reached Dafydd ap Gwilym.

It would therefore be possible, and perhaps acceptable to many, to interpret such a poem as *Cyngor y Biogen* (GDG 63) 'The Magpie's Advice'—the poem in which a busy nest-building magpie turns on Dafydd and roundly rebukes him for his inactive pining for love, as a poem for whose external inspiration—with its exquisite evocation of bird-song in an April woodland after rain—there is no need to look further than to elements already present in the native Welsh tradition. Dr Parry has indeed remarked[17] that the dialogue with the bird could be taken as belonging to a tradition similar to that of the Mabinogi. But this is precisely where the difficulty lies: the difficulty of deciding what in fact is the stimulus behind such a poem as this, utterly unprecedented as it is, as far as we can tell, in earlier Welsh poetry. But there are in fact a number of parallels to it outside Wales, and it is impossible to disregard the significance of these. In Provençal, French, and Latin there are precedents in the type of verse called the *reverdie* (going back as far as William of Poitiers in the late eleventh century, the first Provençal poet): poems of greeting to spring, in which the poet's thwarted love is often contrasted with the joyful mating of birds.[18] Admittedly, the differences from Dafydd's poem are great, and if this were an isolated example one might dismiss the resemblance as being a curious coincidence, but no more. But it is not isolated, and I have shown already[19] that the points of contact with external parallels gain in significance by reference to a number of other French, Latin, and Provençal parallels to themes in Dafydd's poems. Again, Dafydd's repeated controversial exchanges with Friars on matters of behaviour and doctrine (GDG nos. 136, 137, 138) have as their background the widespread criticism of friars in fourteenth-century literature (examples are found in Chaucer

---

[17] *Wales Through the Ages* ed. A. J. Roderick (Llandybïe, 1959), 174.
[18] *Les Chansons de Guillaume IX, Duc d'Aquitaine*, ed. Jeanroy (Paris, 1964), no. X: *Ab la dolchor del temps novel*. See pp. 75–80 above.
[19] Ch. 2, especially pp. 31–6.

and Langland), coming on top of the late thirteenth-century controversy
over the increasing power of the mendicant orders in the University
of Paris, which is reflected in the work of the poet Rutebeuf.[20] There
is also, I find, an interesting parallel in a poem by Dafydd's near-
contemporary Jean de Condé in which he defends minstrels against
the attack made upon them by mendicant friars, and accuses these
of greed and hypocrisy, and it is particularly striking that, just like
Dafydd, he cites in favour of minstrels the precedent of *le roi Davis*[21]—
that is 'Dafydd Broffwyd', the prophet David, to whose authority Dafydd
himself appeals in his vituperative exchange with the Grey Friar (GDG
137, 60).

Then there are the *fabliaux*, those short, episodic, and generally ribald
narrative poems, based upon the timeless literature of jest and anecdote,
which were undoubtedly one of the most widespread sub-literary cur-
rents in medieval literature. These circulated orally in all languages,
and only occasionally received literary form, as they did in a number
of French verse *fabliaux* of the twelfth and thirteenth centuries. A typical
*fabliau* contains the three stock characters of the husband, the young
wife and the lover, and most frequently, the lover is a clerk in minor
orders—compare Chaucer's tales of the Miller, the Reeve, the Friar,
the Summoner, and the Merchant. Throughout Dafydd's work, elements paralleled in the *fabliaux* are widespread, in all those poems which
introduce the figure of *Yr Eiddig*, the 'Jealous Husband', who sometimes
(though rarely with assurance) is equated with Morfudd's husband,
*Y Bwa Bach*. Morfudd herself takes on the conventional role of the young
wife married to an ugly old husband (the theme of 'May and January')
and intrigues with her lover in the typical *malmariée* situation of the
French poems. Dafydd invariably casts himself in the role of the clerk-
lover, and is a leading actor in all those poems of his which reflect
the *fabliau* atmosphere: 'Trouble at a Tavern' (GDG 124), 'The Goose-
Shed' (GDG 126), 'The Bog-Hole' (GDG 127), 'Defaming His Servant'
(GDG 128). This last poem is specifically located at Rhosyr (later Newborough) in Anglesey, and it has been suggested[22] that the last three
poems referred to were all inspired by events, or places, in the vicinity
of this Norman borough: the atmosphere of the boroughs would certainly seem to have been a congenial one for the circulation of *fabliaux*.
Another channel of transmission which seems equally likely would have

[20] As pointed out by Saunders Lewis 'Dafydd ap Gwilym', *Blackfriars* xxxiv (March,
1953), 131 (reprinted in *Presenting Saunders Lewis*, ed. A. R. Jones and Gwyn Thomas
(Cardiff, 1973), 159; E. Faral, *Oeuvres Completes de Rutebeuf* (Paris, 1959–60).
[21] 'Li Dis des Jacobins et des Fremeneurs' 11.9, 18, 25, 54 in Jean de Condé, *La
Messe des Oiseaux et li Dis des Jacobins et des Fremeneurs*, ed. Jacques Ribard (Geneva and
Paris, 1970). Cf. 137, 60, and on the allusion to 'Dafydd Broffwyd' B xxix (1980), 81.
For Dafydd's possible knowledge of *La Messe des Oiseaux* see ch. 2, p. 77 above.
[22] Eurys Rowlands, *Y Traethodydd*, lxxii (1967), 22.

been opened up by the contacts made in the course of the military campaigns at home or abroad, in one of which *Yr Eiddig* is said to have taken part, together with a number of Dafydd's friends and relations (GDG 75). But it is merely the general setting and something of the mood of the *fabliaux* which is reflected in Dafydd's poems; they do not afford any close parallel to the foreign models, though it seems hardly possible that Dafydd would not have been familiar with these licentious anecdotes in one language or another. Though one cannot absolutely exclude the possibility of a written source, we must regard the *fabliau* elements in his work as emanating from a sub-literary tradition whose itinerary there is no means of tracing. As Saunders Lewis once expressed it,[23] there is nothing which can positively be called a *fabliau* in his poetry, but his spirit is frequently not far removed from that of the *fabliaux*.

It is not even improbable that Dafydd could have derived all the stock ingredients of the *fabliaux* from these in their moralized form: that is, from the *exempla* of the sermon literature. One of the best-known of the collections in which these *exempla* were circulated was that known as the 'Seven Sages of Rome', *Seith Doethon Rufein*.[23a] The editor of this work has shown that the stories contained in it circulated orally in Wales for some years before they came to be written down. The Welsh version of the tales is an adaptation rather than an exact translation, and it contains two stories not found elsewhere. We do not know how much older the written text of *Seith Doethon Rufein* may be than the earliest version in the mid-fourteenth century manuscript Jesus College 20, but this is hardly important in view of the anterior circulation of the stories in oral form. The Welsh versions closely reproduce the style and language of the *cyfarwyddiaid* or native story-tellers, and Dafydd must frequently have heard incorporated in sermons many similar *exempla* to these. There are at least two stories in *Seith Doethon Rufein* which definitely reproduce *fabliaux*, since they are based upon the typical three-cornered situation which characterize them: these are *Puteus* (no. 6), in which the guilty wife succeeds in locking her old husband out of the house by pretending that she had drowned herself, and *Tentamina* (no. 14) in which the young wife deliberately wrongs her husband for the sake of her lover by means of three unprovoked injuries, and subsequently incurs the inevitable retribution at the hands of her husband. The sympathy in these moralized *fabliaux* always lies with the outraged husband—whereas Dafydd, in presenting himself as the clerk-lover, calls for the sympathy of his listeners in his repeated unavailing attempts to outwit *Yr Eiddig*. The laugh—if there is one—invariably lies in Dafydd's own discomforture. In this respect, self-mockery is a mainspring

[23] *Blackfriars* xxxiv (1953), 134; A. R. Jones and Gwyn Thomas, *Presenting Saunders Lewis*, (UWP, 1973) 162.

[23a] Henry Lewis, *Chwedleu Seith Doethon Rufein* (2nd edn. UWP 1958).

of Dafydd's humour. And here again it is interesting to compare Chaucer, for both poets affect at will a similar pose of self-depreciation, or of failure through a kind of bewildered incompetence. This humorous pose may arise from the direct and personal relationship which both poets had with their audience, or it may conceivably owe something to Ovid, who maintained a similar pose—or it may in part be a reflex of the unprofessional literary status which both poets enjoyed, and the slightly uncertain and equivocal position as entertainer which both held in consequence. It is worth remembering that it was the keen and unpredictable insight of Iolo Morganwg who first noted the parallels between Dafydd's work and elements in Norman-French poetry, such as we have later come to recognise as elements of *amour courtois*. It was this discovery which inspired him to invent the spurious figure of Rhys Goch ap Rhiccert, together with some attractive poems in the style of the *canu rhydd* or free-metre poetry which he ascribed to him, so that he then described Dafydd ap Gwilym as 'of the school of Rhys Goch.'[24] In his discovery of these affinities with continental literary *genres*, Iolo Morganwg anticipated by more than a century the exposition of a similar discovery by Professor Cowell, the Professor of Sanscrit at Cambridge, as set forth by him in an article in THSC for 1878. The possibility of continental influences of a sub-literary nature on certain of Dafydd's poems which offer undeniable parallels to the types of the *aube*, *pastourelle*, and *serenade* is complicated by the fact that a number of the poems in which such parallels have been traced have now been rejected by Dr Parry from the authentic canon of the poet's work. But in so far as some of these rejected poems may be attributed to poets who were Dafydd's contemporaries, this merely shifts the problem, without removing it. Of the poems which remain within the canon, there can be little doubt that *Uchel y bûm yn ochi* (GDG 129) falls into the category of the *aube*: it consists of a dialogue in which the poet rejects his lady's assertion that the night is over and that dawn has come; but Dr Parry regards the authenticity of this poem as questionable.[25] The other fourteenth-century *aube*[26] which was previously attributed to Dafydd ap Gwilym, is now no longer accepted as his work: in this poem it is, by contrast, the man who points out the signs of dawn to a girl who denies them. *Fal yr oeddwn yn myned / Dros fynydd, gwyr crefydd Cred* (GDG 41) has been rather hesitantly compared by Ifor Williams with the *pastourelle*, but its relation to this type is certainly very slight: the poet encounters a girl as he is crossing a mountain

---

[24] *Gwaith Iolo Morganwg*, ed. Cadrawd (Llanuwchllyn, 1913), 72–4. On Rhys Goch ap Rhiccert see G. J. Williams, *Y Beirniad* viii (1919), 197–226, and p. 57 n above.

[25] GDG² 537.

[26] BDG xcvii. On the two poems see the discussion by Melville Richards in *Eos: An Enquiry into the theme of Lovers' Meetings and Partings at Dawn in Poetry* ed. A. H. Hatto (The Hague, 1965), 568–74.

and she is evidently complacent, promising to meet him at Llanbadarn on Sunday, and then (as is typical in Dafydd's narration of his own love-adventures) she fails him by not keeping her promise. Ifor Williams discerned the features of another *pastourelle* in one of the *apocrypha* poems[27] which has since been rejected from the canon. But by far the most convincing of these alleged parallels to foreign models is certainly *Dan y Bargawd* (GDG 89) 'Under the Eaves' in which the poet begs for admittance to Morfudd's home and describes the bitter weather in which he waits outside.[28] This is certainly the typical situation of the *serenade*, adapted to weather conditions more characteristic of Wales than of Provence, but it remains questionable whether the incident could not, like 'The Magpie's Advice' have arisen spontaneously from the poet's predicament, whether this was real or imaginary, and without any external influence. Clearly all this group of poems need to be studied together whether or not they belong to the canon of Dafydd's work or to the *apocrypha*, and this recommendation would include the very important poem *Claddu'r bardd o gariad* (OBWV no. 61) 'The Poet's Burial for Love', which exhibits striking affinities with anterior French bird-debate poems. Such an investigation could well have the value of bringing out Dafydd's individual characteristics in his treatment of foreign models more clearly than has hitherto been recognised. Taking these poems together it does seem to me that Dafydd's treatment of any foreign models with which he may have been familiar is utterly individual, original and idiosyncratic, and at times even verges on the burlesque.

Professor O'Tuama's recent study of Irish folk-poetry of the sixteenth and seventeenth centuries *An Grá in Amhráin na nDaoine* (1960) offers a thought-provoking and suggestive parallel for the likely channels by which influences from continental *amour courtois* may have been introduced into Wales. Among the specific themes which he identifies in the Irish poems as having French antecedents I find the following to be at least equally characteristic of Dafydd ap Gwilym's poetry:

(i) The association of love-affairs with wild nature; the theme of the escape to the wilderness, and of open-air assignations (the *oed*).

(ii) Allusions to the custom of going to church in order to meet girls (in both cases these are girls of the 'proletariat', i.e. not high-born ladies) (GDG 41, 48, III) also meetings in taverns (GDG 124).

---

[27] *Gwn ledrith un gain lwydraf*, BDG no. clv (see GDG[1] clxxviii).

[28] Cf. ch. 2, p. 85 above. Since writing this, *Dan y Bargawd* has been discussed in David Johnston's percipient article 'The Serenade and the Image of the House in the Poems of Dafydd ap Gwilym', *Cambridge Medieval Celtic Studies* no. 5 (1983), 1–19.

(iii) Various forms of the love-debate, in particular conversations with birds, who are busily engaged in mating, so that the poet compares with them his love-lorn solitude (GDG 63; cf. GDG 36; 115).

(iv) The theme of betrayal; this is more frequently of the man by the woman than of the woman by the man (desertion by either man or woman appears to be a popular rather than an aristocratic theme) (GDG 54, 55, 57, 60, 131, *etc*).

(v) Dream visions; i.e. the man sees the girl in a dream (GDG 39, 66).

(vi) The portrayal of love as a sickness (GDG 45, 84, 106, *etc*.), and the emphasis placed upon the need for secrecy (GDG 34, 74, 78, 129).

(vii) The theme of the *malmariée*, or complaint of a young girl married to an old husband. (This is of course transposed in Dafydd, since he is always his own spokesman, and consequently it is his own complaint that we get, and we never hear what Morfudd thought about the *liaison*.)

Dr O'Tuama notes also the adaptation of foreign conventions to native conditions; e.g. in the *pastourelle* the girl herds cows, not sheep, in Ireland; while in the bird-debates it is the native birds who participate—the blackbird, cuckoo, and thrush, not the nightingale and popinjay (parrot). (Here too, Dafydd's native birds should be compared.)

In suggesting that in the *amhrain grá* or folk-poetry of Ireland we have courtly love in a modified, and indeed in a popular form, borrowed directly from Norman-French in the years following after the Norman conquest of Ireland in 1170, Dr O'Tuama points out that this was a century earlier than courtly influences are manifested in the aristocratic verse or *danta grá* of Gerald Earl of Desmond and his successors, and moreover that the themes listed above are all noticeably absent from the *danta grá*.[29] But he finds a significant analogy to these themes in the medieval English Harley Lyrics,[29a] that is in the unique anthology of secular lyrics brought together in a manuscript believed to have been written at Leominster in Herefordshire about 1320, and whose contents are believed to have been composed at various different places over the previous century. In these lyrics we also encounter courtly love in a modified, popular form, exhibiting many of the features just described: in particular, the unsophisticated association of human moods and emotions, particularly love, with a background of the countryside and of wild nature, the whole treated with a lightness of touch and occasional humour, which are in pronounced contrast to the treat-

[29] Seán Ó Tuama, *An Grá in Amhráin na nDaoine* (Dublin, 1960).
[29a] G. L. Brook, *The Harley Lyrics* (Manchester, 1948).

ment of *amour courtois* on the more usual aristocratic level. It will be remembered that long ago Sir Ifor Williams drew attention to the significance of the Harley Lyrics in relation to the poetry of Dafydd ap Gwilym,[30] pointing out the significance both of their date and of their place of origin, and Saunders Lewis has subsequently re-emphasized this significance.[31] Although I would regard the latter's claim that the lyrics are the work of 'a Welsh-speaking Welshman' as perhaps excessive, yet there is every reason to stress the interest of the collection in relation to the themes of Dafydd ap Gwilym's poetry. The reason for Saunders Lewis's claim was that poems in the collection do in fact contain two probable words borrowed from Welsh—'miles' (W. *mil* 'animal'), and 'wolc' (W. *gwalch* 'hawk'). In one poem we have the earliest and indeed the only allusion outside Wales to the heroine Tegau Eurfron and her love for Caradoc.[32] In addition there are elaborate effects of alliteration and assonance, and something which looks very much as though it might be a transposition of the craft of *dyfalu*, as practised by Dafydd and his contemporaries. In yet another poem the refrain 'Blow, northern Wind, send thou me my sweeting' which suggests a refrain taken from popular oral poetry, has invited an obvious comparison with Dafydd's commissioning the Wind as a *llatai* or love-messenger (GDG 117). It is frequently supposed that the modified forms of courtly love apparent in the lyrics represent a late feature, an adaptation of the convention to the English temperament and to English conditions. But it would seem to me that it is at least arguable, in view of the Irish parallel, that this apparent modification is merely due to the fact that the lyrics represent an older tradition which lay closer to the popular, mainly unrecorded verse of the people. In any case, the significant similarities which the lyrics offer to elements in Dafydd's verse bring out the force of Saunders Lewis's dictum that 'we shall not get a proper idea of the cultural climate of the late Middle Ages in Britain unless we recognise that Anglo-French and Middle English and Welsh were all cheek by jowl in the Welsh Marches and Crown Lordships.'[33] This means, I take it, that we must at all points take into account the probability of a mass of unrecorded verse in all of these languages, in which each one of them is bound to have had an influence upon the others. The kind of fusion of cultures which took place in the orbit of the Norman castles and their surrounding settlements in thirteenth-century Ireland, must have occurred to at least an equal extent in the Norman boroughs which were established in the wake of the Norman Conquest in Wales.

In considering further the probability of un-recorded, sub-literary

---

[30] THSC 1913–14, 149; DGG² xlvii–viii.
[31] *Blackfriars* xxxiv; 133–4; *Presenting Saunders Lewis* 161.
[32] Cf. TYP, 512–14; G. C. Thomas, B xxiv, 1–9. Cf. ch. 5, p. 138–9 below.
[33] Saunders Lewis, *loc. cit.*

channels for the external influences upon Dafydd ap Gwilym's poetry—
and these of course can only be inferential—the Irish parallel adduced
by Dr O'Tuama encourages a fresh examination of the Welsh *canu
rhydd* 'free poetry' (as opposed to *canu caeth*, which was subject to the
rules of *cynghanedd*, and composed in the traditional strict metres). In
Wales, as in Ireland, the manuscript tradition of this popular, unofficial
poetry goes back to the sixteenth and seventeenth centuries. External
influence from English rhythmical song-tunes has been accepted as
having operated upon the development of this verse in Wales (though
it has been disputed, rightly or wrongly, as having had any effect upon
the parallel development in Ireland). In the case of the Welsh *canu
rhydd*, therefore, it would seem a plausible argument that the external
influence from current popular verse in English may have had the effect
of giving a stimulus which had the effect of bringing out into the open
a much older tradition of Welsh verse which had always flourished,
though mainly un-recorded, alongside the *canu caeth*. All authorities
agree that a long history lies behind the very early metres, without
*cynghanedd*, which are employed in the earliest of the free-metre poems
which have come down.[34] It is agreed also that the practice of composition in these metres is to be associated with the various grades which
existed of non-official poets commonly known as *y glêr*. There appears
to be no doubt that this was a development which arose primarily
in south and south-east Wales (though there seems no need to follow
Iolo in his ardent championing of Morgannwg alone as essentially the
home of the *canu rhydd*). W. J. Gruffydd has indeed spoken of the southern
part of the country after the development of the *cywydd* as 'weaving
away in the depths and developing the *canu rhydd* far out of sight'[35]
and thus illustrating his dictum *Y Gogledd sy'n cadw, y De sy'n cychwyn*,
'the North conserves, the South initiates'.

Popular types of poetry in the *canu rhydd* are the *breuddwyd* or dream
(with which one may compare the popularity of the parallel Irish *aisling*),
and the *ymddiddan* or dialogue between a frustrated lover and a bird
(the *reverdie* theme), in which the man asks the bird for advice. The
native birds—lark, cuckoo, thrush, and wren all figure in these dialogues, though the nightingale, more conventionally, is also popular. In
these poems the advice given by the bird always seems to be of a more-or-
less cynical nature (a moralizing tendency consequent upon the Protes-
tant reformation has been discerned here),[36] desertion and broken faith
are frequent themes, and there are references, as in the *cywyddau serch*,
to the stock figure of *Yr Eiddig*, the 'Jealous Husband', and to slanderers.

---

[34] Exx: the metres *awdl-gywydd, cywydd deuair fyrion, traethodl*; see T. H. Parry-Williams,
*Canu Rhydd Cynnar* (UWP 1932), xci–xciv.

[35] *ail ymroes y Dê i weu eto yn y dyfnder ac i ddatblygu'r gân rydd ymhell o'r golwg*, W. J.
Gruffydd, *Llenyddiaeth Cymru o 1450 hyd 1600* (Liverpool, 1922), 68.

[36] D. Gwenallt Jones, *Y Ficer Prichard a 'Cannwyll y Cymry'* (Caernarfon, 1946), 44.

Occasionally *llateion* or bird-messengers play a part[37] (these figure also in the Irish *amhrain grá*, but do not on the other hand, seem to be known in English popular verse). As is the case with the Irish *amhráin grá*, the majority of the love-poems seem to be men's complaints, and this too is interesting in view of the relative scarcity of male love-laments in England and France. There are conventional openings, such as the very common *Fal yr oeddwn* 'As (once) I was', which it is interesting to note that Dafydd ap Gwilym also employs no less than five times.[38]

I would not for a moment suggest that one can exclude the probable influence of the *cywyddau* upon these poems. That would be all the more impossible since we know that there were a number of poets, such as Siôn Tudur, who composed in the traditions both of the *canu rhydd* and of the *canu caeth*. But I do suggest that as regards the subject-matter, no less than the metrical forms, we have to do with a much older tradition which (as in the parallel case of the Irish folk-poetry) goes back ultimately to very early French models, including the popular thirteenth-century cult of poems in which birds debate upon questions of love. If this is the case, and if their prototypes go back as far as the time of Dafydd ap Gwilym, as W. J. Gruffydd suggested[39] might be so, then it would seem reasonable to conclude that Dafydd ap Gwilym derived these and many other themes in his poetry from a popular tradition which had already before his time absorbed many elements from outside sources, and that this tradition continued to exist 'underground' and un-recorded (as did the parallel tradition in Ireland) until it re-emerged when drawn upon again in the sixteenth and seventeenth centuries by the poets of the *canu rhydd*.

Considering the very ancient metrical origins of the popular poetry which emerges in both Ireland and Wales in these latter centuries, it does seem that we have here a repetition of the same phenomenon as that which Calvert Watkins[40] emphasized as having occurred at a much earlier date in Irish. This was the phenomenon presented by the evolution of the syllabic metres out of much older rhythmically alliterative

---

[37] Exx: OBWV no. 103; T. H. Parry-Williams, *Hen Benillion* (Aberystwyth, 1956), 55–7.

[38] As is pointed out by Brinley Rees, *Dulliau'r Canu Rhydd 1500–1600* (UWP 1952), 55–7.

[39] W. J. Gruffydd, *op. cit.* 68.

[40] Calvert Watkins, 'Indo-European Metrics and Archaic Irish Verse', *Celtica* vi (1963), 194 ff, esp. 248. Proinsias Mac Cana further compares the metrical innovations which took place in early Irish with those which appear in the work of Dafydd ap Gwilym and his contemporaries; the metrical innovations being accompanied in both cases by innovations in the subject-matter of poetry. See his 'Conservation and Innovation in Early Celtic Literature', EC xiii (1972), 106–7, and my discussion of this attribute in the Celtic literatures in *Literature in Celtic Countries* (ed. J. E. C. Williams, UWP, 1971), 49–51. Continuity between the rhythmical patterns of the oldest Irish accentual verse and that of the folk-poetry of the last four centuries has also been demonstrated by James Carney, *Ériu*, xxii (1971), 53–63.

verse-forms, under the external impact of Latin hymn-forms: in both cases the innovations consisted in the introduction of new forms out of already established metrical patterns—since metrical forms are slower to change, more conservative and more tenacious in preserving continuity than is the subject-matter of poetry, and more resistant to all kinds of innovation. Even if we had not the important Irish analogy of the *amhráin grá*, there would still be strong reason for believing that new subject-matter inspired from without was already being treated in Welsh before the time of Dafydd ap Gwilym. What Dafydd and his contemporaries accomplished was effectively to unite the two traditions of popular and aristocratic verse, giving *cynghanedd* to the metre of the *traethodl* and taking over with it a freer range of subject-matter, while at the same time giving status to the resulting synthesis by blending with it the established themes and ornaments of aristocratic bardic praise-poetry.

There remain two other points arising out of Dr O'Tuama's book on which I would like to comment briefly for their bearing upon the situation in fourteenth-century Wales. The long survival of the themes of *amour courtois* in an unwritten tradition was materially aided by the essentially oral character of the literary tradition in Ireland. This is of course no less true of Wales; for here, as in Ireland, the foreign literary influences when they came in, encountered and reacted upon a long-established and highly developed native poetic tradition. The popularity in the Irish poems of the theme of love as a sickness and of the *aisling* or love-vision is due to the fact that these themes had already been familiar and had found expression in the native literature as far back as the eighth and ninth centuries, so that it came about that the foreign poems in which these themes were celebrated fell upon fruitful soil, making their impact upon something which was already familiar. It is arguable, I think, that a process of a similar kind may have taken place in the case of Dafydd ap Gwilym's portrayal of birds. The recurrent imagery by which he presents birds as preachers and as poets (endowing them, as it were, with innate qualifications to give advice and to dictate to humans as to their conduct) would seem to indicate the impact of the popular thirteenth-century poems of bird-debate upon a pre-existing and essentially Celtic awareness of birds and animals as sentient fellow-beings—'companions in the world' (as Dr Parry once phrased it),[41] endowed with a special wisdom and engaged in activities parallel to those of humans. In the poetry of both Wales and Ireland this companionable and often affectionate attitude towards birds and animals goes back to a much earlier date than there is any possibility of French influences as having inspired it. This is amply demonstrated by the early nature-poetry in both languages.

[41] *Lleufer*, xii (1956), 125; reprinted in YB IX (1976), 55.

My other point is this. Dr O'Tuama has shown that the themes
of *amour courtois* came into Ireland eventually to emerge in the *amhráin*,
at an earlier date and in a more copious flood than can in any way
account for the appearance of these same themes in the more sophisticated and aristocratic *danta grá* of Gerald Earl of Desmond and his
successors. In a comparable manner, is it not worth considering that
there may have come to Wales two quite separate and distinct waves
of tradition from outside, to be detected on the one hand in occasional
instances in the works of the twelfth-century Gogynfeirdd, and on the
other in the poetry of Dafydd ap Gwilym? Under the first count I
refer of course to the rather ambiguously worded amatory poem
addressed by Cynddelw Brydydd Mawr to Efa the daughter of his
patron Madog ap Maredudd, and to his references in various poems
to the sleeplessness caused by love, to the figure of *Yr Eiddig*, and possibly
also to horses as *llateion* or love-messengers. At an even earlier date
in the twelfth century we have the *Gorhoffedd* or 'Boasting poems' of
Hywel ab Owain Gwynedd and Gwalchmai with their references to
the *eos* or nightingale, and in the case of Hywel, to love for married
women.[42] All these allusions present a considerable problem, because
if as has been suggested, they do really reflect ultimate influences from
the poetry of the Troubadours, then these influences must have reached
Wales at a surprisingly early date, since they are apparently not attested
in the poetry of northern France until they appear towards the end
of the twelfth century in the work of Chrétien de Troyes. Can they
have been introduced into Wales directly from Provence, perhaps via
trade-channels? One piece of collateral evidence may perhaps be relevant here, and that is the fact that Arthurian names of ultimate Welsh
origin appear in Provençal literature (and even further south, in Italy)
in some profusion much earlier than they do in the poetry of northern
France, that is to say, before the middle of the twelfth century. This
seems to corroborate the possibility of some kind of two-way traffic
between Wales and the south of France, by the early years of the twelfth
century.[43] But this is an even more obscure problem of sub-literary
tradition than the problems which relate to Dafydd ap Gwilym's
sources: my point is merely that these influences may have reached
poets in north Wales by a quite separate and earlier channel than the
influences from northern France which reached England and then south
Wales directly in the wake of the Norman Conquest—the influences
which are reflected alike in the Harley Lyrics and in Dafydd ap Gwilym's
poetry. Two quite separate streams of influence could well be involved, so that there is no reason to suppose that Dafydd ap Gwilym's

[42] T. Gwynn Jones, *Rhieingerddi'r Gogynfeirdd* (Denbigh, 1915) compares the *Gorhoffedd*
poems with the *genre* of the Troubadour *vanti*.
[43] Cf. R. G. Gruffydd, YB IV (1969), 25.

love-poetry was directly indebted to the same external influences as those which may have affected Hywel ab Owain Gwynedd, or even that his manifest familiarity with the techniques of earlier bardic praise-poetry need imply a knowledge of the work of any of the court poets of the Gwynedd princes; but rather that this knowledge was indebted to the mainly submerged tradition of bardic praise-poetry which flourished during the same centuries in Morgannwg, Dyfed, and Ceredigion.[44]

---

[44] On this point cf. the remarks of Eurys Rowlands, LlC vii (1963), 230.

# 4. DAFYDD AP GWILYM AND THE BARDIC GRAMMAR

AT THE beginning of the *awdl* which he composed to his uncle Llywelyn, Dafydd ap Gwilym greeted his patron as *llyfr dwned Dyfed* 'Dyfed's Grammar Book' (GDG 12). By this metaphor he implied that his uncle epitomized in himself the total learned inheritance which belonged traditionally to the bards of Dyfed. The word *dwned* derives originally (through the medium of Middle English *donet*[1]) from the name of Donatus, the fourth-century Latin grammarian whose *Ars Grammatica* had a profound influence on the teaching of the schools throughout western Europe during the Middle Ages. But in the Welsh version of the *dwned*, the treatise on the science of grammar—that is, on Latin grammar only very slightly adapted towards the Welsh language—is combined with a lengthy treatise on the metres of Welsh poetry, illustrated by examples.[2] Combined with the prescriptive *Trioedd Cerdd* or 'Triads of Poetry' and the notes listing the ideal terms by which God and the saints and men and women in all walks of society ought to be praised,[3] this indigenous addition to the Grammar greatly exceeds in length the Latin-inspired excursus on grammatical science which precedes it. The allusion in Dafydd's *awdl* to his uncle is the earliest occurrence of the word *dwned* which exists in Welsh, and it is this fact which raises the question which I would like now to examine: Did Dafydd ap Gwilym know the text of the Welsh Bardic Grammar, and can such knowledge have had any influence upon either the content or the style of his verse?

---

[1] GP xcvi, n.

[2] On the Bardic Grammar see Thomas Parry 'The Welsh Metrical Treatise attributed to Einion Offeiriad', PBA xlvii (1961), 177–95. Since the original publication of this article, the following further studies have appeared: Ceri Lewis, 'Einion Offeiriad and the Bardic Grammar', ch. 3 in *A Guide to Welsh Literature*, vol. 2, ed. A. O. H. Jarman and Gwilym Rees Hughes (Swansea 1979): A. T. E. Matonis 'The Welsh Bardic Grammars and Western Grammatical Tradition', *Modern Philology* 79 (1981–2), 121–45.

[3] On this section of the Grammar see Saunders Lewis, *Braslun*, 55–65.

In *Gramadegau'r Penceirddiaid* (1934) G. J. Williams and E. J. Jones prefixed a magistral survey and discussion of the Welsh bardic grammars to a selection of the texts. The selection comprises three of the four basic texts of the Grammar, as redacted in the fourteenth century, with subsequent versions by *penceirddiaid*, such as the *dwned* of Gutun Owain and the *Pum Lyfr Cerddwriaeth* of Simwnt Fychan. It is the four early texts of the Grammar which alone concern the present discussion. These are the texts of the Red Book of Hergest, Llanstephan 3, Peniarth 20 and the incomplete version in Bangor 1.[4] Peniarth 20 is perhaps the earliest inscribed text of the four: it has been shown that it was written in the mid or late fourteenth century.[5] RBH and Ll3[6] are nearly related texts and were both written close to the year 1400; Bangor 1 is of the mid fifteenth century. It is plain that all four texts derive ultimately from a common original, and the closeness of RBH and Ll3 to each other indicates that both may derive from an intermediate copy of this prototype, while the two other MSS derive independently, either directly or indirectly, from the same original text. There are minor variations between the four texts, some of which are in themselves of considerable interest. Since all four are copies of an earlier work, the fact that Peniarth 20 is slightly older than RBH does not in itself prove that this text comes nearest to the common source. As far as the illustrative section on the Welsh metres is concerned, I am not convinced by the argument advanced by Saunders Lewis in favour of the priority of the Pen. 20 text over RBH. But it is fair to observe that Saunders Lewis made no reference in his discussion to the section of the Grammar which treats of the metres. As regards this section at least, I shall presently give the reasons on which I base my conclusion that the text of RBH comes nearest to the prototype of all the four manuscripts.

In RBH the sub-section on the *awdl* metres is accompanied by the statement that a certain 'Einion Offeiriad'[7] (E. the Priest) had 'thought

---

[4] Ed. B ii (1925), 184–200. Some of the *lacunae* in the text have been supplied by the later copies in Peniarth MSS 169 and 191.

[5] On the Peniarth 20 version of the Grammar see Saunders Lewis, *Gramadegau'r Penceirddiaid* (Darlith Goffa G. J. Williams, UWP 1967). The date of the MS is that assigned to it by Thomas Jones in his introductions to *Y Bibyl Ynghymraec* (UWP 1940) and to *Brut y Tywysogyon: Peniarth 20 version* (UWP 1941) and in his inaugural lecture on the same subject (UWP 1953), 7.

[6] On Llanstephan 3 see J. Morris-Jones, THSC 1923–4, 3. This MS is not a copy of RBH, but the closeness of the two to each other emphasizes the fidelity of both to the common original. Yet at least one occasion Ll3 preserves an item paralleled in P20 but omitted from RBH: the important passage on the functions of the different grades of poet, beginning *Ni pherthyn ar brydyd ymyru ar glerwryaeth* (GP 35, 56–7). While giving the same *exempla* as RBH of all the *englynion* and *cywyddau*, Ll3 gives variant *exempla* for two of the *awdl* metres; see p. 114 below.

[7] GP 11, 30.

of' or 'invented' (*a feddyliodd*) the three final examples given of *awdl* metres, those called *Hir a Thoddaid*, *Cyrch a Chwtta* and *Tawddgyrch Cadwynog*. Many years ago Sir Ifor Williams[8] brought forward strong evidence in support of the belief that this 'Einion Offeiriad' was the same man as the Einion Offeiriad who composed an *awdl* in praise of the powerful magnate Sir Rhys ap Gruffudd[9] at some period during the twenties of the fourteenth century. The *awdl* is composed in a strange assortment of eleven different metres, ending with two of the metres which the Bardic Grammar attributes to Einion's 'invention', that is to say *Hir a Thoddaid* and *Cyrch a Chwtta*. Unfortunately the *awdl* has come down in only a single copy, lacking its ending. But as Sir Ifor pointed out, it is extremely likely that the lost ending of the *awdl* is preserved in the Grammar's concluding example, which is that of the metre *Tawddgyrch Cadwynog*, the third of Einion's three 'invented' metres, more particularly because this example ends with the name of 'Rhys ap Gruffudd'. In an important subsequent article[10] Mr Beverley Smith showed that there were three men called Einion Offeiriad living in Wales in the first half of the fourteenth century, and that the one most likely to have been the author of the *awdl* to Rhys ap Gruffudd and also the 'editor' of the Bardic Grammar is the Einion Offeiriad who owned land in the middle of the century in the commote of Mabwynion in the cantref of Is Aeron in Ceredigion—land which he may very likely have obtained as a gift from Sir Rhys ap Gruffudd and which was escheated in the year 1352, presumably as a result of the death of its owner. Nor is it impossible that the 'Einion Offeiriad' who lived in the commote of Is-Gwyrfai in Arfon at this same time was the same man: his death is recorded in 1349, a time when the Black Death was at its height in England and Wales.

The result of the researches of Sir Ifor and of Mr Beverley Smith is to bring Einion Offeiriad's literary activity very close to the circle of Dafydd ap Gwilym, both geographically and socially, spotlighting Einion's connections with people and places with which Dafydd was associated in Ceredigion in the middle years of the fourteenth century. Sir Rhys ap Gruffudd held the position of greatest authority under the Crown among the *uchelwyr* of Deheubarth in the first half of the century, he was also a remote cousin to the poet through his mother Nest daughter of Gwrwared ap Gwilym—the last-named being Dafydd's own great-grandfather.[11] And Dafydd actually refers (GDG

[8] *Y Beirniad* V (1915), 129–34; 'Awdl i Rys ap Gruffudd gan Einion Offeiriad', *Cy.* xxvi (1916), 115–46.

[9] On Sir Rhys ap Gruffudd see R. A. Griffiths, *The Principality of Wales in the Later Middle Ages*, vol. 1, South Wales (UWP 1972), 99–102.

[10] 'Einion Offeiriad' B xx (1964), 339–47. For Einion's association with the commote of Mabwynion see the note by Sir Ifor Williams, B x, 241–2.

[11] GDG xxxii, GDG² xiv; R. A. Griffiths, loc. cit.

75,2) to (Sir) Rhys ap Gruffudd as leading a Welsh army across the sea in support of Edward III in his French wars—one of Dafydd's very rare allusions to contemporary events.[12]

As mentioned above, the name of Rhys ap Gruffudd occurs both in RBH and in Ll3 in the final verse of the Grammar exemplifying the metre *Tawddgyrch Cadwynog*.[13] Further, there is among the examples of the *englyn unodl union* in these two manuscripts an *englyn* in praise of a certain 'Rhys' (no. iv below). I shall be quoting this *englyn* presently in order to draw attention to some other points of interest in it, apart from the probability that it too celebrates Sir Rhys ap Gruffudd. It is notable also that a certain 'Angharad', who is named no less than five times in the *exempla* in the Red Book, appears to have been another flesh-and-blood character: as Sir Ifor showed in the article referred to, she is probably to be identified with the 'Angharad' whom Dafydd ap Gwilym celebrated in his *marwnad* to her (GDG 16). She was the wife of Ieuan Llwyd[14] of Parcrhydderch in the parish of Llangeitho in Glyn Aeron, about ten miles from Strata Florida. Ieuan Llwyd was a man of great prominence in cultural circles in Ceredigion and a member of a family celebrated for its patronage of poets.

But it was not the association of the Bardic Grammar with men and women who were prominent in Ceredigion in the middle years of the fourteenth century and who were also evidently well-known to Dafydd ap Gwilym, which drew my attention in the first place to the significance of the *exempla* in relation to his poetry. Like others before me, I was struck by Dafydd's very close paraphrase of the old three-line *englyn* about the Blackbird (no. xvi below):

> *Chwerdit mwyalch mywn kelli,*
> *Nyt ard, nyt erdir idi,*
> *Nyt llawenach neb no hi* (GP 9).

*(The Blackbird laughs within the copse,/ she does not till the soil, nor is it tilled for her,/ yet none is happier than is she.)*

Dafydd quoted this *englyn*, with the minimum of alteration, as an apologue to justify the care-free life of the *bastynwyr* or itinerant poets

---

[12] In his army went a certain *bygegyr* or 'drone bee' on whom Dafydd wishes perdition, since in the typical role of *Yr Eiddig*, the 'Jealous Husband' we are told that he had frequently chased the poet away from his premises, GDG 75.

[13] GP 11–12, 31.

[14] In an important recent article in NLW *Journal*, xxii (1981) Daniel Huws has shown that a copy of Dafydd's *Marwnad Angharad*, hitherto un-noticed, is to be found on f. 130v of the Hendregadredd manuscript. He would regard this MS as the poem-book of Ieuan Llwyd's family, containing verses addressed to his father, mother, and wife. On the family of Ieuan Llwyd, Angharad, and their son Rhydderch (of D. ap G's 'elegy', GDG 17) see further D. Hywel Roberts, 'Noddwyr Beirdd yn Sir Aberteifi', LlC x (1968), 83–6; D. J. Bowen, LlC viii, 13–14; LlC ix, 60, n. 120.

(he implies that he himself was one of them), implicitly comparing their life with that of the care-free wild birds in the forest:

> Chwerddid mwyalch ddichwerwddoeth
> Yng nghelli las, cathlblas coeth.
> Nid erddir marlbridd iddi,
> Neud iraidd had, nid ardd hi.
> Ac nid oes, edn fergoes fach,
> O druth oll ei drythyllach.
> Llawen yw, myn Duw Llywydd,
> Yn llunio gwawd mewn llwyn gwŷdd (GDG 76, 23–30).

*(The Blackbird, wise and cheerful, laughs/ in the green copse, a mansion of fine song./ No fruitful soil is tilled for her,/ the seed is fertile, and she does not toil,/ yet there is not—little short-legged bird—/ any livelier chatter than is hers./ She is joyful, by Lord God/ making her song of praise in the woodland grove.)*

The *englyn* quoted echoes the familiar words of St Matthew's Gospel, 6,26: *Respice volatilia caeli, quoniam non serunt neque metunt, neque congregant in horreo, et Pater vester caelestis pascit illa.* It is interesting to find that the description of the joyful care-free singing Blackbird recurs twice in closely similar terms in poems of popular origin and of uncertain age which have been traditionally associated with the *clêr*.[15]

Although the four-line *englyn* was common by the twelfth century, it seems likely that the old type of three-line *englyn o'r hen ganiad*, like the one to the Blackbird, continued to be practised by the *clêr ofer* for some centuries afterwards.[16] Behind these *englynion* there lay a long tradition of nature poetry encapsulating gnomic and proverbial state-ments, and this kind of popular verse formed an important element in Dafydd's literary inheritance. It is most interesting that Einion Offeir-iad should have included examples of these archaic *englynion* in his Gram-mar. They were rejected in the succeeding period by the later redactors of the Bardic Grammar.

In the course of an examination of the *exempla* in the early version of the Bardic Grammar it soon became plain that Dafydd ap Gwilym's acquaintance with the verses cited in the Red Book version extended much further than his familiarity with the *englyn* on the Blackbird—that it extended, indeed, to comprise a large number, if not the whole, of those verses which appear to have been contained in the original redac-tion. But before enlarging further on the echoes of these exemplary verses to be found in Dafydd's poetry, I must mention a few essential facts about the *exempla* as a whole. They are divided into four groups:

---

[15] T. H. Parry-Williams, *Hen Benillion* (Aberystwyth, 1956), no. 293 (an *englyn cyrch*); MA² 135a, 5–8 (a *traethodl*). On the metres cf. Parry-Williams, *Canu Rhydd Cynnar* (UWP 1932), lxxxvii–xciii.

[16] CD 319–21; cf. *Canu Rhydd Cynnar*, xci.

(i) *englynion*, comprising fifteen examples of the different kinds of *englyn unodl union*, *cyrch*, and *proest*, together with two examples of three-line *englynion o'r hen ganiad*;[17] (ii) *awdlau*, comprising examples of twelve different metres;[18] (iii) four different kinds of *cywydd*;[19] and (iv) in conclusion an appendix of seven *englynion* illustrating the *beiau gwaharddedig* or 'forbidden faults'.[20] The source of the *englynion* and *cywyddau* are almost entirely unknown (although Peniarth 20 and some later MSS offer a number of tentative and more-or-less uncertain attributions);[21] the occasional differences in wording between the four versions suggests that they are excerpts from poems transmitted orally. Five of the examples illustrating *awdl* metres are from known poems by Gwilym Ddu o Arfon, Casnodyn, Cynddelw Brydydd Mawr, Iorwerth Fychan (the author of a variant given in Pen. 20 only) and Gruffudd ab yr Ynad Coch,[22] while a sixth, as noted above, comes from the lost ending of Einion Offeiriad's *awdl* to Sir Rhys ap Gruffudd. With the exception of the example of *clogyrnach* described as *dull Cynddelw* 'Cynddelw's mode' all these verses are from the work of known poets who were living towards the end of the thirteenth century or the beginning of the fourteenth. In all this gives a total of 38 exemplary stanzas. The most striking thing about the whole collection is their subject-matter: of the 15 four-line *englynion* twelve obviously derive from *rhieingerddi* (poems addressed to girls), so also do five of the twelve *awdlau* and three of

[17] CD 319–27.
[18] CD 331–48.
[19] CD 327–30.
[20] Cf. CD 298–309.
[21] P20 attributes *englyn* 3 to 'Bleddyn Ddu' and a variant of *englyn* 4 to 'Bleddyn Llwyd'. Possibly one or other of these poets could be the *Bleddyn glerddyn glwys* of Gruffudd Llwyd's *Cywydd y Cwest*, IGE[2] xxxix, 1.19. Later MSS ascribe P20's variants of *englynion* no. 5 to Gwilym Ryvel (it is not known in any other source), of no. 6 to 'Llywelyn Moilrawn', and of no. 10 to Gruffudd ab yr Ynad Coch (unattested elsewhere).
[22] On these poets see GP xxviii, and on Iorwerth Fychan T. Parry, *Hanes Llenyddiaeth*, 49. Two *rhieingerddi* are attributed to him, H 324–7 (=MA[2] 279a–280a). His *floruit* is now accepted as *circa* 1300, though Dr John Davies's dating 'about 1360' is quoted GP xxix. Accepting the earlier dating, there now remains no evidence which supports G. J. Williams's contention (*loc. cit.*, endorsed by Parry, PBA xlvii, 182) that some of the *exempla* in the RBH Grammar were composed in the latter half of the C14, however this may be in respect to certain of the variants introduced into the other MSS of this version. In texts other than RBH a few additional *englynion* are quoted in the body of the Grammar (i.e. not among the metrical *exempla*) as follows: *Mi yw'r gwas gweddeiddlas, gwan* (common to Ll3 and P20) GP 25, 45; in P20 two scurrilous *englynion* illustrative of the 'forbidden faults' *Klermwnt abat di-Ladin* and *Trahayarn, trwyn hen gathwrd*, GP 53, and an additional instance of the fault *tin âb, Lloer deket varvret, llwyr vawrvryt—yeuing*, GP 54. Bangor I has an additional example of an *englyn proest, Kerdeis tramwyeis tremynteyrned* (B ii, 193), and gives an additional two-line example of a *toddaid* (B ii, 196). Any or all of these additions may represent ancient material, as is true also of the additional prose passages already referred to, in Ll3 and P20 (n. 6 above). I hope to complete a full edition and discussion of all these fugitive verses in the Grammar at a later date.

the four *cywyddau*, and three also of the five *englynion* illustrating the 'forbidden faults'. That is to say, 23 out of the total of 38 *exempla*—a little under two thirds of the whole. It is fairly certain that all come from men's love-poems, as indeed do all other medieval Welsh love-poems: there is no extant example in which it is a girl who laments her love-sickness and love-longing.[23]

In the subjoined list I give the first lines of the thirty-eight exemplary stanzas as they appear in the Red Book text, noting such variants as are found in one or more of the three other MSS of the early version of the Bardic Grammar, and italicizing all first lines of stanzas which demonstrably come from *rhieingerddi*. Where no such variants are listed, it is because the same stanza occurs throughout all the four texts.

**Red Book of Hergest**
*Englynion* (GP 7–9; cf. 25–8, 46–8):
unodl union:
  (i) *Pei kawn o gyflwr gyfle (broui)—rin*
  (ii) *Dilyneis, klwyfeis, val y'm klyw—deckant*
  (iii) *Un dwyll wyt o bwyl(l) o ball dramwy—hoet*
  (iv) Llawnlwys lys (yw) Rys, Ros genniret—kat
      Variants: P.20: *Prit yw dy dilit, deuliw ewyn—gloyw*
      B.1: *Dydgu degwch llu llathreid dangos—pall*
  (v) Over o iawnder undawt—hwyl anaw
      Variants: P.20: Pan welych llewych lliw gwawr—bit odit
      B.1: Pa wnaf, pa ganaf, gein wawr—lliw goleu
  (vi) *Kathleu eos nos yn oet—y kigleu*
      Variant: P.20: *Nyt gwiw gouyn lliw llewychweith—Tegeu*

unodl crwca:
  (vii) *Kyt ymwnel kywyt, bryt brys*

unodl cyrch:
  (viii) *Hunyd hirloyw y hystlys*

proest:
  (ix) Daeth y ueird heird hard westi
      Variant: B.1: *Yngharat lleuat pob lle*

---

[23] Séan O'Tuama has shown that the same is true for the majority of the Irish *amhráin grá* or traditional love-songs, although there are a few exceptions such as those collected in Douglas Hyde's *Love-Songs of Connacht* and the widely-known love-song *Donall Óg*, which descend from an ancient native tradition of girls' love-songs, going back to the Old Irish period (S. O'Tuama, 'Serch Cwrtais mewn Llenyddiaeth Wyddeleg' ch.3 in *Dafydd ap Gwilym a Chanu Serch yr Oesoedd Canol*, ed. John Rowlands (UWP 1975). A. Jeanroy has argued that love-lyrics put into the mouths of girls are the oldest form of love-lyric in Romance literature, *Les Origines de la Poésie Lyrique en France* (2nd edn. Paris 1969), 150, 157, and Peter Dronke has expressed agreement on this, *Medieval Latin and the Rise of the European Love Lyric* (Oxford, 1965) *passim*.

(x)  *Dy garu, gorhoen eglur*
     Variant: P.20: Pei byw vy llyw, llew, flamdur
(xi)  *Agharat hoew leuat liw*

lleddf broest:
 (xii)  *Kae a geueis da[w]ngeis doe*
(xiii)  *Llawen dan glaerwen lenn laes*

lleddf proest gadwynog:
 (xiv)  *Mynnwn, kyt yt gawn gwc*
 (xv)  *Na'r heul yn hwyl awyrneit*
        Variant: B.1: *Y gyt gwynn vy myt ym oes*


*Englynion o'r hen ganiad:*
 (xvi)  Chwerdit mwyalch mywn kelli
        Variant: B.1: Tri meib gyluaethwy enwir (cf. PKM 76)
(xvii)  Onyt ynat a darlleat—llyfreu
        (absent from B.1)


*Awdlau* (GP 9–12; cf. 28–31, 49–51):
   (i)  Toddaid: Nyt digeryd Duw, neut digarat—kerd
        (Gwilym Ddu o Arfon RP 1226, MA$^2$ 276b)
  (ii)  Gwawdodyn: Daroganaf naf daroganant
        Variants: Ll.3: Meddylyeis y dries o trasyml vryd
                  P.20: *Morwyn a weleis mor drybelit* (Iorwerth Fychan,
                  H 324, 17–20; MA 279a)
 (iii)  Cyhydedd Hir: *Llauaru a wnaf llywyawdyr nef a'e naf*
        Variant: Ll.3: Trindawt parawt pur, traws maws moes eglur
                  (Casnodyn (RP 1237, 8–11; MA$^2$ 288a, 27–8))
  (iv)  Cyhydedd Fer: *Gwan wyf o glwyf yn glaf trymheint*
   (v)  Rhupunt: Trindawt ffawt ffer
                  (Casnodyn RP 1235 8–11; MA 288a, 27–8)
  (vi)  Byr a Thoddaid: Y Gwr a'm rodes rinyeu—ar dafawt
        (Gruffudd ab yr Ynad Coch RP 1161, 5–10, MA$^2$ 271a, 1–8)
        Variant: Ll.3: Thomas a[p] Roppert rwyd par—gwerssyllic
                  (H 350, MA 282b, 11–18)
 (vii)  Gwawdodyn Hir: *Gwan yawn wyf o glwyf yr gloyw uorwyn*
(viii)  Cyhydedd Naw Ban: Wrthyt, greawdyr byt, bit vyg gobeith
  (ix)  Clogyrnach: Y bareu arueu aruoloch ('Dull Cynddelw' H 136,
                  19–20, 9–10, MA$^2$ 162a, 53–4, 41–3)
        (absent from B.1)
   (x)  Hir a Thoddaid: *Gwynuyt gwyr y byt oed uot Agharat*
        (absent from B.1)
  (xi)  Cyrch a Chwtta: *Llithrawd, ys rannawd is rat*
        (absent from B.1)

(xii) Tawddgyrch gadwynawg: Amdyant y ueird, vyrdeu dramwy
(absent from P.20)
Variant: B.l: Mawr yth gereis, mwy yth garaf (cf. CD 346;
*Cy*.xxvi, 125–6)

*Cywyddau* (GP 12–13; 31, 52):
  (i) Deuair Hirion: Breichffyryf, archgrwn, byrr y vlew
  (ii) Deuair vyrryon: *Hard-dec riein*
  (iii) Awdl gywydd: *O gwrthody, liw ewyn*
  (iv) Cywydd llosgyrnawc: *Lluwch eiry manot mynyd Mynneu*

*Y Beiau Gwaharddedig:*
(The Forbidden Faults) (GP 14, 33, 53–4)
  (i) *Gwrthrych eurgreir peir pendefic—yd wyf*
  (absent from B.1)
  (ii) *Gwenn dan eur wiwlwnn, ledyf edrychyat—gwyl*
  (absent from B.1)
  (iii) Pei prynwn seithpwn sathyrgruc—o'th oleu (attributed to
  Gwilym Ryfel, GP 46)
  Variant: P.20: Ar hyt maes yn llaes y llusgir—vchot
  (absent from B.1)
  (iv) *Gwann yawn wyf o nwyf a naws anhun—gwael*
  Variant: P.20: Arglwyd yw aergledyf vn kantref—neu deu
  (absent from B.1)
  (v) Kyrnic llym trychit, llamm trwch—ysgerigyl.

With the doubtful exception of *englyn* no. xv which gives the name
of 'Lleucu Llwyd', and which I shall discuss later, there is no evidence
that any one of the *exempla* in the Red Book belongs to a period later
than the middle of the fourteenth century. In contrast, there is evidence
that some of the *exempla* in the other MSS may belong to a later period.
This possibility relates in particular to the variants in Peniarth 20.
But here I must repeat my initial assertion, based on a comparison
of the *exempla*, that Peniarth 20, with its Gwynedd associations, is
undoubtedly a secondary version of the Grammar: it has excluded all
references to Sir Rhys ap Gruffudd, and it appropriates the three final
*awdl* metres to 'Dafydd Ddu Athro'[24] instead of to Einion Offeiriad—a
claim which is quite incompatible with the evidence furnished by the
appearance of two of the three metres concerned in Einion's *awdl* to
Sir Rhys ap Gruffudd, as was shown by Sir Ifor Williams.[25] As far

[24] On 'Dafydd Ddu Athro' see GP xvii–xxii; *Bywgraffiadur*, 92; *Cy*. 26, 127; Brynley
Roberts, *Gwassanaeth Meir* (UWP 1961), lxxv–lxxx. Only in Peniarth 20 is the Bardic
Grammar associated with his name (GP 51, 65). His name replaces that of Einion Offeiriad
as the author to whom the three last *awdl* metres (nos. x, xi, xii) are accredited.

[25] *Cy*. 26, 115–138. Ifor Williams suggested (p. 121) that the *awdl* was composed between
1314–22; Thomas Parry attributes it to the first quarter of the C14, PBA xlvii, 182;

as I can judge, the nature of the *cynghanedd* in the Red Book *exempla* corresponds broadly with the 'free *cynghanedd*' of the last period of the Gogynfeirdd, according to Dr Thomas Parry's analysis.[26]

It will be seen from the list that the majority of the *exempla* are preserved in all four of the early MSS (except in those instances in which B1 is defective). Variants which differ both from RBH and from each other are to be found in one or—occasionally—in two of the other MSS, as follows: P20 and B1 give variants of *englynion* 4 and 5; P20 has variants of *englynion* 6, 10 and of nos. 3 and 4 of the 'Forbidden Faults'; B1 has variants of *englynion* 9 and 16. Among the *awdlau*, Ll3 gives variants of nos. 3, and 6, B1 of no. 12, while both Ll3 and P20 give different variants of no. 2. A large number of these variants themselves evidently derive from *rhieingerddi*. The *exempla* given of *cywyddau* are the same in all versions, though RBH gives only the first two lines of the *cywydd deuair hirion*. Where the same stanza is given in as many as three of the four MSS, it may be safely concluded that this stanza was present in the archetype from which all ultimately derive. Each variant from it which occurs is individual to one manuscript alone, and therefore may safely be regarded as intrusive. The fact that the *exempla* given in the Red Book are invariably supported by the text of at least one of the other MSS, and that there is no instance in which the Red Book departs by itself from the consensus of the other three MSS, is strong evidence favouring the priority of this version as being nearer than any of the others to the lost archetype. At the same time it is undeniable that there are instances in which one or other of the remaining manuscripts gives a reading or some line or word which is a manifest improvement on the reading of the Red Book, and therefore has strong claims to be regarded as original. (In the examples cited below, such minor emendations based on variant readings are indicated by brackets.) Although the Red Book of Hergest was written some half century after the period when Dafydd ap Gwilym's career is believed to have been at its height, it appears most probable that the prototype from which its version of the Bardic Grammar was derived was composed at some period in the late 20's or early 30's of the fourteenth century, in Dafydd's own native district and most probably during Dafydd's youthful years. And it also seems most probable that the man who either edited or composed the Grammar at this time was Einion Offeiriad. The following discussion therefore concentrates on the *exempla* which are found in the Red Book text.

---

Beverley Smith advocates a date after 1330, B xx, 346*n*. The only real evidence that the *awdl* was composed before the Grammar is the inclusion in the Grammar of no. xii of the *exempla* of *awdl* metres, presumed to represent the lost ending of the *awdl* to Sir Rhys ap Gruffudd.

[26] 'Twf y Gynghanedd' THSC 1936, 154.

Though none of the other *exempla* is so obviously paraphrased by Dafydd ap Gwilym as the *englyn* on the Blackbird, there are several others which merit further discussion for their apparent echoes in his poetry. *Englyn* no. iii is one of these:

> Un dwyll wyt o bwyl(l) o ball dramwy—hoet
> A hut mab Mathonwy,
> Vnwet y'th wneir a Chreirwy
> Ennwir vryt, ryhir vrat rwy (GP 7, 26, 46; Bii, 191).

*(Of like deceitful thought are you from failure of excessive longing,/ to the enchantment of the son of Mathonwy,/ you are formed in a like shape to Creirwy/, of cruel disposition, too long, too great betrayal.)*

In this verse the poet is remonstrating with some girl by comparing her magical allurement and deception to the enchantment of Math fab Mathonwy. The very same accusation is made by Dafydd ap Gwilym against a girl from Dyfed—essentially the land of enchantment, according to the Mabinogi—whose attractions he compares with the magic of Math son of Mathonwy. (The girl may well be Morfudd, though no name is given.) And Dafydd cited the Triads as confirmation of his assertion. He probably quoted them from memory, since his version is an amalgamation of names given in three separate triads[27] as those of well-recognised masters of enchantment:

> Dyn gannaid, doniog annwyd,
> Ddifai dwyll, o Ddyfed wyd.
> Nid dim ysgol hudoliaeth,
> Na gwarae twyll, cymwyll caeth,
> Na hud Menw, na hoed mynych,
> Na brad ar wyr, na brwydr wych
> Uthr afael, wyth arofun,
> Eithr dy hud a'th air dy hun.
> Tri milwr, try ym olud
> A wyddyn' cyn no hyn hud—
> Cad brofiad, ceidw ei brifenw,
> Cyntaf, addfwynaf oedd Fenw;
> A'r ail fydd, dydd da dyall,
> Eiddilig Gor, Wyddel call.
> Trydydd oedd, ger moroedd Môn,
> Math, rhwy eurfath, rhi Arfon (GDG 84, 27–40).

*(Bright girl, endowed with nature's gifts,/ blameless is your deceit, since of Dyfed you are./ It was not in some school of wizardry,/ nor practice of deceit, a constricted argument,/ nor Menw's magic, nor frequent desire,/ nor treachery to men, nor splendid fight,/ terrible*

---

[27] TYP 55–6 (nos. 27 and 28), 250.

*mastery, nor furious intent/ but your own magic and your own address./ Three warriors—it brings me riches—knew enchantment before this:/ battle-experienced, the first upholds his name—/ the gentlest of the three was Menw;/ the second's name (good day for understanding)/ is Eiddilig the Dwarf, a wily Irishman;/ third was, beside the seas of Môn,/ Math, lord of splendid kind, and Arfon's king.)*

*Creirwy* (from *crair* 'treasure' etc.) is named in the *englyn* as a pattern of a girl's beauty, and elsewhere (GDG 123, 19) Dafydd cites the name of this traditional heroine by employing the epithet *Creirwy cret* 'darling of the (whole) Christian world'.[28] And in the next *englyn* (below) he employs the term *kreir cret*.

No. iv of the *exempla* of *englynion unodl union* comes from a praise-poem and not from a *rhieingerdd*:

> *Llawnlwys lys (yw) Rys, Ros genniret—kat*
> *Kedernyt Edelff(l)et,*
> *Llyw diuei, llywyawdyr Dyuet,*
> *Llafyn gynniweir, kreir cret* (GP 7, 26).

*(Most pleasant the court of Rhys, Rhos's place of resort;/ (of) the strength of Ethelfrith in battle/, a perfect lord, ruler of Dyfed,/ an attacking blade, the strength(?) of Christendom.)*

The subject in all probability, if not certainty, is Einion Offeiriad's patron, Sir Rhys ap Gruffudd. Many years ago Sir Ifor Williams pointed out the similarity of the phrase *llywiawdr Dyfed* in this *englyn* to the words which Dafydd ap Gwilym employed to his uncle Llywelyn:

> *Llywiawdr, ymherawdr meiri—hyd Elfed*
> *Llyw yw ar Ddyfed, llawer ddofi* (GDG 12, 37–8).

'Ruler, prince of reeves, as far as Elfed; he is Dyfed's helmsman, subduing many.' For *hyd Elfed* one manuscript[29] (not listed in GDG, but noted by Lloyd-Jones) gives the reading *meiri-Edelffled*, which if authentic, would provide a further indication that Dafydd ap Gwilym knew

---

[28] *Creirwy* lit. 'relic, talisman' etc.; cf. *kreir cret* in the next *englyn* (no. iv) and *creiriau Cred* RP 1215, 33. On the traditional heroine of this name see TYP 311, and p. 139 below. Dafydd names Morfudd *fy nghrair diweirbwyll*, GDG 89, 11.

[29] *BL Addl. 14870*, p. 203. This MS was transcribed by Lewis Morris, and is said (*Rep.* II, 1144) to be the basis of the 1789 BDG, where however the text reads (p. 458) *hyd Elfed*. Lloyd-Jones (G.438) evidently regarded GDG 12, 37 as containing an allusion to the English king, and he cites the reading of Peniarth 49, 66b *hyd Elffled*. If correct, the *englyn* and Dafydd's line are the only recorded instances in which 'Edelffled' is cited in praise-poetry, probably with satirical innuendo. The amended line would then give 'Ruler, prince of reeves of Ethelfrith' (fig. for the king of England?). (The alternative *Elfed* is the commote in Dyfed.)

of this legendary English enemy[30] from the reference in the Grammar. But the evidence of a single late manuscript is insufficient to press. However, as Sir Ifor observed,[31] there was a stronger case for bestowing the epithet *llyw ar Ddyfed* on so prominent and authoritative a figure as Sir Rhys ap Gruffudd[32] rather than on a minor official such as Dafydd's uncle Llywelyn, who was constable only of Newcastle Emlyn. It is highly likely, therefore, that Dafydd borrowed the comparison in these lines from the Grammar.

*Englyn* no. vi contains an allusion to the Nightingale as a bird of love, its plaintive song evoking in the poet memories of former passion:

> *Kathleu eos nos yn oet—y kigleu,*
> *(M)eu gofeu gofalhoet,*
> *Koethlef, herwodef hiroet,*
> *Kethlyd, kein awenyd koet* (GP 7, 26).

*(At [lovers'] tryst by night I heard a Nightingale's song/—mine are sad memories of longing—/a pure voice, suffering the long grief of exile,/ sweet singer, inspired poet of the forest.)*

The allusion here to the lovers *oed* or tryst in the forest is significant. Apart from Gruffudd ap Dafydd ap Tudur, (see below on *exemplum* of *awdlau* no. vii, and n. 46), no other poet among Dafydd's predecessors alludes specifically to the custom or convention of the woodland *oed* (though I am not here forgetting the stories of Myrddin and Trystan). There are other points of interest. Why should the poet of the *englyn* call the Nightingale *herwodef hiroet* 'one who has suffered a long age of exile' or 'who has been in exile for a long period'? The only explanation I can suggest, and that tentatively, is that we have here an echo of the sad tale of the nightingale Philomela in Ovid's *Metamorphoses.*[33] Philomela was daughter to a legendary king of Athens, who caused her to be married to the king of far-away Thrace, and she went there all unknowing that her sister Procne, who had previously been married to the king, was still alive. The two were transformed into birds, the

---

[30] *Edelffled* = Ethelfrith king of Bernicia 593–617, named in the Triads as *Edelffled Ffleissawc*, 'E. the Twister.' See TYP 338.

[31] *Y Beirniad* V, 130.

[32] On (Sir) Rhys ap Gruffudd (*c.* 1283–1356) note 9 above and B xx, 342. He held great power throughout south Wales from the 1320's onwards, and was bailiff of the forest of Snowdon. In 1325 he enlisted 200 men from south Wales to go overseas (cf. n.12), and was on the Crécy expedition in 1346. He was a strong supporter of Edward II and suffered as a result of the latter's downfall in 1327. The *englyn* in the Grammar—not found elsewhere—could well belong to the anonymous sequence of *englynion unodl union* to a certain 'Rhys' which are to be found in H 122b (p. 323). With the expression *Ros genniret* in the englyn (referring to the *cantref* in Dyfed) cf. GDG 94, 31, *O Llanddwyn, dir gyniret*.

[33] Ovid, *Metamorphoses* Bk. 6.

one into a nightingale and the other into a swallow, after Philomela
(or in another version, Procne) had slain her own son and given his
flesh to be eaten by her husband. This is the traditional explanation
for the belief that the Nightingale always sings plaintively and with
longing,[34] or *hiraeth*. The two sisters were *herwodef* 'suffering exile',[35]—
far away from their home in Greece. In one poem Dafydd ap Gwilym
employs a word for the Nightingale which has precisely the same meaning,

> Deholwraig, arfynaig[36] fwyn (GDG 25, 33)

*(Exiled woman, of gentle longing (?).)*

The implication of *arfynaig fwyn* may well be that the Nightingale is
regarded as for ever longing and lamenting, whether for her sister or
for her lost child. Bearing in mind that in all Dafydd's work there
is nowhere else a single allusion to any of the myths contained in Ovid's
*Metamorphoses*,[37] is it not probable that his allusion here to the Nightingale was evoked by the *englyn* in the Grammar? The last line of the
*englyn* recalls the fact that Dafydd describes the Lark as *cethlydd awenydd
winau* (GDG 114, 26). This is the only instance cited in the dictionaries,
other than this *englyn*, in which *awenydd* is used metaphorically for a
bird, rather than in its primary meaning denoting a poet or a prophet.[37a]
In his 'elegy' to his fellow-poet Gruffudd Gryg, Dafydd brings together
both primary and figurative meanings of *awen*: Dafydd envisages his
fellow-poet as a bird, divinely inspired with the *awen*:

> Edn glwys ei baradwyslef,
> Ederyn oedd o dir nef.
> O nef y doeth, goeth gethlydd,
> I brydu gwawd i bryd gwŷdd,
> Awenfardd awen winfaeth,
> I nef, gwiw oedd ef, ydd aeth (GDG 20, 61–6).

*('Bird with pure voice from Paradise,/ he was a bird from the land of Heaven./ From
Heaven he came, sweet singer,/ to sing praise to the forest's beauty;/ an inspired poet,
his inspiration wine-nurtured (fig.);/ he was worthy, he returned to Heaven.)*

[34] H. J. Rose, *A Handbook of Greek Mythology* (London, 1928), 263.

[35] The phrase *herwodef hiroet* is closely paralleled in 'The Cambridge Songs' in the
poem *Musa venit carmine* where we find the lines *Philomela queritur/ antiqua de iactura*, 'The
nightingale laments the ancient wrong' (G. F. Whicher, *The Goliard Poets* 196; H. Waddell,
*Mediaeval Latin Lyrics* 238).

[36] No other example is found of the word *arfynaig*, but Dr Parry compares the various
meanings of *gofynaig* 'hope, confidence, trust, vow, petition' etc.

[37] See *Tradition and Innovation* 28, p. 73 above.

[37a] *Awenydd(ion)* is earliest attested in the famous description by Giraldus Cambrensis
of the inspired poets of Wales, *Descr. Cambriae*, ch. 16.

I pass on now to *englyn* no. xii. This alludes to the *cae* as a lover's gift:

> *Kae a geueis da(w)ngeis doe,*
> *Ku vyd kof, ryt rod eruei,*
> *Yn eilgroes y'm oes a mwy,*
> *Anwylgreir kyweir yw'r kae* (GP 8, 27, 47; B. i, 192)

*(Yesterday I received a* cae, *a sought-for favour,/ dear will be the memory, a splendid free gift,/ a second cross (= emblem, relic) for my life-time and more,/ a dear and well-formed relic is the* cae.*)*

*Cae* is a little difficult, since it can mean many things; sometimes it is a jewel or buckle, sometimes a girdle; a diadem like those worn by the Gododdin warriors, or a garland or chaplet like the *cae bedw* or 'birch-tree garland' which Dafydd alludes to more than once as a lover's gift bestowed on him by a girl[38]—and he claims (perhaps having in mind the poem quoted below) that such a gift is more valuable to him than a *cae* made of gold. Whatever is the precise meaning of *cae* in the *englyn*, the point of interest is that only one other example has come down, anterior to Dafydd ap Gwilym, in which *cae* has the meaning of 'lover's gift'. This is in an *awdl* by Gruffudd ap Dafydd ap Tudur, one of Dafydd's most significant predecessors. Here the *cae* is evidently one of gold, and is bestowed in exchange for a praise-poem:

> *Eur a mein coeluein y cael y kae melyn*
> *da[u] evyn dwy auael,*
> *arwydyon mat y adael,*
> *o rod dawn hoewuod dyn hael.*
> *Rod hael rec auael ry gauas am wawt*
> *y dauawt y diuas*
> *un llythyr llathweith kyweithyas*
> *un lliw ac eur gwiw gae'r gwas.*
> *...Bun ae roes rann einyoes reit,*
> *Bu yn kylchynu kylch eneit* (RP col. 1266; cf. MA[2] 318a).

*('A gift of gold and (precious) stones (is) the yellow diadem,/ two fetters with two clasps,/ omens good to be left,/ by the good will of the generous girl./ A generous gift, a binding gift(?)/ received for my profound praise-poem,/ an emblem(?) of bright companionship,/ the colour of fine gold(is) the lad's* cae./ ...A girl bestowed it, a share of her life's need;/ it encompassed the circuit of (her friend.')*

I would not suggest in this case, that Dafydd is actually quoting from the *englyn* in the Grammar, since his allusions to the *cae bedw* evidently spring from an established convention, but I merely point out that

---

[38] Cf. 'Cae Bedw Madog' GDG 31; also 38, 1; 84, 1; 'Yr Het Fedw', 59. Ifor Williams discusses the various meanings of *cae*, B i (1923), 50–4.

the allusion to the lover's *cae* in the *englyn* fits in very closely with Dafydd's cultural background.[39]

*Englyn* no. xv names a girl called 'Lleucu Llwyd'. I cite it here because it raises one of the outstanding problems relating to the Bardic Grammar:

> Na'r heul yn hwyl awyrneit,
> Na'r lloer nyt gwell y lliwyt,
> Yn llathyrwiw wed, yn llathreit
> Yn llathru no Lleucu Llwyt (GP 8, 27, 48).

*(Neither the Sun on its course, leaping through the sky,/ nor the Moon has been more beautifully coloured/—of bright and comely form, brilliantly shining—/than Lleucu Llwyd.)*

The occurrence of the name 'Lleucu Llwyd' at once suggests an allusion to the girl who bore this name and was addressed by Llywelyn Goch ap Meurig Hen in a passionate elegy, which alone has survived to represent the substantial body of verse which this poet is said to have composed in her honour.[40] If we could accept what I would regard as a strong probability, that the *englyn* in the Grammar is a fugitive survival from this body of verse and is the work of Llywelyn Goch, the question then is whether it is to be regarded as a later addition to the Grammar, composed by a poet who flourished in the second half of the fourteenth century, as was the view of G. J. Williams?[41] I cannot believe it, for the reason that the *englyn* is found in three of the four early manuscripts (in each excepting Bangor 1), and therefore I regard it with assurance as having been present in the archetype. If the *englyn* is indeed the work of Llywelyn Goch, I prefer to adopt a different explanation for it. This is to accept a suggestion of far-reaching implications made by Saunders Lewis,[42] to the effect that we should make a fundamental re-assessment of the relative dates of the earlier *cywyddwyr*. He emphasizes the importance of this *englyn* for his new theory, which is that Llywelyn Goch preceded Dafydd ap Gwilym by several years. If this was the case, it would have been possible for an extract from one of the poems to Lleucu Llwyd to have been included in the Grammar by about the year 1330. Since I first urged the

---

[39] 'Chaplets and garlands of flowers and leaves were worn by both sexes, and the gift of one was a token of love', D. Pearsall, *The Floure and the Leafe* (London, 1962) 27; G. L. Marsh 'Chaplets of Leaves and Flowers', *Modern Philology* iv (1967) 153ff.

[40] DGG² no. lxxxviii; OBWV no. 49. See R. Geraint Gruffydd 'Marwnad Lleucu Llwyd gan Lywelyn Goch Amheurig Hen' YB I (1965), 126–37, especially 129–30.

[41] GP xxviii.

[42] 'Y Cywyddwyr Cyntaf', LlC viii (1965), 191–6, re-printed in *Meistri'r Canrifoedd*, ed. R. G. Gruffydd (UWP 1973), 56–63.

acceptance of Saunders Lewis's theory in my earlier version of this article, important new evidence on the point has been brought forward by Daniel Huws, in the course of his discussion and re-dating of the Hendregadredd manuscript.[43] He has published from this manuscript a stanza (p. 26), hitherto un-noticed, which contains an acrostic of the name 'Lleucu Llwyd'; and he points out that the existence of this stanza strengthens the case for the earlier date of Llywelyn Goch ap Meurig Hen which Saunders Lewis had originally based on the existence of the verse in the Grammar. The name 'Lleucu' comes from that of saint Lucia (Lucy), which means 'light', and the associations of the name with the brightness of sun and moon are given prominence in the *englyn*, just as they are in the *Marwnad Lleucu Llwyd* (*dyn lloer degwch* and *huanwedd haul*). Such images of light are indeed popular throughout the poetry of the Gogynfeirdd, and subsequently in that of Dafydd ap Gwilym.[44] Nevertheless, we should remember that the name 'Lleucu' was one of the most popular names for girls in the Middle Ages,[45] and although the combination with 'Llwyd' gives some measure of probability, there can be no absolute certainty that it is not some other Lleucu who is praised in the *englyn*.

Turning now to the *exempla* of *awdl* metres given in the Grammar, the number of extracts which come from *rhieingerddi* or love-poems is quite as striking as is the case with the *englynion*, although their proportion of the total is rather less—five out of the twelve *exempla*. But in these we find the traditional *awdl* metres used unambiguously for genuine love-poetry, rather than for formal praise-poetry to noble women, as in the *rhieingerddi* of the Gogynfeirdd. Themes which later on appear characteristic of Dafydd ap Gwilym's verse, such as love's wounding, sickness, and sleeplessness, and even of the poet's death for love, are anticipated in several of the verses, as of course they are on occasion in the *rhieingerddi* of the earlier period. From these *exempla* I quote nos. vii, x, and xi.

vii (Gwawdodyn Hir):

> *Gwan iawn wyf o glwyf yr gloyw uorwyn,*
> *Gwae a uaeth hiraeth, brif aruaeth brwyn,*
> *Gwyr vyg kallon donn defnyd vyg kwyn,*
> *Gwnn ar vyrr y tyrr ky(t) bo terwyn*
> *Am na daw y law y lwyn—a bwyllaf*
> *A garaf attaf, atteb adfwyn* (GP 10, 29, 50; Bangor 1, 197).

[43] NLW *Journal* xxii (1981), 1–26. Daniel Huws points out (p. 18) that this stanza strengthens the case for the early C14th dating of Llywelyn Goch. See p. 169 below.

[44] Cf. R. G. Gruffydd, YB I, 133; *Tradition and Innovation* p. 66 above.

[45] Melville Richards, 'Gwŷr, Gwragedd a Gwehelyth' THSC 1965, 39. See further P. C. Bartrum, *Welsh Genealogies 300–1400* (UWP 1974), vol. 6, 482–5. Cf. Beverley Smith, B xx, 339.

*(I am very weak from sickness because of the sparkling girl;/ woe to him who nurtures longing, chief omen of sorrow./ My broken heart knows the nature of my complaint:/ I know it will break soon, though it be passionate,/ because she whom I love, on whom my mind dwells,/ will not come to me beside the grove with a gentle answer.)*

x (Hir a Thoddaid):

> *Gwynuyt gwyr y byt oed uot Agharat,*
> *Gwenvun, yn gyuun a'e gwiwuawr garyat;*
> *Gwannllun a'm llud hun, hoendwc barablat;*
> *Gwynlliw eiry divriw, divris(c) ymdeithyat;*
> *Gwenn dan eur wiwlenn, ledyf edrychyat—gwyl*
> *Yw (v'annwyl) yn y hwyl, heul gymheryat* (GP 11, 30, 51).

*(The joy of the world's men was Angharat's being,/ the fair maid, of one accord in their great love;/ her slight form prevents my sleeping, her speech inspires passion;/ fair hue of unbroken snow, a journey untrodden,/ fair beneath her golden head-dress, of gentle aspect;/ my darling is of gentle nature, the Sun's peer.)*

xi (Cyrch a Chwta):

> *Llithrawd, ys r(y)nnawd (y)s rat,*
> *Llathrgof ynof an(yn)at;*
> *Lloer Gymry, gymreis(c) dyat,*
> *Llwyr y gwnaeth, mygyr aruaeth mat,*
> *Lleas gwas, gwys nas dywat*
> *Lliaws geir hynaws garyat,*
> *Lledyfgein riein llun meinwar*
> *Lliw llewychgar Agharat* (GP 11, 30, 51).

*(It has fled—a blessing for a while—/ the bright memory is disturbing to me,/ of the moon of Wales, of potent aspect./ Good and fine of intent, she has completely/ slain the youth: it is known that she has not spoken/ many pleasant words of love/—Angharad the gentle fair maiden of slender form and lovable aspect.)*

Several words and phrases appear in these examples which are echoed in Dafydd ap Gwilym's poetry, some of them being expressions which are not otherwise of very frequent occurrence. In no. vii the poet complains that the girl will not come to meet him *i law i lwyn* 'beside the grove', that is to come to an *oed* or tryst with him in the woodland; cf. the similar reference in *englyn* no. vi above.[46] In the examples of the metres *Hir a Thoddaid* and *Cyrch a Chwta* we meet with two of the five *exempla* in the Grammar which contain allusions to a certain

---

[46] Both are evocative of the lines of Gruffudd ap Dafydd ap Tudur: *Da y gwnaeth mei dei o'r deil/deuoet dan goet y dan gel/y minneu ui a'm annwyl* (RP 1265, 23–4) 'Well did May make houses of leaves for a tryst for two, secretly under the trees, for me myself and my dear one.'

'Angharad'. In all probability the reference is to Angharad the wife of Ieuan Llwyd of Parcrhydderch, Glyn Aeron, as has been indicated above. If Einion himself was responsible for 'inventing' these two metres, as is claimed in the Red Book text, it is likely that it was also Einion who composed the examples of these two metres in the Grammar, both of which are in praise of 'Angharad'. Whether they are of his own composition or not, the surprising fact is that Einion should choose from love-poems the examples of these metres to be given in his Grammar—and from love-poems which appear to have been dedicated to a particular woman, the wife of one of his influential neighbours among the *uchelwyr* of the *cantref* of Is Aeron. This is all the more surprising since more formal examples of these same metres, and these of his own composition, were at hand in his *awdl* to his patron Rhys ap Gruffudd.[47] Compare now the following passages from the section in the Grammar on the *Beiau Gwaharddedig* or 'Forbidden Faults':

> *Bei ar eglyn yw bot yr vn geir yndaw dwyweith, ony byd deirgweith, ony byd hytgyllaeth neu ysmalhawch karyat yn esgus drostaw ... Ysmalhawch karyat, val y mae yn yr eglyn hwnn:*

> > *Gwenn dan eur wiwlenn, ledyf edrychyat—gwyl*
> > *Y gweleis Agharat,*
> > *A gwann o bryt, erwan brat,*
> > *Y'm gwyl gwylwar Agharat* (GP 14, 33, 53).

*(It is a fault for an* englyn *to have the same word in it twice, unless it occurs three times, and unless there is an excuse for it in eager desire or in foolery of love ... Foolery of love as in this example: Fair beneath her golden head-dress, with downcast look,/ I saw modest Angharad;/ slight of form, a piercing treachery,/ gentle Angharad looks at me.)*

This *englyn* is however an 'exception to the exceptions' in the sense that *ysmalhawch karyat* or 'love's foolery' is called an 'excuse' or exception to the fault of using the same word twice in an *englyn*—and as an illustration we are given an *englyn* in which 'Angharad' is named twice. No doubt the exception, if not the rule itself, are jokes, and *Cerdd Dafod*[48] explains this kind of repetition as a fault in language rather than in metre—the example presumably reflects some private foolery which would have been intelligible only to the immediate circle of the friends of Einion and Angharad herself.[48a] It is not possible for us to comprehend

---

[47] *Cy.* xxvi, 137–8.

[48] CD 305–6. Cf. D. J. Bowen, LlC viii, 13–14.

[48a] Among the prose *exempla* in the grammatical section of the Grammar, GP xxii notes that Hafod MS 24 gives the sentence *Rrrys a Howel a garant Angharad* where RBH and Ll3 gives *Rys ac Einawn a garant Oleudyd* (GP 6, 24). 'Goleuddydd' was the name of the girl loved by Gruffudd Gryg (see GDG 20, 20); her name is found in all texts

the contemporary undertones and their implications. Compare with
it the two *exempla* of *englynion proest* (nos. x and xi):

> x) *Dy garu, gorhoen eglur,*
> *Agharat, gwenwynvrat gwyr,*
> *Hoyw gangen, hy a gyngor*
> *Hawl eneit y direitwr* (GP 8, 27, B. i, 193).

*(To love you, a bright joy,/ Angharad, venomous betrayal of men./ Lively branch, bold
her counsel,/ claiming the soul of a wretched man.)*

> xi) *Agharat hoew leuat liw*
> *(Ynghuryeith) lewychweith law,*
> *Wyf o'th garyat, glwyfgat glew*
> *Ynvyt drwy benyt y'm byw* (GP 8, 27, 47, B. i, 193).

*(Lively Angharad, of the moon's hue,/ I am pining for your love,/ (your) bright handiwork,
a brave battle-wound,/ (I shall be) foolish through its penance while I live.)*

Such *exempla* as these seem to me to cast an extraordinary light on
the intellectual preoccupations and literary interests of Einion Offeiriad.
But I shall come back again to that presently. And since first writing
about this, Daniel Huws has revealed the existence on f. 115 of the
Hendregadredd manuscript of an acrostic *englyn* containing Angharad's
name,[49] and immediately following the *englyn* which contains the name
of Lleucu Llwyd, to which I referred above. As Daniel Huws suggests,
both verses may have had their origin in an *ymryson* or poetic contest
in improvised verse-making—and the same could well be true of the
verses in the Grammar which contain these names. Perhaps the occasion
was some festivity in the home of Ieuan Llwyd? At any rate it seems
a probable conjecture that the Angharad of these verses is the same
as the Angharad of Dafydd's elegy, GDG 16, the wife of Ieuan Llwyd,
(and perhaps also of the *cywydd* GDG 140). It is particularly interesting
that Daniel Huws has brought to light a hitherto-unrecognised copy
of Dafydd's elegy to her in the Hendregadredd manuscript.
  Love-poetry is once again the subject matter of three of the four
*exempla* which illustrate the various kinds of *cywydd* metre in existence
prior to the compilation of the Bardic Grammar:

*Cywyddau* (GP 12–13, 31, 52; B.i, 199):

Deuair Fyrion ii)

---

of the Grammar in the example of a *cywydd llosgyrnog*. One can only speculate as to
which of the two girls' names was the original one in this passage, and what significance
may lie in substituting the one for the other.
  [49] NLW *Journal* xxii (1981), 1–26. See p. 121 above.

> *Hard-dec riein,*
> *Hydwf, glwysgein,*
> *Hoewne gwanec,*
> *Huan debec,*
> *Hawd dy garu,*
> *Heul yn llathru.*

*(Handsome maiden,/ well-grown, fair and pure,/ bright hue of the wave,/ like to the sun,/ easy to love you,/ shining Sun.)*

Awdl Gywydd iii)

> *O gwrthody, liw ewyn,*
> *Was diuelyn gudynneu,*
> *Yn diwladeid, da y len,*
> *A'e awen yn y lyfreu,*
> *Kael itt vilein aradrgaeth*
> *Yn waethwaeth y gynnedueu*[50]

*(If you of the foam's hue/ reject discourteously the lad/ with yellow curls and of good learning,/ his inspiration in his books—/ you will get a villein captive to the plough,/ whose attributes are far worse.)*

Cywydd Llosgyrnog iv)

> *Lluwch eiry manot mynyd Mynneu,*[51]
> *Lluoed a'th uawl, gwawl gwawr deheu,*
> *Llathyrlun goleu Oleudyd,*
> *Lliuawd vy hoen o boen beunyd,*
> *Lludyawd ym hun llun bun lloer byt,*
> *Llet(u)ryt, nyt bywyt, a'm byd.*

*(Like a drift of finely-fallen snow upon the Alps,/ multitudes praise you, splendour of the south's dawn,/ Goleuddydd's shining form of light;/ my joy has flowed away because of daily anguish,/ a girl's form, moon of the world, has prevented my sleep,/ I have sadness, and not life.)*

[50] Peniarth 20 prefixes four initial lines to this extract, unparalleled in the other MSS:

> *Hirwenn, na vyd drahaus*
> *Na ry ysgeulus eiryeu,*
> *Na watwar am dy serchawl*
> *A'th ganmawl ar gywydeu* (GP 52).

*(Tall fair one, do not be proud/ or too neglectful of speech,/ do not mock your lover/ who praises you in poems.)*

Conversely, Peniarth 20 omits the second couplet, common to RBH and Ll3, which significantly contains the word *diwladeid* (cf. n, 53 below).

[51] On *mynyd Mynneu* (*Mons Iovis*) as a name for the Alps, see B xvii, 96–8; TYP 138.

No. iii, the fragment of an *awdl gywydd*, as Sir Ifor observed,[52] echoes
a theme which was popular among the *clerici vagantes* or 'wandering
scholars' in European countries during the Middle Ages: it is the theme
of the scholar's (or clerk's) superiority to the labourer or 'villein captive
to the plough'. (The words *gwladeidd* 'courteous' and its opposite *diwladeidd* 'discourteous, boorish' are among Dafydd ap Gwilym's favourite
words, as was pointed out by Sir Idris Bell.[53]) The example of *diwladeidd*
in this verse is the earliest recorded example of the word, and it is
worth noting that the couplet which contains it is omitted from the
text of Peniarth 20. No. iv, the *Cywydd Llosgyrnog* is a borrowing from
a medieval Latin metre employed by the *clerici vagantes*,[54] but it did
not, like the *cywydd deuair fyrion* and the *awdl gywydd*, continue to be
employed down the ages in the Welsh *canu rhydd* or free-metre poetry.[55]
*Cymeriad llythrennol* (alliteration of initial lines) is a feature of the *cywyddau
exempla* as it is of the *awdlau*. But *cynghanedd* is almost non-existent in
the former.

Here then, are examples of love-poetry embodied in three of the
various types of *cywydd* which were in existence before the time of Dafydd
ap Gwilym. Although I would not put any faith in Iolo Morganwg's
veracity, it is nevertheless interesting to find it recorded in G. J.
Williams's monumental study, that Iolo claimed to have seen in his
youth a manuscript containing verses in the metre of *awdl-gywydd* which
were attributed to Dafydd ap Gwilym.[56]

Before leaving the *exempla* cited in the Bardic Grammar, it is worth
noticing the nature of the images for a girl's beauty which recur throughout. They are the favourite images employed by the Gogynfeirdd—
images of light, of the sun and the moon, of snow, of the dawn and
of the white foam of rivers: the same images, indeed, as were very
popular with Dafydd ap Gwilym. And the names of the girls with whom
these images are associated are also interesting. 'Angharad' has already
been commented upon, it is a name which occurs five times; there
are single examples of 'Generys', 'Hunydd', 'Goleuddydd', and 'Lleucu
Llwyd'; 'Creirwy' is alluded to as one of the heroines in the native
tales, and 'Dyddgu' and 'Tegau' are names used similarly in the variant

[52] 'Dafydd ap Gwilym a'r Glêr' THSC 1913–14, 174.

[53] *Dafydd ap Gwilym: Fifty Poems* (London, 1942), 36. The RBH Grammar's example
of *diwladaidd* (absent from p. 20) and one by Dafydd, GDG 74, 2, are the earliest examples
of the word recorded in G and GPC, though Iolo Goch employs *diwladeiddrwydd*. Dafydd
has four instances of *gwladaidd* and there is one by Llywelyn Goch (DGG[2] lxxxiv, 23).
The examples of both words cited in the dictionaries from RP are all from the work
of poets belonging to the latter part of the C14.

[54] THSC 1913–14, 171–3; DGG[2] lxxvi; cf. CD 330. For the Latin poem *Denudata veritate*
to which Sir Ifor here refers, see now G. F. Whicher, The Goliard Poets, 238.

[55] CD 310–11; on the metre *awdl gywydd* see Parry-Williams, *Canu Rhydd Cynnar*, xc–xci;
on the *cywydd denour fyrion* T. Parry, HLP 129–30.

[56] *Iolo Morganwg* (UWP 1956), 123–4n.

*exempla* in manuscripts other than the Red Book. 'Angharad', 'Lleucu' and 'Dyddgu' are among the most popular medieval names for girls; Hunydd occurs in the early period but is not recorded after the middle of the 14th century, according to the analysis made by Melville Richards.[57] The fact that the names 'Hunydd' and 'Generys' are found together in the *Gorhoffedd* of Hywel ab Owain Gwynedd[58] raises the question as to whether it is possible that some of these girls' names were employed figuratively in the poems from which the *exempla* were derived, in the same way as in England and on the continent imaginary names were sometimes given to girls who were addressed in love-poems. This is particularly probable in the case of 'Tegau', since this name is nowhere recorded of a living woman, but always appears to denote the heroine of romance.[59]

The customary view concerning Einion's activity with regard to the Bardic Grammar is that his contribution consisted in revising and adding to an older body of grammatical material which was used for the purpose of instructing probationary poets, and that since it included a translation of the Latin grammar of Donatus, the name *Dwned* came to be applied by extension to the whole work. It has been tentatively suggested that the translation, with some degree of adaptation, to Welsh may have been the work of an earlier poet and grammarian, possibly of the C13th, called Cneppyn Gwerthrynion,[60] a shadowy figure whose name is associated with the Grammar in some of the later versions. His work may be represented by those sections of the Grammar which are concerned with the letters of the alphabet, and with the parts of speech and syntax: these are a rendering into Welsh of material in the grammars of Donatus and Priscian. The *Trioedd Cerdd* (precepts concerning poets and poetry) which conclude the work, preserve in their form one of the traditional modes of bardic instruction—the systematization of knowledge in triads. It is evident that this section has itself been adapted and renovated, probably by a subsequent editor of the original Grammar, whom it is fair to identify with Einion himself.[61]

---

[57] THSC 1966, 39–40.

[58] *Ll. Hendregadredd* 317, lines 29, 31.

[59] TYP 241; see pp. 138–9 and n. below.

[60] He is alluded to in a list of the famous poets of the previous century in an elegy by Gwilym Ddu o Arfon to a fellow-poet, Trahaearn Brydydd, about 1322 (RP 1230, 7–10). But his name is not actually associated with the Bardic Grammar before the C16; see GP xx–xxi; S. Lewis, *Gramadegau'r Penceirddiaid*, 3; D. M. Lloyd, *Bywgraffiadur* 73.

[61] It seems likely that Dafydd ap Gwilym is quoting from the section on the 'Forbidden Faults' in the Grammar (not from the *Trioedd Cerdd*, as S. Lewis suggests) in a couplet in his Contention with Gruffudd Gryg: *Bustl a chas y barnasom/ Beio cerdd lle ni bo cam* GDG 148, 'Bitter and wrong we have adjudged it to blame a poem where there is nothing wrong'. Cf. 'It is not a fault for an *englyn* to borrow from another *englyn* that is better than it; so long as the *englyn* is without one of the legal faults, it may be judged good if it shows spirit and meaning and imagination' (GP 14, 33, 54).

The latter's activity may therefore have consisted in working over and freshly editing a collection of ancient poetic precepts in the form of triads, combining these with a version of the Latin *dwned*, and making some further additions to the compilation which are entirely his own work. Most probably one of these was the *Prydlyff*[62] which prescribes the manner in which different kinds of men and women are ideally to be praised, each according to his or her social status; and another was the section on the Welsh metres. Although it seems evident that he chose examples of the different kinds of *englynion* and *cywyddau* almost entirely from the work of popular poets, orally current and rarely, if ever, previously committed to writing, yet it seems likely that he added to the collection some examples of his own composition, perhaps including the five stanzas in honour of 'Angharad' which have been discussed above. By far the greater number of the *exempla* are concerned with the subject of love, and indeed Einion's choice of his examples reflects a somewhat astonishing pre-occupation on his part with the kind of verse which is normally associated with the name of the *clêr ofer*. These illustrated a wide range of differently constructed *englynion*—and before Dafydd ap Gwilym the *englyn* was the poetic form most frequently chosen for love-poems—and also four different types of *cywydd*, some of which lingered on for long among the metres of popular poetry. Even in the *exempla* given of the *awdl* metres, the subject of love obviously comes foremost, and Einion's selection of verses, as already indicated, is an amazing choice. The truth needs to be expressed in much stronger terms than those of Glanmor Williams, when he observed that Einion was 'making some concessions to this newer kind of verse',[63] and it comes much nearer to D. J. Bowen's contention that Einion was 'almost one of the *clerici vagantes* himself'.[64] This is an apt and penetrating remark, for whatever was Einion's original motive in redacting the Grammar, his choice of exemplary stanzas reflects his own personal taste in a most revealing manner. His praise-poem to Sir Rhys ap Gruffudd shows him to have been accomplished and able to compose in each one of the recognised *awdl* metres, and even to add to these on his own account, yet in his Grammar he gives equally full representation to the metres which characterized the *clêr ofer*. Love was the favourite theme of these popular, lower-grade poets, as it was apparently for Einion himself and it is interesting to find that their verses not infrequently portray love against a background of wild nature. The standpoint of Einion Offeiriad 'to retain the old but to welcome the new' as Sir Ifor Williams once expressed it,[65] was very much nearer

---

[62] See Saunders Lewis, *Braslun*, ch. IV for a full discussion of this section of the Grammar.

[63] *The Welsh Church from Conquest to Reformation* (UWP 1962) 108, 183.

[64] LlC viii, 15.

[65] Quoted p. 61 above from THSC 1938, 52–3.

to the standpoint of Dafydd ap Gwilym than has until recently been recognised.

Taken as a whole, then, the *exempla* in the Bardic Grammar represent the fullest collection of excerpts that has come down to us of the verse of the so-called *clêr* (though the aptness of this term for popular and lower-grade poets is badly in need of re-consideration) which were in oral circulation throughout Wales during the 13th and 14th centuries.[66] Very little, apart from the excerpts fortuitously preserved in the Grammar, has come down to illustrate the nature of the sub-literary productions of this period. But it seems certain that it was in verse of this kind that there lay the *matrix* or deepest source of inspiration for Dafydd's love-poetry: in their content, in their native metrical techniques and in their inherited poetic vocabulary and stylistic devices. And these fragments show that the themes of continental *amour courtois* were already securely established in Welsh poetry at the time when Dafydd's career began: themes such as sickness and sleeplessness and love's frustrations, all of which strikingly anticipate Dafydd's own complaints and frustrations. Here also we have the *gordderchgerdd o gywyddau teulueidd drwy eiriau amwys* 'seemly love-songs with ambiguous wording'[67] as the Grammar puts it—that is, verses in language which was deliberately chosen because the words were capable of holding more than one meaning—a recognisable characteristic of Dafydd's own technical accomplishment. Here in the Bardic Grammar we have examples of the kind of popular verse of which Dafydd must have encountered numerous unwritten examples.

In this paper I have interpreted the evidence as sufficient to prove that Dafydd was actually acquainted with the *exempla* from popular and normally unrecorded verse which were preserved in the four oldest texts of the Bardic Grammar, of which the earliest is that preserved in the Red Book of Hergest. But here it is necessary to be careful, for the transcription of the Red Book began at earliest in the quarter-century following the presumed life-time of Dafydd ap Gwilym.[68] There can be no doubt but that the Red Book text of the Grammar is a copy of an older text: what was its source, and from whence did it come? If we consider how close are the greater part of the contents of the Red Book to those of the White Book of Rhydderch, it is hard to reject the possibility that the text of the Bardic Grammar in the Red Book derives either from those pages of the White Book which

---

[66] Some of the variant verses culled from the texts of the Grammar, other than RBH, contain allusions to places in Gwynedd and Powys and on the Welsh marches, in addition to Ceredigion and places in Dyfed.

[67] GP 6.

[68] The RBH was written in the late fourteenth century according to Denholm Young, *Handwriting in England and Wales* (UWP 1954), 43; last quarter of C14 and first quarter of C15, RWM II.

have been lost for centuries, or else from a closely related source. Before
the end of the 14th century the White Book was in the possession of
Rhydderch, son of Ieuan Llwyd of Glyn Aeron and his wife Angharad
(it may have even been copied at Rhydderch's own instigation). Rhydderch's home was at Parcrhydderch on the border between the com-
motes of Mabwynion and Penardd, and about ten miles from Strata
Florida, where it is very probable that the White Book was copied.[69]
Dafydd ap Gwilym's *marwnad ffug* or 'fictitious elegy' to Rhydderch
(GDG 17) suggests that there existed a strong degree of intimacy
between the two, although it is likely that Dafydd was the older by
some years. Although there is no certainty that Rhydderch was as well-
informed as to the contents of the Bardic Grammar as he was as to
Cyfraith Hywel[70] (the Welsh Laws), it is worth quoting the words
of Llywelyn Goch ap Meurig Hen in his *awdl* addressed to this same
Rhydderch and to his friend Llywelyn Fychan (who may, incidentally,
have been the abbot of Strata Florida) when he said of the pair:

> *Deallu bard lyfyr da a ellynt* (RP 1309, 20)

*(Well could they understand the bardic book.)*

If the Bardic Grammar was originally contained in the lost portion
of the White Book of Rhydderch (of which the second part was written
in the first half of the 14th century)[71] this would bring its text of the
Grammar very close indeed to the period when Einion Offeiriad is
believed to have 'edited' the work, perhaps at some date during the
1330s. Is it not possible, and even probable, that Rhydderch was the
connecting link between Dafydd ap Gwilym and the source of the Bardic
Grammar in the Red Book, and that this source was to be found among
the contents of Rhydderch's famous book, perhaps compiled at Strata
Florida near his home, and not far either from the home of Einion
Offeiriad in Mabwynion, and during Einion's own life-time?

My suggestion is that Dafydd ap Gwilym discovered *in writing* for
the first time in the Bardic Grammar excerpts from the kind of popular
poetry to whose influence he was peculiarly susceptible. The fact
that such excerpts from love-poems were actually included in Einion's

[69] This is not certain; Strata Marcella is also possible (Denholm Young, *op. cit.* 43).
On the *Llyfr Gwyn Rhydderch* and its history through the centuries see the introduction
by R. M. Jones to the new edition of the tales and romances (UWP 1973) especially
xiii.

[70] 'He (Rhydderch) was an expert in Welsh legal procedures, and was called upon
as *dosbarthwr* (mediator) in Carms. and Cards. between 1380 and 1392'—R. A. Griffiths,
*Principality* 117. It is extremely probable that Rhydderch was Dafydd ap Gwilym's informant on the Welsh legal system, with which he was obviously conversant.

[71] RWM I, 305. Part of the MS was written in the last quarter of C13, the remainder
in the first half of the C14. Daniel Huws would date the whole to the mid C14.

treatise alongside excerpts illustrating the honoured and respected *awdl* metres, gave them a recognised place among the essential elements in bardic instruction. Further proof of this is to be found among the large number of words, lines, and parallel ideas which are to be found in the Grammar to those which occur in Dafydd's poetry.[72] And perhaps it would not be over-imaginative to suggest that the *englyn* which commemorated the exultant, laughing song of the Blackbird among the trees had so immediately penetrating an effect upon the poet as to turn this Blackbird into the essential symbol which inspired his fantasy of escape from a life spent in the confined dwellings of ordinary mortals to the blessed life of limitless freedom enjoyed by the wild birds in their forest solitudes.[73]

[72] In addition to those instances already discussed, I note the following: among the *exempla* of *awdlau* metres listed above (pp. 121–2), no. iv rhymes *heint/goueileint* as in GDG 11, 21–3; 94, 13–14 (later poets who employ the same rhyme occur in RP 1249, 5–6; 1275, 23–4). With the first line of no. 10 of the *awdlau* examples (p. 122) cf. *Gwynfyd gwŷr oedd ganfod gwen*, GDG 40, 10, and with the fourth line of the same stanza cf. *hoen eiry di-frisg*, GDG 33, 18. With the third line of no. 11 of the *awdlau* examples (p. 122) cf. *O ddyad twyll ydd wyd di*, GDG 84, 25, and with the sixth line, *fal gwr hynaws*, GDG 141, 8. The Red Book Grammar alone employs *kyfanhedu* in the infrequent meaning of 'entertainment': *Tri pheth a berthynant ar deuluwr, kyuanhedu, a haelyoni, ac eruyn da yn deulueid* (GP 17), where Ll3 substitutes *digrifwch* (and P20 omits the whole entry). It is relevant to compare GDG 137, 66 and 76 for Dafydd's use of *cyfanheddu* and *cyfanheddrwydd* in this perhaps unfamiliar and newly-coined sense. (In DGG² 203, Ifor Williams quotes the definition of Siôn Dafydd Rhys of *cyfanheddu* as *llawenhau dynion a difyrru'r amser*). For Dafydd's fondness for the words *gwladaidd* and *diwladaidd*—paralleled in the third example in the Grammar of *cywyddau* (p. 125)—see n. 53 above.

[73] With this possibility in mind it is interesting to compare the following (if unreliable) note by Iolo Morganwg: *Ym Maes y Crugiau ar lann Teifi y mae Gramadeg o waith Dafydd ap Gwilym, medd Ben Simon o Lyfr Iago ab Dewi*, for which the source is given as *Llyfr Brechfa* (see Llanover MS C52, 85; also *Iolo Manuscripts*, ed. Taliesin Williams (1878), 94). For what it is worth, this note contributes to the evidence for Dafydd's familiarity with the Bardic Grammar.

# 5. ALLUSIONS TO TALES AND ROMANCES

LITTLE difficulty is presented by the task of surveying Dafydd ap Gwilym's allusions to secular narrative, since these have all been conveniently listed in Dr Parry's comprehensive index to *Gwaith Dafydd ap Gwilym*. Nevertheless, a survey of the poet's allusions both to indigenous Welsh narrative and to such foreign literature as was available to him in translation points the way to some interesting conclusions with respect to Dafydd's cultural inheritance. These conclusions form an appropriate sequel to those reached earlier with respect to Dafydd's indebtedness to the Bardic Grammar. (In the following analysis the numbers refer in each case to the number of the poems in GDG):

## THE MABINOGI

It is evident that Dafydd was acquainted with all the tales in the 'Maginogion' collection, with the exception of 'The Dream of Rhonabwy[1] and there is also some slight uncertainty with respect to 'Lludd and Llefelys'.[2] Although Dafydd alludes to characters from each one of the Four Branches, it is clear that the story of Pwyll and Pryderi as told in the first Branch was the one nearest to his heart. He describes his uncle Llywelyn as *ail Bryderi* (12, 40), he alludes to *Gwri Wallt Euryn* (12, 35), and causes Hiraeth ('longing') to trace its descent to *Gwawl (fab hud) fab Clud* (92, 26; cf. *ail Clud* 13, 29). The land of Dyfed is called *Bryderi dir* (150, 32). R. Geraint Gruffyd has suggested that in the line *Pellenig pwyll ei (=un?) annwyd* (122, 7–8) Dafydd is comparing

---

[1] See n. 62 below.
[2] Lines 31–4 of *Cywydd y Sêr* (DGG[2] no. 40; OBWV no. 64) have been interpreted as alluding to this tale, but the authenticity of this *cywydd* is at present *sub judice*. See n. GDG[2] 200 and S. Lewis, LlC ii, 201; *Meistri's Canrifoedd* 44. But it seems at least equally probable that the allusion here refers to the story of the burial of the dragons in a stone chest at Dinas Emrys as told in *Brut y Brenhinedd*; see BD 103. There is a similar ambiguity in Dafydd's description of the Fox as *draig unwedd daroganair* (22, 34) which may be a reminiscence either of *Lludd and Llefelys* or of the *Brut*.

the Cock Thrush to the hero Pwyll.[3] The tale of 'Manawydan' is recollected in Dafydd's allusions to Dyfed as *bro yr hud* and *gwlad yr hud* (13, 2, 17; 15, 2); in another instance his explanation of a certain girl's enchantment is that she originates from Dyfed (84, 23–8), and in the same vein he compares her tantalizing fascination to *ail rhyfel Llwyd fab Cel Coed* (11, 46).[4] The heroine Branwen is commemorated in a unique citation of her name as a standard for a girl's beauty (40, 14), and her story as told in the second Branch is further recalled in his description of Rhosyr or Newborough as *pair dadeni pob rhi rhydd* (134, 28).[5] The central character of the Fourth Branch is commemorated in Dafydd's allusion to *Math* (*fab Mathonwy*) as *rhi Arfon* (84, 42). He is here quoting from a triad, as I have indicated below, but his words imply that he was familiar with more of the story of Math fab Mathonwy than is contained in the triad—he knew, at any rate, where Math's story was located.

TRIOEDD YNYS PRYDAIN

In GDG 84, 35–42, *Math* is listed with *Menw* (*ap Teirgwaedd*) and *Eiddilig Gor* as *tri milwr . . . a wyddyn' cyn no hyn hud* ('three warriors who once knew enchantment'). This is a citation of TYP no. 28 *Teir Prif Hut* ('Three Great Enchantments of the Island of Britain') but in a form slightly different from the one extant[6]—there is nothing in the triad to support Dafydd's description of *Eiddilig Gor* ('the Dwarf') as *Gwyddyl call* (84, 40) 'a wily Irishman'. In his *cywydd* no. 51 *Teir Gwragedd a'i gwedd fal gwawn* Dafydd once more gives a direct quotation of the triad, *Teir Gwraged a gavas pryt Eva yn tri thraean* (TYP no. 50) 'Three Women who received the beauty of Eve in three third-shares'. The three were Diadema, Polixena, and Helen of Troy, and the triad is based ultimately on the Welsh translation of *Dares Phrygius*, of which the text is to be found in RBH.[7] From the same source comes TYP no. 47 *Tri dyn a gauas Kedernit Adaf* 'Three Men who received the Strength of Adam', and Dafydd drew upon this triad to obtain names worthy of comparison

---

[3] YB X̄ (1977), 182. If this interpretation is correct, a similar possibility arises in connection with Dafydd's description of Ifor Hael as *pellgardd pwyllgall* (7, 19); is it not equally likely that *pwyll* here is to be regarded as the proper name?

[4] Both *kelcoet* (an older spelling) and *kilcoet* occur in this name; cf. WM 466, 1 = RM 110, 8, and note PKM 247.

[5] In B viii, 301 W. J. Gruffydd proposed that the lines *Tydi a bair . . . dadeni byd* (27, 5–6) should be amended to *Tydi yw pair . . .* This emendation has been accepted by Dr Parry (though not by Ifor Williams, DGG² 42, 5). In my note in *Selections*, p. 21 I have given my reasons for rejecting the emendation and retaining *a bair* with DGG³, following the reading of the majority of the MSS. An additional note in GDG² 556 discusses further emendations to this line proposed by Eurys Rowlands, LlC v, 126–30.

[6] See n. to triad 28, and cf. TYP Appendix IV, 4.

[7] See TYP xxiv–v, 122–30. There can be little doubt but that triads 47–50 were originally present in the White Book.

with his patron Ifor Hael, these are *Ector* (*Echdor*) or Hector, Samson, and *Ercwlff* or Hercules. But there is one triad to whose fame Dafydd himself has undoubtedly contributed very largely—TYP no. 2 *Tri Hael Ynys Prydein* 'Three Generous Men of the Island of Britain', *Rhydderch*, *Nudd* and *Mordaf*. These were three heroes of the 'Old North' to whom the epithet *Hael* 'the Generous' traditionally belongs. In a famous metaphor Dafydd endowed his patron with the same epithet:

> *Rhoist ym swllt, rhyw ystum serch,*
> *Rhoddaf yt brifenw Rhydderch* (GDG 7, 9–10).

*(You gave me treasure, as a pledge of love,/ I give you (in return) Rhydderch's great name.)*

He was able to depend upon his audience to recognise at once the point of his comparison, since he could rely upon his hearers' familiarity with the Triads. For obvious reasons this triad was the most popular of all among the poets, and like many of his forebears and contemporaries, Dafydd makes several references to the proverbial generosity of one or other of the *Tri Hael*: *Nudd* (5, 26); *Rhydderch* (10, 19; 15, 42); *Mordaf* and *Rhydderch* (25, 3).

CULHWCH AND OLWEN

It is obvious that Dafydd is referring to the story of Ysbaddaden Pencawr—though he does not actually name him—when he reproaches Gruffudd Gryg: *Ped fai ffyrch ... dan aeliau dyn anolesg* (154, 15–18)[8] 'if there were forks beneath the brows of the sprightly man'—it would be easier for Dafydd to wound him. I have already noticed Dafydd's allusion to Menw ap Teirgwaedd, a character belonging to the tale, in the triad of Great Enchantments (TYP 28; cf. GDG 84, 31, 38), and in the Contention he describes himself as *mwynwiw gystlwn Menw* (152, 53) 'of the gentle kindred of Menw'.

Apart from these specific allusions to the tale of *Culhwch*, Dafydd displays a general knowledge of Arthurian tradition in its Welsh form, citing the names of *Gwalchmai* (21, 2), *Cai Hir* (21, 53; cf. *iawnGai angerdd* 114, 13 'of the genuine attribute of Cai');[9] *Arthur* (5, 14; 147, 35); *Gwenhwyfar* (82, 33); *Melwas* (64, 23, 29); *Huail*[10] (*fab Caw*) (14, 40)—on these two last see below under 'Unknown Tales'. These allusions indicate Dafydd's wide knowledge of Arthurian material, including the

---

[8] See Dr Parry's note, GDG 553; WM 477–9.
[9] In THSC 1946, 298 Dr T. J. Morgan suggests that the English word '(musical) key' and not the name of *Cai* is present in this allusion.
[10] See in particular Thomas Jones, 'Chwedl Huail ap Caw ac Arthur', *Astudiaethau Amrywiol a gyflwynir i Syr Thomas Parry-Williams*, ed. Thomas Jones (UWP 1968), 48–66; TYP 408–10.

contents of *Brut y Brenhinedd*, the Welsh version of Geoffrey of Monmouth's *History*. From the latter work it is probable that he derived the name of Arthur's father *Uthr* (Pendragon) (16, 51; 84, 33) and of his mother *Eigr* (see below under 'Heroines of the Romances'); his allusion to the contention between the two brothers *Brân* and *Beli* (79, 44; cf. BD 33); *Caer Droea* (140, 24); *gwlad Gamber* as a name for Wales (84, 70); and possibly *Llŷr ennaint* (11, 43).[11] Dafydd is also well informed with regard to the genealogies—he cites the names of *Beli (Mawr)* (12, 43); *hil Brân* (15, 9); and describes the people of Wales as *cenedl Gwinau Dau Freuddwyd* (15, 6).[12]

THE DREAM OF MAXEN

There are no explicit allusions, but there are two which are conjectural. In a poem addressed to Dyddgu (45, 23–4) we find:

> *Rhyfedd gan Ddoethion Rhufain*
> *Rhyfeddod pryd fy myd main.*

*(Rome's Wise Men would have marvelled at it—/ the wonder of my slender darling's grace.)*

It is known that the tales in *Saith Doethion Rhufain*, the 'Seven Wise Men of Rome' circulated over Wales through oral channels, and since the oldest written text dates from the mid-fourteenth century,[13] it would have been possible for Dafydd to have known of the proverbial 'Wise Men' from either written or from oral sources. But in this particular context, which is a love-poem, I think it is at least equally probable that Dafydd called to mind those other *doethion Rhufain* who in the tale of Maxen Wledig were summoned to the emperor of Rome to interpret for him the dream in which he had seen Elen, the girl he loved, in the midst of her family at Caernarfon (WM 183, 18–23). If Dafydd had made some specific allusion elsewhere either to SDR or to 'The Dream of Maxen' it would have been a help towards deciding which alternative is most probable, but there is none which can be regarded as certain. Many years ago Saunders Lewis advanced the suggestion that 'The Dream of Maxen' had inspired Iolo Goch's description of the home of Sir Hywell y Fwyall in Cricieth (IGE² IX),[14] in which the sleeping poet sees in a dream a wonderful castle with girls embroidering

---

[11] See BD 30 and Dr Parry's note, GDG 445.
[12] EWGT 39, 59 etc. On Beli Mawr as a dynastic ancestor see TYP 281–2.
[13] Henry Lewis, *Seith Doethon Rufein* (UWP 1958). The MS Jesus 3 (=20) was written in the middle of the fourteenth century (see B xv, 110 note, being), a copy of an earlier text. The text is also found in the Red Book. The stories circulated orally in Wales, and are presented entirely in the style and manner of the native *cyfarwyddiaid*.
[14] *Y Llenor*, v (1926), 157. See p. 163 below.

silk and young men playing draughts—and that on awaking it is explained to him that it was the castle of Sir Hywel that he had seen. Saunders Lewis later extended the same argument to another dream-poem, Dafydd ap Gwilym's *Cywydd y Cloc* (66).[15] The resemblance in this case is general rather than particular, in that Dafydd receives in a dream a vision of a girl he had once loved. But I think it is far less likely that this poem was inspired by 'The Dream of Maxen' than is the case with the poem of Iolo Goch.

## THE THREE ROMANCES

Dafydd shows some degree of acquaintance with each of the three tales. In particular there is the striking apologue, drawn from *Peredur*, of the bird killed on the snow as illustrating the contrasting colours of black, white, and red (45, 33–52; note that the slain bird is for Dafydd a blackbird, rather than a duck as in the original tale).[16] A further echo of an episode in the same tale is found in GDG 85, 41 when Dafydd complains of the sticks (*llysgon*) thrown at him as a sign of his humiliation as a disappointed lover, recalling the similar phrase used to describe Peredur's humiliation on his first arrival at Arthur's court.[17] The episode of the *cae niwl* or 'hedge of mist' in *Geraint ab Erbin* probably accounts for Dafydd's reference to his sigh as *cae niwl hir feddwl* (109, 14) 'long reflection's mist-hedge'. Eurys Rowlands[18] has suggested that there is a recollection of the romance of *Owain* in GDG 91, 36, where Dafydd compares an icicle to the spikes of the famous portcullis which in this story slices the hero's horse in two. In addition Dafydd shows his familiarity with the names of the heroines of both *Owain* and *Geraint* (see the following section).

## HEROINES OF THE ROMANCES

*Eigr*, the mother of Arthur, is the most popular of all the heroines with whom Dafydd compares the girls whom he praises; there are 15 allusions to her in GDG. The second in popularity is *Enid*, the heroine of *Geraint* (7 allusions), and she is followed closely by *Luned*, from the tale of *Owain* (5 allusions). As mentioned above, Dafydd quotes (51,

---

[15] LlC ii, 206; *Meistri'r Canrifoedd* 51. In *Selections*, 123 I have given my reasons for rejecting I. C. Peate's suggestion that Dafydd could have been in any way indebted to Froissart's poem *Li Orloge Amoureus* (composed between 1365–70, according to Armel Diverres—by letter). The earliest European clocks have been discussed in relation to Dafydd's poem by Gareth Evans, *Y Traethodydd* cxxxvii (1982), 7–16, with the suggestion that *Y Cloc* may be by a later poet.

[16] For the original tale see WM 140 (quoted GDG 481), and cf. n. 65 below.

[17] Cf. WM col. 122 (*Mab.* 187), *ar hynny y harganuot o'r teulu a dechreu y dyfalu a bwrw llyscon idaw* 'thereupon the household caught sight of him and they began to make fun of him and throw sticks at him.'

[18] YB III (1967), 32–3.

12) a triad which names three classical heroines—Helen of Troy, Polixena, and Diadema—whose names come ultimately from *Dares Phrygius*. Once he describes a girl as *Elen ail* (141, 2), and this may refer to either of the two Elens, either the Greek princess or the native *Elen Luyddog* of the 'Dream of Maxen'.

There are six allusions to *Esyllt*, beloved of *Trystan* (*Drystan*), the romance heroine whose story in its Welsh form has only been preserved in fragments.[19] It is possible, as D. J. Bowen has suggested,[20] that in one poem Dafydd re-echoes the exultant *englyn* which Esyllt declaims at the end of the *Ystorya Trystan* after hearing Arthur's judgement that she shall be allowed to go with Trystan while the leaves are on the trees (and therefore for ever, since some trees are evergreen), and live with her husband March 'when there are no leaves upon the trees'. In his poem he places the stock figure of the *Eiddig* in the place of March:

> *Eiddig, cyswynfab Addaf*
> *Ni ddawr hwn oni ddaw'r haf*
> *Rhoed i'w gyfoed y gaeaf,*
> *A rhan serchogion yw'r haf* (24, 31–2).

*(The Jealous Husband, Adam's bastard son,/ need not be anxious till the Summer comes./ Winter was given for those of his like age/ the gift to lovers is the summer time.)*

If this suggestion is correct it is valuable evidence with regard to the date of the *Ystorya Trystan*—or at any rate as to the date of Esyllt's final *englyn* which forms its climax:

> *Tri phren sy dda eu rhyw,*
> *Celyn ac eiddew ac yw*
> *A ddeilian' ddail yn eu byw—*
> *Trystan piau fi yn ei fyw.*[21]

*(There are three trees of good kind,/ the holly and the ivy and the yew,/ which keep their leaves while they live:/ Trystan shall have me while I live.)*

---

[19] For refs. to the Welsh material relating to the story of *Drystan* (Trystan) and *Esyllt* see TYP 329–33, and notes to *Drystan, Essyllt, March m. Meirchawn*; also my discussion of the story THSC 1953, 32–60, and some further comments by O. Padel in *Cambridge Medieval Celtic Studies I* (1981), 53–80. The *Ystorya Trysan* has been translated by R. L. Thomson in *Leeds Medieval Studies no. 2*, ed. Joyce Hill (Leeds, 1977). Additional MSS versions of this text have been published by Jenny Rowlands and Graham Thomas, *NLW Journal*, xxii (1982), 241–53.

[20] B xxv (1972), 21–2. On *cae Esyllt* as a frequent metaphor used by the poets for a treasure see D. J. Bowen, *Barddoniaeth yr Uchelwyr* (UWP 1957), 105; GPC 382.

[21] B v (1931), 121; xxv, 22. Variant versions of this stanza (which is possibly the nucleus of the whole) are found in the texts of *Ystorya Trystan* printed in *NLW Journal*, xxii.

Before leaving this point, it is interesting to notice how Dafydd compares himself (or his poetic *persona*) with Trystan:

> *Unfryd wyf yn y fro deg*
> *A Thrystan uthr ar osteg* (33, 7–8)

*(I am of one mind, in the fair land,/ with Trystan, famous in verses.)*[22]

It is also relevant to recall here the comparison made in the disputed *Cywydd y Sêr*:

> *Neithiwr, hir ffordd gam orddu*
> *Fal Tr(y)stan am feingan fu.*

*(Last night, on a long dark crooked road/ I was like Trystan for his slender fair one.)*[23]

The two allusions taken together testify to the poet's (or poets') idea of Trystan as a man who was perpetually wandering over the country-side seeking to arrange a tryst or *oed* with his love Esyllt—an idea which is anticipated in the Triads.[24] This is essentially the way of life which Dafydd himself purports to be leading in so many of his poems. However this may be, it is evident from various sources, that the romance of Trystan and Esyllt was popular in Wales in the four-teenth century.

OTHER LEGENDARY HEROINES

Dafydd also refers to a number of heroines who appear to have been well-known in Welsh tales belonging to an oral tradition from which virtually nothing has survived, although they seem to have been at least equally popular as Eigr, Luned, Enid, and Esyllt.

There are eight allusions to *Indeg*, daughter of *Garwy Hir* (see below under 'Unknown Tales'). An early triad[25] makes her 'one of Arthur's three mistresses'—with two companions whose names and stories are unknown.

Seven allusions are to *Tegau*, elsewhere known as *Tegau Eurfron* ('Gold Breast'). In GDG 52 Dafydd compares Morfudd to the 'Three Splendid

---

[22] *Gosteg*, i.e. *cân*, *cerdd*. One of the meanings is 'a series of connected *englynion*' (GPC) which would suit well with the *Ystorya Trystan*. The other meaning of *gosteg*, 'silence', is clearly inappropriate here.

[23] DGG[2] no. xl; cf. OBWV no. 64, lines 15–16. (It is fair to point out that the MS reading is *trwstan*, which Ifor Williams interprets as 'Trystan' (DGG[2] 200), but Dr Parry interprets as the adj. 'awkward', thus rejecting any connection with the romance hero).

[24] TYP no. 26 *Tri Gwrddfeichiad* 'Three Powerful Swineherds.'

[25] TYP no. 57; for further refs. see TYP 413.

Maidens of Arthur's Court'—*Tegau*, *Dyfyr*, and *Enid*. But this triad comes only in a late manuscript: the earliest source for it is in one of the rhetorical exercises in prose—*Araith Ieuan Brydydd Hir*,[26] dating from the fifteenth century. Dafydd's grouping of the three names together suggests that he was familiar with similar material, whether in oral or written tradition.

*Dyfyr* (*Wallt Euraid* 'Golden Hair') has three references only. Apart from frequent references to her by the poets[27] nothing whatever is known of her.

*Fflur* also has three citations. All that we know about her is that she was loved by Caswallawn fab Beli.[28]

*Creirwy* (123, 19)[29] was daughter of Ceridwen in the story of Taliesin and was loved by *Garwy Hir*. Patrick Ford cites *Crairw* and *Creirfyw* as variants of her name in some texts of the *Hanes Taliesin*, and Ifor Williams accepts *Creirfyw* ('lively darling') as the meaning of the name, but *Creirwy* is the form favoured by the poets. Dafydd seems likely to have derived this name from a verse in the Bardic Grammar:[30] there is no other evidence that he knew of the *Hanes Taliesin*.

TALES FROM IRELAND

The tale of *Culhwch and Olwen* gives evidence for the knowledge of Irish narrative tradition in Wales, and this makes it the less surprising that Dafydd ap Gwilym knew the names of two heroines who do not, however, appear in that tale in the famous list of characters present at 'Arthur's Court'. These are *Derdri* (139, 21) and *Nyf* (84, 69; 71, 24; 98, 56; 129, 8). Deirdre was a heroine famous in the Ulster Cycle of tales, as the girl who eloped with Naoise and who was slain with her lover by the king, Conchobar mac Nessa, who had intended her for his own bride. Her flight with Naoise and his brothers through many wild and mountainous tracts of Ireland and Scotland is one of the central tales in the Ulster Cycle. Dafydd's citation of the name of Deirdre is the earliest to be found in Welsh, although Gruffudd ap Maredudd also mentions her: the references by both poets thus corroborate the evidence for some knowledge of the Ulster stories in Wales. *Nyf* is

[26] D. Gwenallt Jones, *Yr Areithiau Pros* (UWP 1964), 30 (from Peniarth MS 218), pp. 99–103. Cf. TYP no. 88 *Tair Rhiain Ardderchog Llys Arthur* and TYP 512–14 on *Tegau Eurfron*; also Graham Thomas, 'Chwedlau Tegau Eurfron a Thristfardd bardd Urien Rheged' B xxiv (1970), 1–9 (for summary see TYP² 564–5).

[27] Further refs. can no doubt be added to those listed TYP 335.

[28] TYP 352–3, and in particular Ifor Williams's note on the story of Fflur and Caswallawn, THSC 1946, 41–3.

[29] 'A Fragment of the *Hanes Taliesin* by Llywelyn Siôn' EC xiv (1974–5), 451–60; I. Williams, *Chwedl Taliesin* (UWP 1957), 4.

[30] See above p. 116 and n.

mentioned by more than one poet: Sir Ifor Williams argued[31] that her name is derived from the Irish *Niamh*, beloved by Oisín son of Fionn mac Cumhaill: she enticed Oisín to an enchanted island, like Ynys Afallach, somewhere across the western seas. Unfortunately a certain ambiguity arises from the fact that *nyf* is also an old and poetical word for 'snow', so that it is frequently uncertain which of the two meanings is the one intended by the poets.[32]

Next, *Cuhelyn*. In GDG 25, 41 the Nightingale is described as *chwaer Guhelyn*; in another poem (143, 39) Dafydd alludes to *ysgwyd Guhelyn* 'C's shield'. Here again there is a slight difficulty because, as Dr Parry points out,[33] the name *Cuhelyn Fardd* is found among Dafydd's early ancestors: it might therefore not be impossible, though surprising, for Dafydd to call the Nightingale 'Cuhelyn's sister'. But in respect to 'Cuhelyn's Shield' there is a more acceptable possibility. J. Morris-Jones[34] regarded *Cuhelyn* as the Welsh equivalent of the name of the Irish hero Cú Chulainn (although *Cocholyn* appears elsewhere in an early poem[35] as the Welsh equivalent of this name). Interestingly enough, two other poets also make references to *ysgwyd Guhelyn*: these are Prydydd y Moch in reference to the shield of Llywelyn Fawr,[36] and Iolo Goch in a poem giving thanks for a dagger.[37] It is therefore worth asking whether there is any ancient tale which can explain these three allusions to the fame of Cú Chulainn's shield. And it so happens that there is: many years ago the following anecdote was published with translation from an early Irish manuscript:[38]

'*Dubhan* was the name of Cú Chulainn's shield, and this is how it was made. It was enacted among the men of Ulster that each one of them must own a silver shield with a special device carved upon

---

[31] For allusions by the poets to *Derdri* and *Nyf* see TYP lxxxii, n.; further allusions can be added. Ifor Williams derived the name *Nyf* from *Niamh* (the Irish heroine loved by Oisín); DGG² 187; IGE² 360. Gwyn Thomas has suggested in B xxviii, 405 that Dafydd's comparison of Morfudd to Deirdre in GDG 139, 21 shows actual acquaintance with the story of the Irish heroine who eloped with her lover from the aged king Conchobar (on the passage see *Selections* 64, n.). These names entered Welsh oral tradition in a manner similar to those of the Irish heroes at Arthur's Court in *Culhwch and Olwen*, on which see P. Sims-Williams, B xxix (1982), 591–620.

[32] Cf. Davies's Dictionary (1632): *Nyf, pl.a Nef, caeli, orum. Est etiam nomen proprium mulierum apud antiquos. Et vid. an Nivem significet: gwynbryd nyf cyn dattawdd. Ior.G.*

[33] GDG p. 547. On Cuhelyn Fardd see above pp. 13, 15 and the edition by R. Geraint Gruffydd in SC x/xi, 198, 209 of the praise-poem addressed to him in BBC 9–17.

[34] *Cy.* xxviii, 273.

[35] BT 66–7. See edition and discussion of this poem by P. Sims-Williams, 'The Evidence for vernacular Irish Literary Influence on early mediaeval Welsh Literature', *Ireland in Early Mediaeval Europe*, ed. D. Whitelock et al. (Cambridge, 1982), 235–57.

[36] *ysgwyd ball guall guhelyn* (H 281, 25–6).

[37] IGE² 58, 30.

[38] Trinity College Dublin MS, H 17, 664. Published with translation by R. I. Best, *Ériu*ᵛ (1911), 72. See also E. O'Curry, *Manners and Customs of the Ancient Irish* (London, 1873) ii, 329. See n. on *Cuhelyn*, G 185.

it, and each of these devices must be different from the others. When Cú Chulainn asked the smith, whose name was Mac Endge, to make for him such a shield, the smith replied that he had no device left which he could use, since he had already used up all the designs he knew upon the shields of the other Ulstermen. Cú Chulainn was very annoyed, and threatened to kill the smith. While the smith was trembling with fear, there appeared all at once a marvellous man (no doubt one of the gods) who at once drew a design in the ashes which were upon the floor, with a wonderful fork which he had in his hand, and which was called *Luaithrinne* ('ash-engraver'—a kind of compasses?), and afterwards Mac Endge copied this design on Cú Chulainn's shield.'

Evidently, therefore, there was some magic significance attached to Cú Chulainn's shield. And the allusion to it by three Welsh poets as a great marvel gives some support to Morris-Jones's belief that *Cuhelyn* is a variant form for the name of the Irish hero Cú Chulainn. These three allusions are a valuable addition to the evidence for the knowledge of some of the Old Irish tales in medieval Wales.

TRADITIONS OF THE 'OLD NORTH'

The significance for Dafydd ap Gwilym of the Welsh legendary background of northern tradition was that *yr hen Ogledd* symbolized generosity and patronage given to poets, combined with national independence and opposition to the English invader (see above on the triad of the *Tri Hael*). There must have been a certain nostalgia in Dafydd's presenting himself as *ail Daliesin* (10, 34) 'a second Taliesin' enjoying the same kind of patronage from 'Ifor the Generous' as Urien Rheged was believed to have extended to the historical Taliesin:

> Rhoddaf i hwn, gwn ei ged,
> O nawdd rugl, neuadd Reged,
> Bendith Taliesin, wingost,
> A bery byth heb air bost (9, 33–6).

*(I bestow on him—I know his bounty—/ of ready patronage (like) the hall of Rheged,/ Taliesin's blessing, wine-provider,/ which without boasting will endure for ever.)*

Ifor Hael is portrayed as the enemy of the English and of the men of Deira—the Northumbrian settlers who opposed the Britons in the North—(5, 23, 42); Ifor 'will not endure the Deirans' (*Deifr ni oddef* 8, 27), and causes them to be laid dead on biers (*Deifr ar esyth* 11, 10).[39] It is interesting to find that Dafydd—like Cynddelw before him—knew as much as this about the historical Taliesin: he never connects

[39] Cf. p. 62 above for Dafydd's description of his uncle Llywelyn as *Deifr helgud* (13, 13) 'pursuer of the men of Deira.'

Taliesin with Elffin and Maelgwn Gwynedd of the mythical story which evolved around the name of the famous poet, as do a number of other poets both before and after Dafydd.[40] It is intriguing to speculate as to how much genuine recollection of the 'Old North' may have survived down to the fourteenth century in Welsh cultural tradition.

In his fictitious elegies addressed to contemporary poets, Dafydd compares his poetic inspiration (*awen*) to that of Taliesin (20, 2) and of Myrddin (19, 27), the two prophetic poets who stood at the beginning of the tradition and whose names are frequently coupled together. Both poets appear also to have enjoyed a certain reputation as lovers,[41] according to *Yr Wylan* 'The Seagull':

> *Och wŷr, erioed ni charawdd*
> *Na Myrddin wenieithfin iach*
> *Na Thaliesin ei thlysach* (118, 22–4).

*(Ah men, neither Myrddin with his goodly flattering speech, nor Taliesin ever loved one of fairer form.)*

Myrddin as a lover suggests some knowledge of the cycle of poems referring to his story preserved in the Black Book of Carmarthen,[42] as well as in RBH. Myrddin's reputation as a prophet of future events seems also to be indicated, somewhat ironically, in Dafydd's description of the Echo, *Y Garreg Ateb*:

> *Mwy y dywaid heb beidiaw*
> *Ar ael y glyn ar ôl glaw*
> *No Myrddin sonfawr mawrddig,*
> *Fab Saith Gudyn, y dyn dig* (130, 5–8).

*(It says more without ceasing,/ on the hill's brow, after the rain,/ than noisy Myrddin with great passion,/ son of Saith Gudyn, that angry man.)*[43]

Dafydd makes no allusion to the other early poet, Aneirin, although Gruffudd Gryg in his elegy to him compares Dafydd himself to Aneirin.[44]

---

[40] For the allusions by the poets both to the 'Taliesin of history' and to the 'Taliesin of legend' see TYP 510–11.

[41] Resemblances in the legends which grew up concerning these two poets have been pointed out by I. Williams, *Chwedl Taliesin*, but the subject needs further investigation.

[42] For refs. and discussion see A. O. H. Jarman 'Daroganau a Chanu Myrddin', *Llyfr Du Caerfyrddin* (UWP 1982), xxxiv–xl; idem, 'The Welsh Myrddin Poems' ch. 3 in R. S. Loomis (ed.), *Arthurian Literature in the Middle Ages* (Oxford, 1959).

[43] On *saith gudyn* (a proverbial expression) see Dr Parry's note, GDG 538.

[44] GDG p. 428.

THE 'LLYWARCH HEN' POETRY

The evidence is doubtful, yet suggestive. Dafydd cites the name of *Pyll* (12, 42) the name of one of the sons of Llywarch Hen, but otherwise very rare.[45] His allusion to *Llŷr ennaint* (11, 43) suggests a reminiscence of CLIH iii, 6c: *kell llyr kein ebyr gwyr glawr*—though *llŷr* here is not a personal name but a figurative name for the sea, like the Irish *ler*. This seems likely to be the case also in Dafydd's allusion, especially since generosity in bestowing drink is the significance of both expressions. In the line *Rhydain hen, y rhed yn hwyr* (148, 54) 'the aged deer runs slowly' Dafydd is echoing Llywarch's lament about his old age, *Eidyl hen, hwyr y dyre* (CLIH 11, 13c). In his prayer to St Dwynwen Dafydd quotes the proverb *Nid adwna ... Duw a wnaeth* (94, 23–4): the same proverb is cited CLIH VI, 29c, *Nyt atwna Duw ar a wnel*. But apart from these details there is nothing but suggestive echoes of a generalized kind, in the way in which Dafydd treats particular themes such as that of ruined and abandoned homesteads (13, 49ff.; *Yr Adfail* 144); or of old age and the loss of youth (90, and perhaps 106), to raise the question whether he had in the back of his mind the lamentations of the old Llywarch. The allusions are much less explicit than is the case with the reminiscences of the Taliesin poetry.

UNKNOWN TALES

*Ysgolan.* GDG 50, 52 contains the line *Ysgolan wyf, nis gwyl neb* 'I am Ysgolan, whom no one sees'. A poem in the Black Book of Carmarthen alludes to the story of *Ysgolan ysgolhaig* ('Y. the Scholar'); it appears that a story concerning this character was known in both Wales and Brittany in the Middle Ages.[46] But the fragmentary allusions to the tale which have survived throw no light on the meaning of Dafydd's allusion to his invisibility.

*Ystudfach.* A single reference to him in GDG 137, 71 implies that he was an early bard, and William Salesbury connects him with Myrddin and Taliesin and the unknown Meugant; apart from this, the allusion remains completely obscure.[47]

*Huail (fab Caw)* GDG 14, 40. There are many scattered allusions to the enmity between Huail,[48] said to have been a ruler in Scotland,

---

[45] The index to EWGT lists two instances of *Pyll* in addition to those to the son of Llywarch Hen. There is a further instance in the Gododdin, CA line 357.

[46] GDG 486–7. For a full discussion of the story of Ysgolan see A. O. H. Jarman 'Cerdd Ysgolan' YB X (1977), 51–78; ibid. *Llyfr Du Caerfyrddin*, lx.

[47] W. Salesbury, introduction to *Oll Synnwyr Pen* (1547). Cf. GDG 540–1; *Meistri'r Canrifoedd* 135; RWM II, 109.

[48] On *Huail* see n. 10 above, and Hugh Williams's edn. of the Life of Gildas by the Monk of Ruys, *Gildae De Excidio Britannicae* (London, 1899), 323 ff.

and King Arthur; also concerning his father *Caw* who is connected with Pictland[49] and the region of the Grampians, and his brother Gildas. *Gwenhwyfar and Melwas.* In GDG 64, 19—26 Dafydd compares his state of frustration beneath the window of the girl he loves with the state of Melwas who climbed successfully through a window at Caerlleon to meet with Gwenhwyfar, succeeding where Dafydd himself failed;

> *Ni bwyf hen o bu o hud*
> *Ffenestr â hon un ffunud,*
> *Dieithr, hwyl dau uthr helynt,*
> *Yr hon ar Gaerlleon gynt*
> *Y dôi Felwas o draserch*
> *Drwydi heb arswydi serch,*
> *Cur tremynt, cariad tramawr*
> *Gynt ger tŷ ferch Ogfran Gawr.*
> *Cyd cawn fod pan fai'n odi*
> *Hwyl am y ffenestr â hi,*
> *Ni chefais elw fal Melwas,*
> *Nychu'r grudd yw, nacha'r gras.*

*(May I not grow old if there was ever formed by magic/ a window of like kind to this,/ except for the one that Melwas once—a terrible predicament in the career of two—/ climbed through once in Caerlleon/ without fear and from great love (an enormous trial of excessive love)/ beside the home of Ogrfran the Giant's daughter./ Although while it snowed I might make/ progress on the opposite side of the window from her,/ I did not win such advantage as belonged to Melwas;/ my cheek's affliction was my only grace.)*

The story of Gwenhwyfar's violent abduction by Melwas 'king of the summer country' (Somerset) was known early in the twelfth century, and is summarized in the *Life of Gildas* by Caradog of Llancarfan[50] (where the story of Huail fab Caw is also to be found). There is also a sequence of obscure *englynion* of uncertain antiquity concerned with the story; evidently in Welsh tradition Melwas played the part afterwards taken over by Lancelot.[51] *Ocuran Gawr* (sic) is named in the triad of the *Teir Prif Riein Arthur* (TYP 56) which oddly triplicates the name of Arthur's queen[52] giving her a choice of three different fathers.

---

[49] For the story of *Cau Pritdin* 'Caw of Pictland' see *Life of St Cadoc* ch. 28, ed. and trans. Wade-Evans, *Vitae Sanctorum Britanniae* 82–4, where Cau is interpreted as *cawr* 'giant'; TYP 301–2. His home was *ultra montem Bannauc* which has been interpreted as 'beyond the Grampian mountains' (CLIH 156–7).

[50] Hugh Williams, *Gildas* 408–10.

[51] TYP 380–5; B viii, 203–8; *Speculum* xiii, 38–53. Cf. Brynley Roberts 'Rhai Cerddi Ymddiddan', *Ast.H.* 284.

[52] The name of Gwenhwyfar's father belongs solely to Welsh tradition (it is not known to Geoffrey of Monmouth or to the continental romances); see TYP 363–4. Eurys Rowlands has argued (LlC vi, 241) that Dafydd's form *Ogfran* and not *Gogfran* is the earlier

*Garwy.* In GDG 48, 15 Dafydd refers to what was evidently a known story about the loves of Garwy Hir, father of *Indeg* and allegedly the lover of *Creirwy*:[53]

> *Ni bu mor lud hud a hwn*
> *Anad gwyr annwyd Garwy;*

*(Never was there such persistent charm as this,/ beyond the passion of men like to Garwy.)*

The fame of Garwy's love-story is substantiated by a number of references by the poets, but its details have not survived.

*Gwgon Gleddyfrudd.* Dafydd alludes twice to this legendary hero of Ceredigion (46, 67–8) and he was evidently familiar with *Castell Gwgawn* as a local landmark. The existence of a story known to him is indicated by a cryptic allusion in his eulogy of Morfudd as *Chwaer ... i ferch Wgon farchoges* (34, 29–30) 'sister ... to the daughter of Gwgon, horse-woman' (if this is the same person). Gwgawn Gleddyfrudd is commemorated in a triad[54] and in the genealogies, and may have been a historical character who lived in the ninth century. Although *Gwgon* is a common man's name, I have found no other mention of him by any other poet.

*Gwaeddan.* GDG 84, 21–2 (addressed to an un-named girl):

> *Gyrraist fi yn un gerrynt*
> *Gwaeddan am ei gapan gynt;*

*(You drove me on a like short chase/ As Gwaeddan once, in pursuit of his cap ...*

Nothing is known of this intriguing story, though Dr Parry notes that *Gwaeddan* is found in several early instances as a personal name.

*Dinbyrn.* In Dafydd's satire of Rhys Meigen *nid ail Dinbyrn* (21, 76) the comparison is used disparagingly. Apart from Einion fab Gwalchmai's allusion to Llywelyn fab Iorwerth as *angert Dinbyrn* (H 39, 29) 'of the passion of D.' there is no other known reference to this character.

To list these obscure references to unknown characters and stories adds a little more to the rich body of evidence for the wealth of Dafydd's inheritance of tales and traditions which cannot be elucidated from extant written sources and were probably never written down, but were still orally current over wide parts of Wales in the fourteenth century.

---

form of the name, though *Gogbhran Gawr* occurs in Siôn Dafydd Rhys's list of Welsh Giants, *Cy.* 27, 134. *Ocuran Gawr* is named only in WR texts of the triads and copies based upon them; it is unknown in the 'Early Version'.

[53] On *Garwy* see GDG 484; TYP 354.

[54] TYP no. 60, which is found only in the WR version. For further refs. see G 675–6, 389–90.

BELIEFS CONCERNING GWYNN AP NUDD AND THE HOUNDS OF ANNWN

These beliefs are prominent in Welsh folklore, and the number of Dafydd's allusions to them are significant. They have been studied in detail by Eurys Rowlands,[55] who shows that Dafydd's attitude to Annwfn and everything connected with it is hostile, partly because its associations are with winter and lack of fertility. I shall therefore merely list the allusions here, without further discussing them.

(The Owl):

> *Anos cûn y nos a wna*
> *Edn i Wyn fab Nudd ydyw* (26, 22, 40).

*(He incites the Hounds of the Night;/ He (the Owl) is the bird of Gwyn fab Nudd.)*

(The Peat Bog):

> *Pysgodlyn i Wyn yw ef*
> *Fab Nudd, wb ynn ei oddef!* (127, 29–30).

*(It is the fish-pond of Gwyn fab/ Nudd; alas that we suffer it!)*

In answer to Grufudd Gryg:

> *O syrr, lle'i gwesgyr gwasgwyn*
> *O'm dawr, Gwyn ap Nudd i'm dwyn!* (150, 51–2).

*(If he is angry, when the Gascon horse pursues him, may Gwynn ap Nudd abduct me if I care!)*

The Mist:

> *Tyrau uchel eu helynt*
> *Tylwyth Gwyn, talaith y gwynt* (68, 31–2)

*(Troublesome high towers belonging/ to the family of Gwynn, the province of the wind.)*

> *Gwaun dalar Gwyn a'i dylwyth* (68, 40)

*(the heathy headland of the family of Gwynn.)*

> *Anardd darth lle y cyfarth cûn*
> *Ennaint gwrachiod Annwn* (68, 43–4).

[55] 'Cyfeiriadau Dafydd ap Gwilym at Annwn', LlC v (1958–9), 122–4. For an edition and discussion of the dialogue between Gwyn ap Nudd and Gwyddno Garanir in BBC see Brynley Robert's, *Ast.H.* 311–18; LlC xiii, 283–9.

*(Unsightly fog in which the dogs are barking,/ ointment of the witches of Annwn.)*

There should certainly be added to this list a further allusion to the 'hounds of Night' in Dafydd's *Aube* (129, 32) in which the poet answers the girl's complaint that dawn has come, since she can hear the dogs outside barking, with the rejoinder that it is only the 'hounds of Night'; that is the *cŵn Annwn* who accompany Gwyn ap Nudd on his hunting expeditions through the forests at night:

*Cyni a wna cwn y nos.*

*(The Hounds of Night are fighting.)*

CONTINENTAL WORKS TRANSLATED INTO WELSH

*Tales of Charlemagne.* Dafydd compares his sword to *Cyrseus*, which was the sword of Otfel, and also with *Hawt-y-Clŷr*, the sword of Oliver (143, 24, 44).[56] But as Chotzen points out, there are several lists of the swords of famous heroes to be found in the manuscripts; e.g. in Llanstephan 28, where the swords of Arthur, Ulkassar (Julius Caesar), Roland etc. are listed by their appropriate names. Dafydd could therefore have derived the names in the poem to his sword from such list:[57] to cite them does not necessarily imply that he was acquainted with the romances from which they are derived. Yet when Dafydd compares Gruffudd Gryg to *Gwenwlydd* (*Ganelon*) (149, 4) Roland's betrayer, it does imply some fuller knowledge of the story. The Charlemagne tales were translated into Welsh for the first time in the second half of the thirteenth century and the beginning of the fourteenth, and several different but incomplete translations have come down including those in the Red Book. It is therefore quite uncertain from whence Dafydd could have derived his knowledge.

*Dares Phrygius.* Dafydd alludes to *Ercwlff* (5, 25) and to *Ector, Echdor* (5, 14, 41)—names which certainly became known in Wales through the medium of this text, of which the earliest extant copy is in RBH. From *Dares Phrygius* also comes the names of the three classical heroines named in GDG 51, where Dafydd is quoting from a pre-existing triad of the women who shared in Eve's beauty. The names *Ercwlff* and *Ector* could well have been derived from the same group of triads,[58] which are preserved only in the Red Book and manuscripts derived from it. Once more, therefore, there is no need to conclude that Dafydd

---

[56] Cf. IGE² 57, 12 where Iolo Goch makes a similar comparison of a dagger with *Hawd-y-Clŷr*.

[57] Chotzen, *Recherches* 140; RWM. II, 464. For *Gwenwlydd* see YCM 113, GDG 550.

[58] TYP nos. 47–50; ibid. intro. xxiv.

knew the text of *Dares Phrygius*, since he was plainly familiar with the group of triads in the Red Book.

*Amlyn and Amig.* Dafydd compares the grief of Llywelyn Fychan for his friend Rhydderch ab Ieuan Llwyd to the grief of *Amlyn* for *Emig* (sic):

> *Och Amlyn o'i dyddyn dig*
> *Alaeth mamaeth, am Emig* (17, 15–16)

*(Amlyn's cry from his afflicted home, for Emig, like a foster-mother's grief.)*

Iolo Goch also quotes the story in his elegy for Llywelyn Goch ap Meurig Hen (IGE² 42, 34–43, 1–2): *Mi ac ef, ail Amig oedd,/ Amlyn wyf* 'We two, he was a second Amig, and I am Amlyn'.[59] The elegy was composed towards the end of the 14th century. The only text of *Amlyn ac Amig*, which was translated from French and Latin versions, is that of the Red Book (cols 1085–1115).

Apart from some of the Charlemagne romances, which are a little earlier, all the above texts were translated into Welsh during the fourteenth century.[60] The forms of the proper names which Dafydd uses bear witness to the fact that he was quoting them from the Welsh translations rather than from their French or Latin originals. All these translations are found in the Red Book of Hergest (though *Campeu Charlymaen* is only one of several tales of Charlemagne). But since it is almost certain that this great compendium of verse and prose was not compiled until a date subsequent to Dafydd's life-time, the question arises, from whence did he acquire his knowledge of these tales? No texts of *Dares Phrygius* or *Amlyn ac Amig* are earlier than those of the Red Book, while of the Charlemagne tales there are parts in the White Book of Rhydderch which corresponds closely with the Red Book version. Dafydd must therefore have derived his knowledge from some older source—and what source is more likely than those pages of the

---

[59] On the significance of this allusion see S. Lewis, *Meistri'r Canrifoedd*, 58. Towards the middle or latter half of the 14th century there are further refs. to the story by Meurig ab Iorwerth RB 1373, 32 and by Rhisierdyn RB 1290, 41. See *Kedymdeithyas Amlyn ac Amic* ed. Patricia Williams (UWP 1982). *Amis e Amilun* was very popular in the 13th and 14th centuries, and an English version was based on the Anglo-Norman text in the second half of the C13, which remained popular in the next century; see M. D. Legge, *Anglo-Norman Literature and Its Background* (Oxford, 1963), 115–21.

[60] It is worth noting that Dafydd makes no allusion anywhere to the characters of *Y Seint Greal*, which was translated towards the end of the 14th century (the earliest text is Peniarth 11)—although this does not of course prove that the French prose romances including those of the 'Vulgate Cycle' were not translated from French into Welsh during the life-time of Dafydd ap Gwilym. (See Creidwen Lloyd-Morgan, 'A Study of *Y Seint Greal* in relation to *La Queste del Saint Graal* and *Perlesvaus*', D.Phil. thesis, Oxford 1978); ibid. 'Nodiadau Ychwanegol ar Achau Arthuraidd a'u Ffynonellau Ffrangeg', *NLW Journal* xxi (1980), 329–39.

White Book of Rhydderch which have been missing from the manuscript for centuries? It is evident that Dafydd's allusions to the Triads correspond more closely with the version of these which is found in the White Book and the Red Book (WR) than in that which I have called the 'Early Version'. The group of triads based on *Dares Phrygius*, for instance, appears only in the WR version. I have suggested earlier[61] that Dafydd derived his obvious knowledge of the Bardic Grammar from a text which must have been the *exemplar* of the Red Book version, and in this case also, what manuscript is this more likely to have been than the lost pages of the White Book—the celebrated possession of the man to whom Dafydd composed his 'elegy'—in all probability during his subject's life-time—Rhydderch ab Ieuan Llwyd.

If the White Book of Rhydderch was indeed Dafydd's source of knowledge, not only of the Bardic Grammar but also of the triads of classical heroes and heroines, of *Amlyn ac Amig* and of the Charlemagne romances, what other texts are there which would have been accessible to him by means of the literary treasure which was in the possession of his friend? Was it from the pages of the White Book that Dafydd ap Gwilym obtained his knowledge of the Four Branches of the *Mabinogi* and of the other tales and romances?[62] And was it also from this manuscript that he came to know of the 'Seven Wise Men of Rome' and perhaps also of the poems concerning *Llywarch Hen*? Three facts have recently struck me as being relevant to this suggestion. Firstly, in describing the Owl (GDG 26) he says of her:

> *A 'i gwedd, wyneb pryd dyn gwâr*
> *A 'i sud, ellylles adar.*
> *Pob edn syfudr alltudryw*
> *A 'i baedd, pond rhyfedd ei byw?* (26, 31–4).

*(With her face, like to a gentle mortal,/ and her form, she-fiend of birds./ Each unclean bird of alien kind/ will harass her, is it not strange she lives?/*

Is not Dafydd here using words which are closely similar to those with which Gwydion addresses Blodeuwedd in the *Mabinogi: bot gelynyaeth y ryghot a'r holl adar. A bot anyan udunt dy uaedu, a'th amherchi y lle i'th*

---

[61] Ch. 4 above. It is also relevant here to draw attention to the elegy (whether genuine or fictitious) addressed by Gruffudd Llwyd to the same Rhydderch, IGE² xxxviii, which alludes consecutively to several texts which are present in RBH but which may have been present on the lost pages of Rhydderch's famous MS—the White Book. See my note B xxix (1980), 81–3.

[62] It is significant that Dafydd does not refer in any place to the tale of 'The Dream of Rhonabwy'. According to Daniel Huws (in conversation) it is unlikely that this tale exactly filled the missing leaves in WB corresponding to the length of the tale in RBH, as Gwenogvryn Evans claimed in his introduction to WB pp. x–xi.

*gaffant*[63] 'may there be enmity between you and all the birds. And may it be their nature to harass and dishonour you wherever they may find you'. The verb *baeddu* (var. of *maeddu*), rare in early times,[64] and meaning 'to beat, harass, maltreat', etc. appears in both extracts, and re-inforces the suggestion that there is a connexion between them. A similar conclusion seems to be invited by Dafydd's citation of the incident of Peredur and the blood-drops on the snow (GDG 45). In his note Dr Parry has drawn our attention to the fact that in the line *Gwaed yr edn gwedy r'odi* (45, 51) Dafydd uses the same early verbal construction *r'odi* (for *ry odi*) exactly as in the corresponding passage in the tale of *Peredur* in the White Book *kawat o eira gwedy ryodi*.[65] Thirdly, I have indicated above that Dafydd employs names from the first Branch of the *Mabinogi* more frequently than names from any of the other Branches. When in the Contention he threatens Gruffudd Gryg he says, *O doi di i'r Deau dir/ Ti a fydd ... Broch yng nghod* (152, 44–6) 'if you come to the land of the South, you will be a Badger in a Bag'—an obvious allusion to the episode of the 'badger in the bag' in *Mabinogi Pwyll*.[66] Considering the extreme scarcity of the allusions to the merciless game of 'Badger in the Bag'—other than these two the only one which has come down is that in Davies's Dictionary of 1632—is it not likely that here too Dafydd is directly quoting from the text of the White Book? No certainty on this matter is possible, but it may well be that others will notice further apparent echoes in Dafydd's poetry of the actual wording of the text of the *Mabinogi* as it has come down.

There is one other allusion made by Dafydd, which is interesting from an entirely different point-of-view, and which I would like to mention before closing. When he compares his patron Ifor Hael to *Ffwg* (6, 37) we have the only instance in which he alludes to a figure who was famous in Norman historical legend belonging to the Marches but not, so far as is known, by means of any Welsh version of his story. *Fulk* or *Fouke fitz Waryn* was an outlaw in the reign of King John, and a member of a powerful family of Marcher lords, owners of the castle of Whittington in Shropshire, and long-lasting enemies of their neighbours across the border, the princes of Powys. It is difficult to explain the very numerous allusions to *Syr Ff(a)wg* by poets of the fourteenth

---

[63] PKM 91, 11–13; see I. Williams's note, 301–2.

[64] GPC records no example before the 16th century.

[65] WM col. 140 = RM 211, 12. In his apologue, Dafydd has substituted a blackbird for the duck slain on the snow in the original, perhaps because for him and his contemporaries the blackbird's hue was a conventional colour-comparison for a girl's beauty.

[66] PKM 17, 12; *Mab.* 15. Davies's *Dictionary* (1632) gives under *gwarau*: '*gwarae broch ynghod, lle y rhoe'r trechaf y llall mewn cod*', 'the game of Badger in the Bag, when the strongest one puts the other in a bag.'

and fifteenth centuries[67] except on the supposition that a wealth of folklore had grown up concerning him before the end of the thirteenth century, and that he was looked upon on both sides of Offa's Dyke as the romantic symbol of an outlaw. About 1320–30 a semi-imaginary 'history' of him was written in Anglo-Norman prose, and this in its turn was based upon a lost poem in the same language, possibly the work of a cleric belonging to Ludlow in the second half of the thirteenth century. The earliest allusions to him in Welsh are those by Dafydd ap Gwilym and by Iolo Goch.[68] There can be little doubt that all the allusions by the poets to *Sir Ff(a)wg* are derived from folklore current throughout the length and breadth of the Welsh Marches.[69] The story of *Fouke fitz Waryn* exists only in a single manuscript, so that it appears that it never had any very extensive circulation—for instance, it appears to have been quite unknown in France. It is most improbable that the Welsh poets knew of the fame of *Syr Ff(a)wg* from a written 'history', of which the copies must always have been rare and hard to come by, or that they knew of the Norman poem which preceded it. Like Gwyn ap Nudd, then, he was for Dafydd a hero of folk-tradition, and not a figure known from such Welsh or continental romances as he seems likely to have become acquainted with through written sources.

This is not the place to discuss Dafydd ap Gwilym's references to Biblical characters, or to the native saints of both north and south Wales—Dewi, Brychan, Cynfelyn, Cyndeyrn, Mordeyrn, Dwynwen, Deinioel, Beuno, Cadfan and Cybi—or to *Cyfraith Hywel*, the native legal system, or to the poet Ovid—the only foreign poet of whom Dafydd gives evidence of so much as having ever heard the name.

[67] These are conveniently collected in G 505; add the allusion by Gruffudd ap Maredudd to *(g)wyr ffwc*, RP 1314, 25.

[68] IGE², 11–12: *Llys Ffwg yn llawes y ffordd,/ Llety'n braff, lled hen Brifiordd.* Alan Roberts has suggested to me (by letter) that the allusion here is to an incident recorded towards the end of the Anglo-Norman text which tells that Fulk caused the highway to be deflected in such a way that it should pass through his own estate, so that he might be enabled to extend hospitality to travellers. But he could give no elucidation from the Anglo-Norman text which would explain Iolo's other allusion (IGE² 75, 18) where he compares a ship to *Sarff oer megis march Syr Ffwg*, 'a cold serpent like Sir Fulk's horse.'

[69] This is also the conclusion reached by Chotzen, *Recherches* 140. The most recent editors of the tale of *Fouke le fitz Waryn*, C. A. Robson, E. J. Hathaway, P. T. Ricketts, A. D. Wilshere (Oxford, Anglo-Norman Texts Soc. 1975), suggest (p. xxxii) that Hawyse, mother of Fulk III and a haughty and forceful character, was probably the ultimate source for most of the stories which were in circulation concerning her son. See also M. D. Legge, *Anglo-Norman Literature*, 171–5. On the allusions in the tale to fighting between Fulk and Owain Cyfeiliog (which are completely unhistorical) see Gruffydd Aled Williams, B xxvi (1974), 35–6.

# 6. THE EARLIER *CYWYDDWYR*: DAFYDD AP GWILYM'S CONTEMPORARIES

THE following lively fragment[1] describing a horse is quoted, in whole or in part, in each of the four early versions of the Bardic Grammar as an example of the metre *cywydd deuair hirion*, which was to become the increasingly favoured medium of fourteenth-century poets:

> *Breichffyrf, archgrwn, byr ei flew,*
> *Llyfn, llygadrwth, pedreindew,*
> *Cyflwydd coflaid, cyrch amcaff,*
> *Cyflym, cefnfyr, carn geugraff,*
> *Cyflawn o galon a chig,*
> *Cyfliw blodau'r banadlfrig.*

*(Strong of foreleg, round-chested, short-haired,/ Sleek, keen-eyed, thick-haunched,/ Victorious darling, greedy for oats,/ Swift, short-backed, firm and hollow-hoofed,/ Fulfilled in spirit and in flesh,/ One hue with the flower-tips of the broom.)*

This is evidently an excerpt from a poem of request or thanks for the gift of a horse, but beyond this the authorship and provenance of the fragment are equally unknown. If we knew by whom and at what time the lines were composed, this knowledge would be of the greatest value towards elucidating the origin of the *cywydd*. Metrically, these lines are a crude and inadequate illustration of the metre as it came to be developed by Dafydd ap Gwilym and his contemporaries. Only the first and the third of the three couplets of which it is composed have end-rhyme between accented and unaccented syllables, such as later became obligatory, and *cynghanedd* appears only in an incipient or rudimentary form, most evident in the alliterating initial words of the last four lines. Apart from the predilection for compound words in describing the horse, there is little that can be related to the art of *dyfalu* as this was developed in the poetry of Dafydd ap Gwilym.

[1] GP 12, 31, 52; B ii, 199.

Yet the lines are a fair example of the verse-type known as the *traethodl*, which was practised by the poets of subordinate status known collectively as the *clêr*, to whom Dafydd ap Gwilym as has been seen, acknowledged a somewhat ambivalent allegiance.[2] The *cywydd* came into being in direct descent from the *traethodl*, by the endowment of the latter with full *cynghanedd*, and the tightening up of the rule as to the asymmetrical final rhymes. Except in occasional instances, such as his dialogue with the Grey Friar (GDG 137), which is composed in the looser form of the *traethodl*, the *cywydd deuair hirion* was Dafydd's choice for all those kinds of verse which departed radically in their subject-matter from the older tradition of praise-poetry—for verses of familiar personal address to friends and to his patron Ifor Hael, and above all for poetry concerned with the love-theme in its various aspects, most characteristically set against a background of wild woodland scenery. Yet with hindsight we can see that the literary development in fourteenth-century Wales, which was at least as far-reaching in its consequences as were Dafydd's thematic innovations, was this very transference into the medium of the *cywydd* of all the traditional apparatus of praise-poetry, as this had been practised by previous generations. Without this development, which secured lasting prestige for the *cywydd*, the poetry of love and nature might not itself have persisted, in the way that it did, to remain a lasting and recognisable constituent in the poetic tradition of Wales.

Since Dafydd ap Gwilym adhered to the traditional *awdl* for his 'genuine' praise-poems and elegies,[3] he cannot with any probability be regarded as the innovator responsible for the adaptation of the *cywydd* to *canu mawl*. Some other powerful influence must be postulated as having lain behind the emergence, in the middle years of the fourteenth century, of *cywyddau* paying tribute to patrons, and recreating within the new medium all the inherited concepts of the *awdlau* of the Gogynfeirdd. The verse of five poets needs to be considered in relation to that of Dafydd ap Gwilym, if we are to obtain anything approaching to a correct perspective of his achievement. These were Iolo Goch, Llewelyn Goch ap Meurig Hen, Gruffudd Gryg, Madog Benfras and Gruffudd ab Adda, all of whom appear to have been closely contemporary with each other[4] and also with Dafydd himself. References in contemporary legal documents place this beyond reasonable doubt in

[2] See p. 44n. above.
[3] GDG nos. 11–16, and cf. ch. 2 above.
[4] The belief that the first three poets named were contemporaries of Dafydd ap Gwilym was expressed by T. Gwyn Jones as long ago as 1911 (*Y Beirniad* i, 11–12), and it is coming to be increasingly recognised; see Saunders Lewis 'Y Cywyddwyr Cyntaf', LlC viii (1965), 191–6, reprinted *Meistri'r Canrifoedd*, 56–63; D. J. Bowen LlC viii, 10–11 and n. 91. See also ch. 4 above.

the case of Madog Benfras[5] and Gruffudd Gryg,[6] showing that they may be presumed to have reached man's estate by the year 1340: these two, in addition to Gruffudd ab Adda, were certainly known personally to Dafydd. It is a significant and striking fact that all five of these pioneer poets of the *cywydd* belonged to north or north-east Wales: not one of them, like Dafydd himself, belonged to the south. Iolo Goch came from the Vale of Clwyd, Gruffudd Gryg from Anglesey, Llywelyn Goch ap Meurig Hen from Merionydd, Madog Benfras from Marchwiail near Wrexham in Powys, and Gruffudd ab Adda also from Powys. The likelihood that all five were closely contemporary with Dafydd himself has been obscured by the fact that whereas there are no certainly datable poems by Dafydd composed after the 1350's, Gruffudd Gryg was still composing in the 1370's, and probably later, while Iolo Goch and Llywelyn Goch, whose earliest *cywyddau mawl* of certain date belong to the 1350's, were still active in the final decades of the century: both speaking of themselves in their last poems as being very old men. These two, it would seem, may actually have survived to reach their eighties—a remarkable attainment in the fourteenth century. All five had passed away before the end of the century, and did not live to witness Glyndŵr's revolt.

All of these poets composed love-poems in the *cywydd* form.[7] Indeed, all the main types of *cywyddau* composed by Dafydd ap Gwilym are represented in the work of one or other of them: by all there are *cywyddau* of love and of love-complaint addressed to girls; there are poems showing affinity with the Continental *fabliaux* (Madog Benfras and Iolo Goch), *llatai* or love-messenger poems (Gruffudd Gryg and—probably—Llywelyn Goch) and poems abusing friars (Iolo Goch), besides religious *cywyddau* (all of them but Madog Benfras and Gruffudd ab Adda) and fictitious *marwnadau* addressed by them to Dafydd as well as by him to them (Madog Benfras and Gruffudd Gryg). The poetry that has been preserved in the name of each of these poets is very much smaller in quantity than is the accepted canon of Dafydd ap Gwilym. Of the five, Iolo Goch has by far the largest number of poems ascribed to him, and is second in stature only to Dafydd himself, though very different from him in the main features of his verse. On the existing evidence, Madog Benfras is the least distinguished of the five, though it is he who is the most plainly under the influence of Dafydd ap Gwilym, without

[5] A. N. Palmer 'Records of the Bailiwick of Wrexham 1339 and 1340', *Arch. Cam.* v (1888), 258–62; idem. 'Notes on certain Powysian Poets', *Cy.* xxi (1908), 132 (quoted GDG lvii–viii, abbreviated GDG[2] xxxvi).

[6] See n. 16 below.

[7] The work of Dafydd's contemporaries has been collected in DGG[2] and IGE[2], and a number of their poems are included in OBWV. A single *cywydd serch* by Iolo Goch is found in RP 1407–8. (A new edition of the poems of Iolo Goch is in preparation by David Johnston.)

distinctive inspiration of his own. But much of his verse, and indeed of that of the others, may be presumed to have been lost, or may perhaps in a few instances be recoverable among the 'apocryphal' *cywyddau*, now rejected by Dr Parry from the canon of Dafydd ap Gwilym's own work. There exists in the manuscripts the same kind of confusion with regard to the authorship of individual poems by these poets as is the case with Dafydd himself, and their verse—again like his—has in the main survived only in late copies which have suffered all the vagaries of both scribal and previous oral corruption.

Yet among the poems which may with confidence be ascribed to these poets there have come down a handful of highly original and exceptional *cywyddau* which deserve to be placed on a par with Dafydd's finest work: Gruffudd Gryg's *cywyddau* 'To the Moon' and 'To the Wave', Gruffudd ab Adda's poem to the Birch-tree uprooted and placed as a may-pole in the town of Llanidloes, Iolo Goch's praise of the labourer or ploughman, his dialogue between the Soul and Body (which effectively burlesques the old convention of such dialogues, to describe a *taith clera* or bardic circuit between the homes of his patrons), and his vivid description of the miseries of a sea-journey in his satiric *dyfalu* of a ship. There is also Llywelyn Goch's celebrated *marwnad* (elegy) for his beloved Lleucu Llwyd, to which I shall return later. Mutual influences are discernible in a marginal degree between all these poets, yet except for Madog Benfras all the poets mentioned show on occasion strong and impressive originality.[8] In addition to these poems, which may indeed, like Dafydd's *cywyddau*, be classified as 'personal poetry', three of the five poets composed *cywyddau* of a kind which is quite unparalleled in Dafydd's work: that is, *cywyddau mawl* and *marwnad*, or formal praise-poems addressed to patrons, including also a *dadolwch* or placatory poem asking for forgiveness for offence from his patrons (Gruffudd Gryg), and poems of asking and thanks for the gift of a horse, a dagger, and for generous hospitality (Iolo Goch) and for a greyhound (probably by Llywelyn Goch, but uncertain authorship). These are all versetypes which are attested at an earlier date in the *awdlau* of the Gogynfeirdd.[9] Metrically, the verse of these poets tends to be 'coupletstructured' more often than it is 'sentence-structured' with tmesis (*lorymadrodd*—with *sangiadau*), in the manner favoured by Dafydd ap Gwilym. Where the device of *dyfalu* occurs, it is almost always used pejoratively' rather than 'positively' by these poets (whereas Dafydd

[8] This judgement may seem harsh in view of the fact that the canon of Madog Benfras's verse can hardly as yet be regarded as established. Yet his published poems include none of the quality of those by his contemporaries mentioned above.

[9] The only asking poem (for a horse) by one of the Gogynfeirdd is by Llywarch Llaety (before 1160) (H 294–6, MA$^2$ 280b); Lloyd-Jones concluded from the fact that it is in *englynion* that it is the work of a *bardd teulu*, CPWP 9. Gruffudd ap Dafydd ap Tudur (*c.* 1300) has a poem asking for a bow (RP 1253–4, MA$^2$ 319a).

ap Gwilym employs it in both ways), and mainly with the purpose of satirizing the various impediments to love's game. A notable exception, however, is Iolo Goch's remarkable 'positive' *dyfalu* of the Plough in his *cywydd* to the Labourer:

> A cradle which tears the trailing broom,
> a gentle creel which yet can shred the plain.
> His praise is cherished, a holy relic,
> a heron who opens a quick furrow.
> A basket of the wild land, henceforth to be cultivated
> with a coulter in wisely-ordered state.
> A gander of the untamed acres,
> true it is that grain will be had from his skill.
> He drives forth crops from the heavy tilth,
> a fine young boar, rootling the ground.
> He must have his knife and his food
> and his table under his thigh.
> He goes unwillingly over small stones—
> a lad who flays with leg outstretched.
> His snout is active daily
> in a fair hollow beneath the oxen's feet.
> He would often sing his hymn—
> his wish is to follow the plough-chain (IGE², XXVII; OBWV 53).

But this is in every respect a remarkable poem: the fact that it is unmatched in the work of any other of the early *cywyddwyr*—except by Dafydd ap Gwilym himself—in its 'positive', rather than negative and 'pejorative', use of the device of *dyfalu*, lends force to my earlier suggestion that the main origin of this device is to be found in the elaborately figurative language of bardic satire—witness, for instance, Dafydd ap Gwilym's satire of Rhys Meigen (GDG 21). Iolo Goch was apparently inspired to compose his praise of the Labourer by the words of the *Elucidarium*, a popular twelfth-century theological treatise, which was translated into Welsh in the *Book of the Anchorite of Llanddewifrefi*[10] and appeared in 1346. In a well-known passage of this work the author assigns the *clêr* (meaning, in this case, poets in general) to perdition,[11] and contrasts them with the humble tillers of the soil, who shall be blessed because they feed the populace by the sweat of their brows. Iolo paraphrases the text of the *Elucidarium*: (*Lusudarus hwylus hen* or 'good old Lucidarius' is for him a person) when he quotes this authority as saying: 'Blessed is he who from boyhood holds the plough with his

---

[10] J. Morris Jones and J. Rhŷs, *The Elucidarium and other tracts from Llyvyr Agkyr Llandewivrevie* (Oxford, 1894).

[11] *Pa obeith yssyd yr cler? Nyt oes yr un kannys oe holl ynni y maent ygwassanaethu y diawl* = Habent spem joculatores? Nullam: tota namque intentione sunt ministri Satanae (ibid. 40,203).

hands'—and he goes on to expand upon the virtues of the labourer—he trusts in God, he pays his tithes and receives God's bounty in recompense; he is hospitable and generous to all; he does not utter an opinion on any subject but one which concerns his own craft; he dislikes all disputation and all warfare; he does not rob anyone or claim the least thing unjustly; he prefers humbly to follow the plough, rather than to be an 'Arthur' despoiling castle towers. And yet *nid bywyd, nid byd hebddaw ef* ('there is no life, nor world without him'). As in Dafydd ap Gwilym's *cywydd* to the Wind of which Iolo's poem contains some verbal echoes (GDG 117), the picture of the Labourer is built up by a series of negative statements: the Labourer's virtues are expressed mainly by a list of the things he does *not* do. In both poems the catalogue of negatives indicates a deftly implied criticism of their opposites: in The Wind this is aimed against the 'restrictive practices' of the alien officers who administer the foreign legal system; in Iolo's poem it is obviously directed against those in high places who rob and persecute, pursue unjust claims, fail to dispense charity and hospitality, are too ready with their opinions—or interference—in matters which do not concern them, and above all, who prosecute warfare. These are the sins which may pertain to the great and powerful ones of the earth, and it is surprising to find such a minutely detailed list in the work of a poet who was a pioneer in composing *cywyddau mawl* to just such temporal magnates as might on occasion be accused with some justice of committing them. Yet no doubt Iolo's idealized portrait of a character who embodied the opposite of all these sins was intended for a clerical rather than for a secular audience. The poem 'Piers Plowman' by the English poet Langland invites an obvious comparison; it appeared about 1370, but we have no means of knowing whether or not Iolo's *cywydd* preceded it in date of composition. The social upheavals consequent upon the Black Death are likely to have been a contributory cause behind both poems.

Another characteristic of the verse of these poets which is also significantly characteristic of Dafydd ap Gwilym's poetry is their use of personification. In the passage which has been quoted from Iolo's *cywydd* to the Labourer the plough is personified as *gŵr* and *gwas*, 'a man' and 'a lad', and 'he must have his knife and his food, and his table under his thigh'. For Gruffudd Gryg the Moon is *mursen* ('a coy wench'), while Gruffudd ab Adda's Birch-tree is poignantly addressed as if it were a sentient and suffering creature:

> Green birch-tree with bedraggled tresses, you have been long exiled from the hill-side; a lovely tree in the forest where you were reared, green-mantled, you are now a traitress to the grove. Your enclosure made a lodging for me with my darling in the short nights of May ... Now no longer do you meditate on love, and your branches up aloft stay dumb. In your entirety, and at whatever cost, you have gone from the green

upland meadow, an honoured miracle, to the town, by a swift exchange. Though your favoured eminence may seem good, in Llanidloes town, where crowds assemble, yet may I not approve, my birch-tree, either your abduction, or your present company, or your home; it is no good place for you, with long face, to bear forth new leaves. Every town-garden is able to have feathery green—was it not rash, birch-tree, to bring about your fading there—a wretched pole, beside the pillory? Have you not come, at the very time of putting forth leaves, to stand at the barren centre of the cross-roads? Although they say your station is pleasant, birch-tree, yet it were better by far to be a roof above the brook. No bird sleeps or sings, with slender voice, in the fair precinct of your topmost branches, owing to the great clamour of the people about your tent, sister of the shady trees ... You have been made over to bartering, and you have the look of a woman merchant; everyone will point his finger at your suffering, with joyful chatter, as you stand in your grey dress and your worn fur, amidst the trivial merchandise of the fair ... You will no longer shelter the April primroses; no more will you have concern for the valley's birds, though once their kind protector ... Choose one of the two, captive branches—your burgess-hood is artless—either to return home to the woodland, or to wither yonder in the town (DGG² LXV; OBWV 54).

Here again, as in Iolo Goch's *cywydd* to the Labourer, the undertones are all but audible: beneath the sensitive evocation of the birch-tree's beauty in its natural woodland setting, which is rarely matched even by Dafydd ap Gwilym, lies a general suspicion and rejection of the crowded life of the boroughs, with their often predominantly alien population ('your burgess-hood is artless'[12]), and again at an even deeper level there is the poignant realization of beauty's frailty and life's transitoriness.

Another characteristic which more than one of these early *cywyddwyr* share with Dafydd ap Gwilym is an expertise in the embodiment of colloquial dialogue in their verse, undaunted by the restrictions imposed by *cynghanedd* and by the *cywydd*'s obligatory rhyme-scheme: good examples are Iolo Goch's 'Dialogue between the Soul and the Body' (IGE² XXVI) or the poem in which he abuses his beard ('like a hedge-hog's coat') for acting as an impediment to his love-making (IGE², II). Yet a third feature which is also characteristic of Dafydd is their manner of presenting themselves as leading actors in their poems of incident, as does Madog Benfras in his *fabliau* poem 'The Saltman' (DGG² LXX) and Iolo Goch when—again like Dafydd—he tells how he was pursued by *Yr Eiddig* (IGE² XXI), the stock figure of the 'Jealous Husband'

---

[12] *Disyml yw dy fwrdeisiaeth. Disyml* can mean both 'noble, dignified' etc. (here used ironically) and 'artless, innocent' (GPC). Perhaps 'naïve' comes nearer to the meaning in this instance.

as the result of a game played with nuts by which he played at fortune-telling with the man's wife.[13]

We do not know how these poets stood in relation to each other with respect to the early development of the *cywydd*. Any conclusions which are to be reached concerning this must be based upon the poets' own statements, and in particular upon what they have to tell us concerning their own attitudes towards Dafydd ap Gwilym. Some indication of these may perhaps be deduced from the 'elegies' composed for Dafydd by Gruffudd Gryg, Iolo Goch, and Madog Benfras,[14] and—more importantly—from the eight *cywyddau* of the *ymryson* or poetic controversy which took place between Dafydd ap Gwilym and Gruffudd Gryg.[15] This poet came from the commote of Llifon in the *cantref* of Aberffraw in the west of Anglesey. Evidence brought to light from a legal document[16] some years ago by Mr E. D. Jones would place the probable date of Gruffudd's birth several years earlier than was hitherto supposed, and this earlier dating casts a somewhat different light upon the controversy between the two poets from that in which it had been regarded previously. No longer do we have a young poet from Gwynedd, the stronghold of the poetic 'establishment', challenging the poetic innovations made by his senior from the more volatile south; but instead, an argument between two contemporaries relating to differences in the basic assumptions of each concerning the subjects proper to be celebrated in poetry.[17]

An 'elegy' (undoubtedly a mock elegy)[18] composed by Gruffudd Gryg to Dafydd ap Gwilym regularly follows the *ymryson* in nearly all the manuscripts, and is best regarded as a poem composed to form a gracious termination to the controversy. Gruffudd forgives Dafydd for his harsh words, expresses regret for their dissention, admits that he himself

[13] Dr Parry comments on the degree to which the early *cywyddwyr* composed upon similar themes, and on the similarity of their language, GDG xcviii–c. Cf. also D. J. Bowen, LlC viii, 196–7.

[14] GDG pp. 422–30. I conclude that all these poems belong to the strange convention of complimenting living contemporaries by composing fictitious elegies to them.

[15] See above pp. 46–50.

[16] *NLW Journal*, x (1957), 230–1. Gruffudd Gryg was son of Cynfrig ap Gruffudd Foel whose family owned land at Tregwehelydd, half a mile to the north of Llyn Llywenan. The deeds are mortgages relating to the years 1336 and 1338, but it appears that at some time after the original date Gruffudd's name has been substituted for that of his brother Iorwerth. Whatever may be the reason for this substitution, the deeds serve to establish the dates by which both Gruffudd and his brother had reached man's estate, and indicate that Dafydd and Gruffudd were more nearly contemporaries than has hitherto been recognised. The earlier dating for Gruffudd is further corroborated by the existence of *englynion* attributed to him in Hendregadredd; see D. Huws, NLW *Journal* xxii (1981), pp. 17, 24.

[17] On the Controversy see above, pp. 68–70 (GDG nos. 147–54). D. J. Bowen argues that it took place early in Dafydd's career, LlC viii, 9–11.

[18] GDG p. 427.

has been partly in the wrong, and acknowledges his debt to Dafydd—
*Disgybl wyf, ef a'm dysgawdd* ('I am his pupil, he instructed me'). Dafydd
is *paun Dyfed* ('the peacock of Dyfed'), he is in the direct line of descent
from Taliesin, Myrddin, Aneirin, and the most famous of the Gogynfeirdd;
and Gruffudd claims that he would prefer satire from Dafydd's lips
rather than praise from those of any other poet. It is clear that Gruffudd
regarded Dafydd as a master of the *cywydd serch* or new love-poetry,
yet none the less he placed him within the central tradition of Welsh
poetry, as one who worthily perpetuated the tradition inherited from
the Cynfeirdd or earliest poets. A parallel attitude is expressed by Iolo
Goch and by Madog Benfras[19] in their *marwnadau* for Dafydd: for both
he was *pensaer yr ieithoedd* ('architect of words', literally 'languages'),
and *pensaer gwingerdd* ('architect of song'), he was *athro pawb* ('everyone's
teacher'), and by his death, according to Iolo, the *cywydd* will be reduced
to a sorry state. Madog Benfras describes Dafydd as *digrif* ('amusing'),
and as *tegan rhianedd* ('the darling of girls'), and prays that Mary and
Jesus will forgive his levity; yet he too describes Dafydd as a worthy
transmitter of the traditions of Aneirin and Taliesin. None of these
poets offer any suggestion that they regarded Dafydd as the *inventor*
of the *cywydd*; indeed, Iolo Goch appears to give pride of place to Llywelyn Goch ap Meurig Hen in this respect, describing him in another
so-called 'elegy' as *primas cywydd Ofydd* ('the primate of Ovid's *cywydd*'),[20]
to be praised above all for his love-poetry: when a court-
audience requests a song, no other *cywydd* but one by Llywelyn Goch
will satisfy it, and in his verse no single word is misplaced; he is compared to the prophet David, who like Llywelyn, was a sinner in love
who afterwards repented. The force and immediate application of all
these compliments and innuendos would surely have been lost had
not their subject been still alive to take note of them, and I think it
is only natural to conclude that it was to the living Dafydd, or to the
living Llywelyn, that all these poems were addressed. This is no less
obviously the case, I think, with the *cywyddau marwnad* addressed by
Dafydd to Gruffudd Gryg, Madog Benfras, and Gruffudd ab Adda:
the presumption is, indeed, that all such 'elegies' addressed during
the early *cywydd* period by one poet to another are 'fictitious' elegies,
addressed to men who were still living. The choice of the *cywydd* for
compositions of this kind is an indication that they are not serious,
but that they are to be regarded as friendly and admiring compliments
to their subject, for almost invariably they contain touches of humour
which betray their fundamental levity. They subscribe to certain recurrent conventions; one is the expression of regret that such-and-such
a despised poet (a certain unknown 'Bleddyn' is alluded to in this way

---

[19] GDG pp. 422–6.
[20] IGE² XV.

in Gruffudd's elegy for Dafydd) was not removed from the world instead of the subject of the elegy; another is a prayer for divine forgiveness on behalf of their subject for his frivolity in composing love-poetry. As in much medieval poetry, levity goes hand-in-hand with seriousness (in this case with genuine admiration and affection), as when Dafydd ap Gwilym in his 'elegy' for the poet-musician Gruffudd ab Adda[21] follows up his marvellously sustained image of a nightingale singing enchantingly in an orchard, only to be struck wantonly by an arrow, with the abrupt assertion that the poet was killed with just such a 'discourteous' blow ( *pond oedd wladeiddrwydd?* ) as if one were striking off the head of a goose. Even Gruffudd Gryg's poem to the Yew-Tree above the grave of Dafydd ap Gwilym[22] comes under suspicion for similar reasons, as well as on grounds of general probability: the poem echoes closely Dafydd's own *cywydd* to that other evergreen, the Holly; both take the form of a direct address to the tree concerned, and of both trees it is claimed that they will provide secure 'houses' for the poet, and both will share the additional advantage that their leaves will not be nibbled away by goats! Even Iolo Goch's comparison of Llywelyn Goch, in his eloquent tribute to him, with the prophet David who also sinned in love and subsequently repented, undoubtedly has a greater ring of authenticity if we are to believe that the poet was at the time still in the land of the living. These early *cywydd* poets were not as yet fully enfranchised from an inherited tradition, in that the *awdl* still retained for them the *aura* of its ancient prestige as the preferred medium alike for formal elegy and for the expression of genuine grief in bereavement, as I have already suggested in discussing Dafydd ap Gwilym's employment of the two media. The same probability that a *cywydd marwnad* enshrines a familiar personal tribute to a living friend is applicable to Dafydd ap Gwilym's address to Rhydderch ab Ieuan Llwyd; and very probably also, as D. J. Bowen has suggested,[23] to Gruffudd Gryg's 'elegy' for Rhys ap Tudur of Penmynydd.

This convention of addressing elegies to the living, which appears so strange to present-day readers, seems to have been employed primarily for the purpose of making familiar, semi-humorous addresses by one poet to another. Outside this relatively well-defined category, there is frequently no possibility of distinguishing among the compositions of fourteenth-century poets between the 'fictitious' and the genuine *marwnad*. Soon after 1356 we have Iolo Goch's *cywydd marwnad* to Sir Rhys ap Gruffudd,[24] securely dated by the death of its subject in that year. This was followed after twelve years by the same poet's *cywydd*

---

[21] GDG 18.
[22] GDG pp. 429–30; *Y Llwyn Celyn* GDG 29. See *Selections* pp. 23–4.
[23] LlC viii, 11, no. 91.
[24] IGE[2] IV.

*marwnad* to Tudur Fychan of Penmynydd (1367),[25] and later again
by his elegy to Tudur's sons Ednyfed and Goronwy (1382),[26] and by
his dramatic and moving elegy to his friend and principal patron Ithel
ap Robert, archdeacon of St Asaph[27]—a poem which Saunders Lewis
has acclaimed as one of the poetic masterpieces of the century. There
can be no doubt but that all these are sincere and genuine elegies,
each one a formal composition in honour of a man who wielded great
power and authority, whether local or national. These are praise-poems
which in their language, metaphors and concepts—in everything but
in their metrical form—reproduce the tradition of the *canu mawl* of previous generations, employing the linguistic archaisms and all the familiar imagery of the traditional *awdlau*. Like Dafydd ap Gwilym, Iolo
is believed to have been a man of good birth and standing who had
taken minor religious orders. It is evident that he possessed deep learning and wide knowledge of biblical and classical sources, of divinity
in translation (the *Elucidarium*), as well as of all branches of the native
Welsh tradition as expressed in earlier poetry, in triads and romances,
in saints' lives, in genealogy and in heraldry. There is also that 'subtle
over-plus' of poetic vision which is characteristically his own: a remarkable power of evoking atmosphere and of conveying with intensity the
sense of an impressive occasion; as in his portrayal of the immensely
long funeral *cortège* which accompanied Ithel ap Robert to his burial,
led by the high cross waving like a ship at anchor in the March gale
of rain and wind, or his description of the darkness which overcast
all Anglesey upon the death of the sons of Tudur of Penmynydd.

No less strong an affiliation with the whole range of techniques of
the Gwynedd court poets who were his predecessors is apparent in
Iolo Goch's many other *cywyddau mawl*: ironically enough, the earliest
of these whose authenticity is without doubt may well be his remarkable
*cywydd* in praise of Edward III (composed after 1347),[28] in which after
praising the king for his victories in France and Scotland, including
Crécy (1346), Iolo takes it upon himself to impress upon the king his
responsibilities, urging him to undertake a crusade to the Holy Land.
It seems incongruous to meet here with all the age-old formulas: Edward
is described as *anian Bedwyr* ('of the nature of Bedwyr'); he is the defender
of Windsor, a lion, a boar, and a leopard. From every point-of-view
this is a surprising poem: why was it composed at all? D. J. Bowen
suggests that this may perhaps have been due to the instigation of
Sir Rhys ap Gruffudd,[29] a strong supporter of the king, to whom Iolo's
*marwnad* attests his allegiance: one wonders, however, in what form,

[25] IGE² V.
[26] IGE² VII.
[27] IGE² VIII. Cf. S. Lewis, YB III, 11–27, *Meistri'r Canrifoedd* 64–79.
[28] IGE² III.
[29] D. J. Bowen, LlC ix (1966), 62.

if at all, its import was ever communicated to the king. But here, in
what may well be the earliest of all *cywyddau mawl*, is a poem of assured
technical accomplishment and of unquestionably serious intention; the
earliest extant example (to be followed later by Iolo's urgent advice
to Sir Roger Mortimer on the occasion of his coming-of-age)[30] of a
succession of *cywyddau* in which poets ventured to offer weighty ideologi-
cal, practical, or political advice to their patrons.

Iolo's gift for selecting the essentials of a scene and projecting them
with an almost photographic immediacy is to be seen no less in certain
of his praise-poems than in his elegies. It is most noticeable, however,
in those of his *cywyddau* in which praise is offered to a patron by means
of praising the splendour of his home; as in Iolo's minutely detailed
description of Owain Glyndŵr's court at Sycharth,[31] or his description
of Cricieth castle when 'Sir Hywel of the Axe' was its constable.[32]
This is a poem-type which has an illustrious ancestry, leading as far
back as the ninth-century 'Praise of Tenby' in the *Book of Taliesin*,[33]
and precedents for it in the older metres must presumably have been
known to Iolo. Yet he gives to this type of poem a new orientation
by presenting his description of Cricieth in the form of a dream, and
in doing so he evokes in the plainest terms, the closely similar description
of the heroine's home as Caernarfon, seen in a dream, which occurs
in the tale of *The Dream of Maxen*:

> I see in the first place, truly, a fair large fortress yonder by the sea;
> a splendid magnificent castle, with men at tables, a rampart, and a blue
> sea against a wall of comely stone. There are sea-waves about the womb
> of the tower of dark aspect; music of flutes and pipes; a lively warrior
> and a man of note; sprightly maidens weaving pure and shining silk; proud
> men on the fortress's floor playing chess and backgammon on a dais. And
> a grey-haired man, a very savage Twrch Trwyth in battle, passing from
> his hand to mine, like this, a gold-chased goblet containing sweetly-tasting
> wine, with a fair tall black standard on the turret-top, bearing three identi-
> cal white flowers with silver leaves—he was a noble warrior (IGE² IX).

The main cause for the transference in Gwynedd of the traditional
techniques of court-poetry from *awdl* to *cywydd* must be sought in the
rapid social changes which followed the conquest, but the obscurity
which surrounds the successive stages in this change is thrown into
relief by the fact that whereas Iolo Goch composed a *cywydd marwnad*
to Tudur ap Goronwy of Penmynydd (d. 1367), his younger contemporary Gruffudd ap Maredudd was at the same time composing an elegy

---

[30] IGE² XVI. See Eurys Rowlands 'Iolo Goch', *Celtic Studies in Memory of Angus Matheson*,
ed. J. Carney and D. Greene (London, 1968), 124–46.

[31] IGE² XIII.

[32] IGE² IX.

[33] Ifor Williams, *The Beginnings of Welsh Poetry*, ed. R. Bromwich (UWP 1972), 155–72.
See p. 135 above.

to him in the form of an *awdl*;[34] also that Llywelyn Goch ap Meurig Hen addressed an *awdl*[35] to the powerful magnate Sir Rhys ap Gruffudd, whose death in 1356 was subsequently celebrated by Iolo in a *cywydd marwnad*. The possibility can certainly be excluded that Iolo Goch's *cywyddau mawl* owe anything initially to the example of Dafydd ap Gwilym: appearing as they do in mature and assured form in the middle years of the century, the date assigned to the earliest of these is by itself sufficient to discredit such a supposition. The only possible influence which would need to be considered would be that from Dafydd ap Gwilym's four polished *cywyddau* to Ifor Hael,[36] and the date of these in relation to Iolo's *cywyddau mawl* is purely a matter of conjecture. And the Ifor Hael poems offer no sufficient explanation: the *cywydd* was for Dafydd the obvious medium for such poems of familiar personal address to a generous friend and patron; three of the four were composed, apparently, in response to particular incidents of a trivial nature: a journey planned or deferred, the gift of money in the fingers of a glove. Their whole manner and tone is entirely different from that of the genuine *cywydd mawl*: their originality consists in the way in which recognisable concepts from the new love-poetry have been blended with the inherited praise-formulas[37]—the mutual dependence of poet and patron, praise of the patron's home, the poet's deserved reward compared with that given by Urien Rheged to Taliesin. It is, on the other hand, with the formal *awdl* which Dafydd addressed to Ifor[38] that Iolo Goch's *cywyddau mawl* and *marwnad* deserve rather to be compared—with the essential difference that Iolo has transferred into the new medium all the traditional techniques known to him from the *awdlau* addressed to the Gwynedd princes. Nor does it appear that any other of the earliest group of *cywyddwyr* but Iolo Goch composed sincere and genuine *marwnadau* in the form of the *cywydd* (the only other questionable example being Gruffudd Gryg's supposed *cywydd marwnad* to Rhys ap Tudur[39]— but this is in all probability a 'fictitious' *marwnad*, as has already been seen, and one whose penultimate lines link it with the Ifor Hael poems rather than with genuine elegy[40]). We have no evidence that Iolo Goch had any predecessor in making the transference of serious praise-poetry from *awdl* to *cywydd*: as far as our existing knowledge will take us, the

[34] RP 1212–3.

[35] RP 1301–2.

[36] GDG nos. 7–10.

[37] D. J. Bowen comments on the manner in which images from nature are introduced into the *cywyddau* in praise of Ifor Hael (e.g. GDG 9, 47–54); LlC v (1959), 170.

[38] GDG 5.

[39] DGG² LXXX; see n. 23 above.

[40] Lines 49–60 refer to Gwynedd's deprivation: there will be no more joyful entertainment or meetings in the forest with girls, or birds in the birch-wood; no one but *Eiddig* will be happy. These lines resemble closely lines 29–36 in Dafydd's 'elegy' to Gruffudd Gryg (GDG 20).

*cywydd mawl* originated with Iolo Goch in Gwynedd, just as the *cywydd serch* originated with Dafydd ap Gwilym in Dyfed. Both innovations were of equal magnitude, and were comparable in their far-reaching implications.

But already from the early years of the fourteenth century, and in a sense from a very much earlier date, love-poetry in *awdl* and *englyn* metres was being prefigured, and to some degrees overtly expressed, by such poets as Gruffudd ap Dafydd ap Tudur, Goronwy Ddu, Casnodyn, and Hywel ab Einion Llygliw,[41] as well as by a number of anonymous poets, of whose work we get a fleeting glimpse in the *exempla*, chosen to illustrate the various forms of *awdl* and *englyn*, which are to be found in the four early texts of the Bardic Grammar.[42] This was, indeed, an inevitable and natural development from the *rhieingerdd*, with its exalted ancestry going back to the earliest *Gogynfeirdd* in the twelfth century: it is nevertheless worth setting on record that elements of *canu serch* such as we associate with Dafydd ap Gwilym, in the form of notions borrowed from international love-poetry—love's sickness and sleeplessness, and the like—had penetrated the *awdl* and were very frequently celebrated in *englynion*, at a much earlier date than that at which serious *canu mawl* or praise-poetry had become acceptable in the form of the *cywydd*. Of Iolo Goch's two love-poems, one is the unique *cywydd* to a girl preserved in the *Red Book of Hergest*:[43] Iolo here follows closely the traditional pattern of the *rhieingerdd*, but betrays the source of his inspiration (including, perhaps, that of the licence expressed in the last lines) by closely reproducing several lines from a poem to a girl by Hywel ab Owain Gwynedd.[44] The poem is in almost all respects closer to the *rhieingerdd* tradition than it is to the *cywyddau serch* of Dafydd ap Gwilym. Yet Iolo's *cywydd marwnad* to Dafydd testifies to his recognition of his contemporary's high poetic status—*athro pawb oedd* ('he was everyone's teacher')[45]—thus magnanimously acknowledging in general terms his debt to Dafydd, though the nature and extent of this debt are by no means readily apparent. Parallel usages in vocabulary and in imagery are indeed more easily recognisable as between Iolo and Gruffudd Gryg on the one hand, and between Iolo and Llywelyn Goch ap Meurig Hen on the other; though in the instances which occur, there is no means of telling which poet it was who borrowed from the other.

---

[41] Much of the work of these poets is contained in RP. For further references see D. S. Evans, *A Grammar of Middle Welsh* xxviii–ix; H. Lewis and E. J. Jones, *Mynegai i Farddoniaeth y Llawysgrifau* (UWP 1928).

[42] See ch. 4 above.

[43] IGE² I, RP 1407–8.

[44] *Caraf amser haf, amsathr gorwydd* etc. (H. 318; OBWV no. 24). Cf. S. Lewis, 'Iolo Goch', *Y Llenor* (1926), 158.

[45] IGE² XIV, 1.26.

It is to Llywelyn Goch ap Meurig Hen that Iolo Goch gives obvious priority, in his *marwnad* for him,[46] as master of the *cywydd serch*, and he expressly names the woman with whose name that of Llywelyn has become indissolubly linked: it will, he says, be pleasing for the prophet David in Paradise to listen to *cerdd Lleucu Llwyd* ('the poetry of Lleucu Llwyd'); and Llywelyn, like David, will win forgiveness from God for the sinful love of which he has repented at the last. Llywelyn himself reiterates the name of Lleucu Llwyd more than once, as that of the supreme object of his song: in his *cywydd* to the Snow[47] he expresses his gratitude to his two nephews, Hywel and Meurig, for their generosity in providing him, an infirm old man, with comfortable winter-quarters in his old age; his pleasant occupation, he says, will include reading with them the laws and historical texts of their country, and composing verse 'comparing Lleucu Llwyd to a beautiful rose in a fair garden, to bountiful Mary, or to the splendid sun'. The name of Lleucu Llwyd was no pseudonym to conceal the identity of an un-named girl, but like Dafydd ap Gwilym's Morfudd and Dyddgu, she was evidently a real woman, and—again as in the case of Dafydd and Morfudd—behind Llywelyn's allusions to her there appears to lie just such another story of a passionate and frustrated liaison with a married woman. The points of similarity between Llywelyn and Dafydd ap Gwilym go much further than this: both were by birth *uchelwyr* (Llywelyn belonged to the important family of Nannau, near Dolgellau)[48] who did not depend upon their verse for their subsistence, and—significantly—both composed a group of *awdlau* in praise of patrons. Both, indeed, seem to have made a similar distinction between what they regarded as the proper function of *awdl* and *cywydd*, employing the *awdl* for serious, and in the main, formal praise-poetry and for devotional poetry, while the *cywydd* was used by both in the main for poetry of a more light and intimate nature.[49] The tone of Llywelyn's address to his nephews is in many ways reminiscent of the tone of Dafydd ap Gwilym's *cywyddau* to Ifor Hael.

Yet there appears to be a virtually insurmountable difficulty in applying any such hard-and-fast distinction as to the themes accepted as proper to *awdl* and *cywydd* when considering what is undoubtedly Llywelyn Goch's most famous poem, his *cywydd marwnad* to Lleucu Llwyd.[50] It is very difficult to doubt the sincerity of the passionate cry of grief which permeates this poem. Yet against all the internal suggestions,

---

[46] IGE² XV, OBWV no. 52.

[47] DGG² LXXXV. Cf. p. 120 above.

[48] DGG² p. civ: but cf. Bartrum, *Welsh Genealogies 300–1400*, I, 77.

[49] RP 1301–1310 gives examples of both *awdl* and *cywydd* by Llywelyn Goch; other examples of both types of poem remain in manuscript, see *Mynegai i Farddoniaeth y Llawysgrifau*.

[50] DGG² LXXXVIII; OBWV no. 49.

Dr Thomas Parry has preferred to regard the lament as belonging to the convention of 'fictitious' *marwnadau*,[51] and as having been addressed to the poet's mistress while she was still living, and in the absence of positive evidence on either side it is difficult to reject this view out-of-hand. The poem is composed in the form of a direct address by the poet to the dead girl, in which he bids her to rise up and answer his complaint of love:

> Pale girl in the oaken coffin, sad is my condition after you. Fair of form, Gwynedd's candle, though you be in the captivity of the grave, rise up, my soul, open the earth's dark door, reject a long-lasting gravelly bed, and give me answer, fair one. I am here at your grave—sun's beauty—a worn man grief-stricken for your loss, Llywelyn Goch who sounded the bell of your praise. I am a groaning poet, walking in affliction, the servant of strong passion ... But you, mute, lovely girl, would give me no answer from the deep pit, silent, solemn, and loveless ... I will go from Gwynedd today—I care not where, lively girl with the moon's beauty—if you were alive, by God I would not go. I do not mind where it is that I may see you again, whether it be upon the Mount of Olives (i.e. at the day of Judgement) where love's bonds are cast aside, bright one, Lleucu with the wave's fairness. You have ensured that I will be there, fair bright-hued maiden, sleeping too long in a stone enclosure ... Woe is me for the weight of earth and soil upon the mistress of beauty, woe that a coffin should guard you, a dwelling of stone between you and me, chancel of church and robe of rock, the weight of earth and a wooden garment. Woe is me for the fair girl of Pennal, it is a harsh dream that a roof of earth covers your brow, a strong oaken lock (begetter of bitter grief), heavy door of oppressive bondage on the fair-browed one, the earth between me and her countenance, an enclosing wall with hard black lock, with a latch—farewell, Lleucu (DDG² LXXXVIII; OBWV 49).

The direct address, the exclamatory style, the torrential outpouring of grief and reproach to the dead girl for her silence, and for breaking troth with her lover by her death, is wholly in the style of the keen, or extemporary dirge, as this has been traditionally practised in Ireland[52] and elsewhere. It gives to Llywelyn's *cywydd* an effect of vivid reality and spontaneity, which argues forcibly in its favour as a genuine expression of grief in bereavement. As W. J. Gruffydd pointed out some years ago,[53] it is also strongly reminiscent of the form of a *sérénade*, in which the lover shivers outside his lady's window, and begs for admittance (Dafydd ap Gwilym's *Dan y Bargod* 'Under the Eaves', GDG 89, may be compared), and as such Llywelyn's lament formed the model

---

[51] OBWV p. 544, note.
[52] It is relevant to compare the Irish keen, 'A Lament for Art O'Laoighaire', no. 62 in *An Duanaire: Poems of the Dispossessed*, ed. and trans. S. O'Tuama and Thomas Kinsella (Dublin, 1981).
[53] 'Y Farwnad Gymraeg', *Y Llenor* xviii (1939), 34–45.

for a number of subsequent *marwnadau bun* or *cywyddau* which were ostensibly composed in tribute to dead girls. A no less significant parallel to Llywelyn's elegy was however indicated more recently by Dr Geraint Gruffydd:[54] it is the parallel with Dafydd ap Gwilym's *awdl farwnad* to his uncle. In this *awdl*[55] the poet similarly addresses the dead man directly, and reproaches him for his *mudandod* or silence and inability to answer. Dr Gruffydd suggests that Llywelyn Goch may actually have been influenced by his knowledge of this poem; though this suggestion once more brings to the fore our ignorance as to their relative dates. Whether the points of resemblance between the two poems be fortuitous or not, Llywelyn's composition of a lament for a dead girl within the framework of a *sérénade* is a remarkable instance of the fresh adaptation of a poetic convention of foreign origin to a new and highly original purpose—and this once more invites a fruitful comparison with similar achievements by Dafydd ap Gwilym. A further question is, if the elegy is 'genuine', why should Llywelyn have composed it in the form of a *cywydd* and not of an *awdl*? Here one may compare not only Dafydd ap Gwilym's elegy to his uncle, but also his *awdl farwnad* to a woman—Angharad, the wife of his neighbour Ieuan Llwyd of Glyn Aeron—which shows verbal resemblances to Gruffudd ap Maredudd's *awdl farwnad* to Gwenhwyfar of Anglesey,[56] and obviously shares with it the inheritance of a common tradition: a tradition in which one might well expect that Llywelyn Goch also would have composed. There are at once no clear answers and many answers to this question, in a century in which the new *cywydd* was gaining gradual acceptance, with Iolo Goch, as an alternative medium for serious elegy. If the *Marwnad Lleucu Llwyd* is 'genuine', it is unique in the fourteenth century in being a *cywydd marwnad* addressed to a woman; and that is perhaps the nearest that we can get to a reason for its form.

That the *marwnad* was but the final *cywydd* in a sequence of poems addressed to Lleucu Llwyd which have not come down, but which were above all responsible for Llywelyn's fame in his own day, is evident both from the poet's own allusions to them, and from Iolo Goch's comparison of Llywelyn's sinful love with the love-story of the prophet David. All this is corroborated by the words of Llywelyn's *awdl gyffes* or 'recantation' (a poem which powerfully recalls the *marwysgafn* or death-bed poem of a forerunner, Meilyr Brydydd[57]), in which the poet makes a line-by-line comparison between God's goodness to him and his own sins; these include his unlawful love for Lleucu and his

---

[54] 'Marwnad Lleucu Llwyd' YB I (1965), 126–37. See further G. Ruddock, 'Amwysedd ac Eironi ym Marwnad Lleucu Llwyd', YB IX (1976), 61–79.

[55] GDG 13.

[56] RP 1318–21; OBWV no. 38 (extract).

[57] OBWV no. 20.

expression of this in poems to her:

> I performed continual rape, incurring Thy rebuke ... I neglected Heaven
> and men of faith; I performed *llateiaeth* (i.e. 'sent messages of love'); I
> dishonoured true religion ... I made in writing (*ar draethawd*) a *cywydd*
> of false praise (*geuwawd o gywydd*), comparing Lleucu of the snow's hue,
> to the like of Mary; I performed hidden adultery ... I confess to Thee,
> who knowest all things, the wrongs that I did, skilful in words ... I broke
> the burden of my faith daily ... I broke the Ten Commandments, the
> covenanted safeguard of religion, God's unbending Law for all lands ...
> Because of Thy crown of thorns, because of Thy chastisement, because
> of Thy love, hear, Lord, my song ... Because of Thy very certain death
> upon Thy bier, and Thy wise resurrection the third time, before my final
> day of death (grant me) Thy reconciliation (RP 1301).

If Llywelyn's lost poems to Lleucu included *englynion* as well as *cywyddau* (and no love-poetry other than *cywyddau* are anywhere ascribed to him), then it is possible, and has indeed been suggested by several scholars, that a stray stanza from one of them has been preserved in the early version of the Bardic Grammar, as an example of the measure known as *englyn lleddfbroest gadwynog*.[58] Saunders Lewis has pointed out the significance of the consequences which would follow, if indeed the *englyn* is the work of Llywelyn Goch ap Meurig Hen. This poet has been commonly regarded as a younger contemporary of Dafydd ap Gwilym (though the traditional dates assigned to his *floruit* should be put back at least into the 1350's, in view of his *awdl foliant* to Sir Rhys ap Gruffudd[59]). But this evidence would mean that he was already composing love-poetry in *englynion* at least a decade before the time at which we have any sure evidence that Dafydd ap Gwilym was composing *cywyddau*, since the 'archetype' from which each of the four early texts of the Bardic Grammar derive is now generally concluded to have been redacted early in the 1330's. Llywelyn Goch would then be a contemporary—perhaps even a slightly older contemporary—of Dafydd ap Gwilym, and his verses to Lleucu Llwyd would date from as early a period as that at which we have any knowledge of the earliest *cywyddau*.

This leads us back to the lines descriptive of a horse, which were quoted from the Bardic Grammar at the beginning of this chapter, and which purport to illustrate the measure *cywydd deuair hirion*. Among the early *cywyddwyr*, Iolo Goch is the only one to whom *cywyddau gofyn* or 'poems of asking' for horses are attributed. The two that have come

---

[58] S. Lewis, 'Y Cywyddwyr Cyntaf' (see n. 4 above); D. Huws, *NLW Journal*, xxii (1981), 18. See ch. 4 above.

[59] RP 1301–3. Rhys ap Gruffudd was also the patron of Einion Offeiriad, the redactor of the Bardic Grammar. This may add some measure of support for the belief that the work of Llywelyn Goch is included in the Grammar.

down[60] belong to Iolo's old age; they are in the form of a circumstantial, familiar, and humorous address to his patron the archdeacon Ithel ap Robert, recalling their youth together, and begging him for the gift from his stud of a decent sober horse suited to carrying an infirm old man—not a horse so weak that he would fall down under the burden, or one that jibs, or one that will not stand still while being shod, or a frisky young horse whose mane has not yet grown, who would start off on his own 'like a long-haired goat' leaving the poet behind or else clinging precariously to the saddle—if such a horse were to trip and cause him to bite his tongue, it is Poetry which would suffer. One of the two *cywyddau* is in the form of a dialogue between the poet and the old horse who has died, and he thus addresses him:

> You were a fair, stout, straight-legged courser; it is sad you will never be so again. You were the best of runners, and it is sad and grievous after you to see the place where you were reared empty, and your manger without food. What can I do to obtain a large and gentle steed to carry me? It is wearisome for a feeble old man to have to walk without resting, lacking the gift of a horse—but whom I should ask in Is Conwy, I do not know (IGE² XVIII).

The old horse is made to reply with the obvious answer, that the poet should go and ask Ithel ap Robert for a replacement, and this he does with success: the only remaining difficulty being to obtain a mounting-block, since he is 'heavy and stooping like a hunchback', and then to avoid anything—like the noisy turning millwheel—which might startle or impede the new horse, as they ride on the familiar journey home. The whole tenor of these poems leaves the reader in no doubt as to Iolo Goch's particularly strong feeling for horses, and as to the striking wealth of his vocabulary for describing the *minutiae* of their behaviour (good or bad), and as to his knowledge of the various ailments which might befall them—knowledge which was widespread in his day, no doubt, but which is nowadays an almost obliterated technology.[61] Saunders Lewis has pointed out that in Iolo's description of the kind of horse which he would wish to have there is to be found the phrase *carn geugraff*[62] ('hollow-hoofed'), which occurs also in the descriptive lines quoted above from the Bardic Grammar. These lines also include the rare compound *amcaff* ('greedy'), of which the only other example attested from the fourteenth century is in a pejorative description of a dog, in a satire which is also by Iolo, preserved in the *Red Book*

---

[60] IGE² XVII and XVIII.

[61] More than a century later this knowledge was preserved in 'A Welsh Treatise on Horses', ed. C. O'Rahilly, *Celtica v*, 145–60, from Peniarth 86 (sixteenth century), 139–50. The treatise is based closely on Leonard Mascall's *Book of Horses* (London, 1587). The words for the diseases of horses are derived from English.

[62] *Carn geugraff mewn rhaff yn rhwym*, IGE² p. 53, 1.9.

*of Hergest.*[63] Saunders Lewis therefore concludes that the lines in the Grammar which are the earliest extant example of a *cywydd deuair hirion* may quite possibly be a quotation from an early poem by Iolo Goch.

These suggestions as to the authorship of the two examples of *englyn* and *cywydd* in the earliest version of the Bardic Grammar have much to recommend them, and their acceptance would confirm the conclusion that both Llywelyn Goch and Iolo Goch were Dafydd ap Gwilym's close contemporaries in the second quarter of the fourteenth century, and that the early evolution of both *cywydd serch* and of *cywydd mawl*—poems of love and poems of conventional praise in the new *cywydd* metre—are likely to have been closely contemporaneous developments, and are to be attributed to the activities of a group of poets rather than to any single innovator. And in so far as we can identify individually the pioneers of this development—and it may be that our lack of evidence is responsible for giving an inaccurate impression—the impelling force which instigated the evolution of the *cywydd* appears to have come from the poets of Gwynedd, whose 'security of tenure' was most quickly and catastrophically affected by the loss of patronage from their native princes which followed upon the break-up of the old society in the last decades of the thirteenth century.

---

[63] *huuen amkaff*, 'greedy for cream', RP 1291, 30–1.

# INDEX

Aberystwyth, 11, 12
*aisling*, 100, 102
*alba, aube*, 41, 44, 87n., 96, 147
*amhráin grá*, 101, 102, 103, 111 and n.
*Amlyn and Amig*, 148
*Amores* (Ovid), 72–3, 75, 76n., 88, 103
*amour courtois*, 68, 96, 97, 102, 129
Aneirin, 50, 59, 142, 160
Angharad, wife of Ieuan Llwyd, 16
    and n., 108, 123 and n., 124–5, 128
Anglesey, 30, 44, 49, 65, 94
Anglo-Norman literature, 75, 76, 96;
    *see Fouke fitz Waryn*
*An Grá in Amhráin na nDaoine*, 97
Arthur, 46, 144
Arthurian Names, 103, 134
*arblastr* (cross-box), 83
*areithiau*, 80
*Ars Amatoria* (Ovid), 71–2, 73
*Annwfn, cŵn Annwfn*, 146–7
Arnold, Matthew, 53, 80n.
*Athrodi ei Was* (GDG 128), 44, 94
*awdl, awdlau*, 14, 46, 61, 105, 106, 107,
    110, 128, 153, 161, 162, 168; *exempla*
    of, 112–13, 126, 131 and n.
*awdl gywydd*, 125–6
*awenydd*, 118

Bangor, 17, 18; Bangor Cathedral, 72
Bardic Grammar, the, 2, 39, 60, 68,
    89, 92, 105 ff., 132, 149, 165, 169,
    *see Gramadegau'r Penceirddiaid*
*Barddoniaeth Dafydd ap Gwilym* (*1789*),
    51, 57 and n., 59, 70n,

Basaleg, 20
Bell, Sir Idris, 60, 126
Birds, 76, 77, 78, 79, 80, 81, 82, 92,
    100, 102, 117–18, 131; Bird-
    debates, 75, 77, 78, 79n., 81, 97, 98,
    102; Bird-song, 77; Birds' 'Latin',
    78
Blackbird, 7, 77, 79, 92, 108
Black Book of Carmarthen, the, 142
Black Death, 24, 107, 157
Black Prince, 13
Bowen, D. J., 22n., 29n., 61n., 85n.,
    128, 159n., 161, 162
Branwen ferch Llŷr, 133
*Breuddwyd Maxen*, 76, 135–6, 163
*Broch yng nghod*, 150
Brogynin, 11, 12, 29
*Brut y Brenhinedd*, 2, 135, *see* Geoffrey
    of Monmouth

*cae*, 119; *cae bedw*, 74, 119; *cae Esyllt*,
    137n.
Caernarfon, 17, 54
Cai Hir, 90, 134
'Cambridge Songs', The, 79
*canu caeth*, 100; *canu mawl*, 89, 101, 153,
    162; *canu rhydd*, 60, 78, 80, 87, 100,
    101
Casnodyn, 110
Ceredigion, 104, 107, 110
Charlemagne tales, 147, 148
Chaucer, 41, 53, 56n., 60, 77n., 81,
    93, 94

Chotzen, Th. M., 58, 64n., 66n., 74n., 77n., 84n.
Chrétien de Troyes, 70, 103
Cneppyn Gwerthrynion, 127 and n.
*Claddu'r Bardd o Gariad* (OBWV, no. 61), 51, 78
*Clêr, Y Glêr, clêr ofer*, 44 and n., 67, 87, 91, 100, 109, 128, 129, 153
*clerici vagantes*, 126, 128
Clerk *versus* Knight controversy, 44, 75, 78
Cock Thrush, the, 6, 36, 54
Courtly Love, 69, 70, 73, 74, 79, 81, *see amour courtois*
Cowell, E B., 57, 58n., 96
Creirwy, 115–6 and n.
Cuhelyn Fardd, 13 and n., 15, 140
*Culhwch ac Olwen*, 79, 134–5, 139
currency, names for, 83, 84 and n., 85
*Cwm Bwa*, 29
*cynghanedd*, 8, 9, 87, 100, 102, 152, 153
Cynddelw Brydydd Mawr, 20, 50, 64, 67, 103, 110, 141
*Cyfraith Hywel* (native legal system), 2, 90, 130, 151, *see* Welsh Laws
*Cyngor y Biogen* ('The Magpie's Counsel'), 37, 41, 79, 87 and n., 93
*cywydd, cywyddau*, 2, 3, 8, 12, 17, 27, 46, 47, 49, 52, 63, 65, 68–70, 72, 76–8, 80, 87, 113; *cywydd*, metre, 68, 82, 87, 91, 110, 124–5, 152; *cywydd deuair fyrion*, 124–5, 126; *cywydd deuair hirion*, 90, 114, 152–3, 169; *cywyddau mawl*, 154, 163; *cywyddau serch*, 65, 165, 171; *cywydd bun*, 49; *cywydd gofyn*, 39; *cywydd llosgyrnog*, 125, 126; *cywydd marwnad*, 161
*Cywydd y Sêr* (OBWV no. 64), 51, 85
*Cywydd y Cloc* (GDG 66), 136
*Cywydd yr Eira* (OBWV no. 65), 51

*Dafydd Broffwyd*, 94
Dafydd Ddu Athro, 113 and n.
*Dan y Bargawd* (GDG 89), 42, 85, 97 and n., 167
*danta grá*, 98, 103
*Dares Phrygius*, 133, 137, 147, 148, 149
Deheubarth, 107
*deildy*, 4, 35, 83

*Derdri*, 139
Desmond, third Earl, *see* Gerald, Earl of Desmond
Donatus, 105, 127
Dreams (symbolic), 72, 100; dream belief, 76, 77, 98
*Dream of Maxen (Breuddwyd Maxen)*, 135–6, 137
Dronke, P., 76n., 79n., 111n.
*Drystan, Trystan*, 117, 137, 138
*dwned*, 105, 106, 127; *llyfr dwned* 14
Dwynwen, St, 30 and n., 36, 143
Dyddgu, 27, 28 and n., 29, 65, 67, 85, 166
*dyfalu*, 37, 39 and n., 40, 42, 52, 66, 80, 82, 99, 152, 155–61
Dyfed, 22–3, 91, 104, 115, 132, 133
Dyfi, river (GDG 71), 72, 75, 77

Edward III, 11, 108, 162
*Edifeirwch*, (GDG 106), 56
Efa, d. of Madog ap Maredudd, 103
*Eiddig*, the, 33, 44, 66, 94, 100, 103, 108n., 137, 158
*Ei Gysgod* (GDG 141), 41
Einion Offeiriad, 105n., 106–7, 109, 110, 113–14, 123, 127–8, 130
English, medieval, 8, 14, 15, 83, 105
Elen, wife of Robin Nordd, 28
Elfed, 116, 128
*Elucidarium*, 156, 162
*englyn*, 14, 46, 61, 63, 108, 109; *englynion*, gnomic and proverbial, 2, 92, 110; *englyn o'r hen ganiad*, 109, 110, 112
*eos*, 103, 117; *eos Dyfed*, 22, *see* Nightingale
*exempla*, 5, 95, 108, 109, 113, 114, 124, 165

*fabliaux*, 2, 3, 44, 66, 94, 154
*fflwring* (florin), 84
'Forbidden Faults', the, 110, 111, 113, 123, 127n.
*Formulae* (poets') for ideal beauty, 66 and n.
*Fouke fitz Waryn (Syr Ffwg)*, 150–2
Fox, The (GDG 22), 81
France, 31, 44, 68, 71, 101, 103

French influences, 93, 102; French poems, 75, 76, 77, 79, 83, 87, 94; French beast-epic, 81
Friars, 66, 93; *see* Grey Friar, the,

*Galw ar Ddwynwen* (GDG 94), 52
Geoffrey of Monmouth, 89
Gerald, Earl of Desmond, 60 and n., 98, 103
Gilbert de Clare, 74
Gilbert Talbot, 13
Giolla Brighde Mac Con Midhe, 72n.
Glamorgan, 74, 91
Glyn Davies, J., 81n.
Glyndŵr, Owain, 163
Gnomic poetry, 109
Gododdin, the, 119
*gofeirdd*, 64
Gogynfeirdd, 61, 66, 69, 90, 103, 121
*Gorhoffedd* poems, 103, 127
Goronwy Owen, 52
*Gramadegau'r Penceirddiaid*, 14n., *see* Bardic Grammar
Grey Friar, the, 19, 50, 79, 94
Griffiths, R. A., 16n.
Gruffudd ab Adda, 16, 82, 84, 153–4, 155, 157–8, 161
Gruffudd Gryg, 11, 16, 22, 23, 46, 47–50, 52, 63–5, 68, 69–70, 79, 83, 85, 118, 142, 147, 153–4, 155, 157, 161
Gruffudd ap Dafydd ap Tudur, 48, 69n., 117, 119, 122n., 155n., 165
Gruffudd ab yr Ynad Coch, 110
Gruffudd ap Maredudd, 56n., 63n., 67, 139, 163
Gruffydd, W. J., 8, 60, 64n., 71n., 88, 100, 101
Gruffydd, R. G. G., 87n., 90n., 103n., 132
Guillaume de Lorris, 73, 74, 75
Gutun Owain, 106
*gwayw, gwewyr*, 68n.
Gwalchmai, 90, 134
Gwalchmai (poet), 103
Gwenhwyfar, 144–5
Gwernyclepa, 20, 24
Gwgon Gleddyfrudd, 145
Gwilym Gam, 12, 13

Gwilym Ddu o Arfon, 110
Gwilym ap Gwrwared, 13
*gwladeidd*, 126
Gwynfardd Dyfed, 13 and n., 15, 90
Gwynedd, 48, 67, 104, 113, 164
Gwyn ap Nudd, 146–7

Harley Lyrics, the, 79n., 98–9, 103
Hendregadredd MS., *see* Manuscripts
*Hengerdd*, 90
Hopcyn ap Thomas, 11
*Huail fab Caw*, 143–4
Huws, Daniel, 108n., 159n., 121, 124
*Hwsmonaeth Cariad* (GDG 87), 31, 52, 74–5, 77
Hywel ap Goronwy, 17, 29
Hywel Dda, 14
(Sir) Hywel of the Axe (*H. y Fwyall*), 163
Hywel ab Owain Gwynedd, 48, 67, 69, 91, 103, 104, 127, 165

Ieuan Llwyd of Glyn Aeron, 15, 16, 108 and n., 123
Ieuan ap Gruffudd ap Llywelyn, 28n., 29
Ifor Hael, 20, 21, 22–5, 61, 62, 90, 141, 150, 164, 166
Ifor ap Llywelyn, *see* Ifor Hael
Imagery (Dafydd's poetic), 82, 85–6
*Immacallam in dá Thuarad*, ('Colloquy of the Two Sages'), 64n.
Indeg, 90, 138
Iolo Goch, 12n., 67, 69, 85n., 91, 135–6, 140, 148, 153 ff.
Iolo Morganwg, 11n., 13n., 24, 51, 57n., 96, 100
*Iomarbhaigh na bhFileadh*, ('The Contention of the Poets'), 64n.
Iorwerth Fychan, 110
Ireland, 15, 46, 63, 90, 100, 101, 102
*I'r Llwyn Banadl* (OBWV no. 63), 51
Irish Poetry, 2, 60–1, 62, 66n., 72n., 78n., 97, 101; Irish keen, 167; Irish hermit verse, 80 and n., 102
Ithel ap Robert, 170

Jackson, K. H., 64n., 80n.
Jarman, A. O. H., 15n., 142n.

Jean de Condé, 76n., 77, 94
Jean de Meun, 73, 81
Jenkins, David, 12, 29
Jones, David (Llanfair) *see*
 Manuscripts: Book of David Jones,
 Llanfair
Jones, D. Gwenallt, 51
Jones, T. Gwynn, 64n., 66n., 67n.,
 69n., 84n., 103n
Jones, G. Hartwell, 57
Jones, W. Lewis, 58, 71n., 87n.

Latin, 93, 102; Latin grammar, 105;
 *see* 'Birds' Latin'
Langland, 94, 157
Lewis, Saunders, 19, 45, 61n., 66n.,
 84, 88, 94n., 95, 99, 106 and n.,
 120–1, 135, 162, 169
Lewys Glyn Cothi, 23, 24n.
Llanbadarn Fawr, 11, 12, 40, 72, 97
Llanddwyn, 30
Llanllugan, 31
*llatai*, 31, 36, 37, 66, 99; *llateion*, 76,
 101, 103
Lleucu Llwyd, 113, 120–1, 124, 166,
 168–9
*Lludd and Llefelys*, 132
*Llwybr Adda*, 12n.
*Llyfr Ancr Llanddewifrefi*, 19n.
*Llyfr Gwyn Rhydderch*, 16; *see* White
 Book of Rhydderch
Llywarch Hen (poetry), 143, 149
Llywelyn ap Gruffudd (Last Prince),
 11
Llywelyn ap Gwilym, 13n., 14, 62, 90,
 91, 105, 116–7
Llywelyn Goch ap Meurig Hen,
 56n., 85n., 120, 148, 153–5, 164 ff.,
 169

*Mabinogi*, the, 2, 93, 115, 132–3, 149;
 *Mabinogi Pwyll*, 49; *Mabinogi Math
 fab Mathonwy*, 115, 133
Macrobius, 76
Madog Benfras, 16, 22, 69, 83, 153–4
Madog ap Maredudd, 64
Magpie, the (GDG 63), 41, 79; see
 *Cyngor y Biogen*
*malmariée* poems, 87, 94, 98

Manuscripts: Bangor MS. I, 106;
 Llanstephan 3, 106,
 Hendregadredd, 121, 124, 159n.;
 Book of David Jones, Llanfair, 17,
 18n., 49n.; Peniarth 20, 106, 113;
 Peniarth 28, 17
*marwnad, marwnadau*, 49, 52, 62, 63,
 82, 89; *Marwnad Gruffudd Gryg*, 49
*Marwnad Angharad* (GDG 16), 108 and
 n.; *Marwnad Lleucu Llwyd*, 62n., 121
Medieval debate poems, 70
*La Messe des Oiseaux*, 76 and n., 77
*Merched Llanbadarn* (GDG48), 3, 12
*Metamorphoses* (Ovid), 73, 117, 118
Middle English, 83, 105; *see* English,
 medieval
'The Mist' *Y Niwl*, (GDG 68), 39
Morfudd, 12, 23–33, 35, 40–42, 46,
 49, 53, 65, 67n., 68, 75, 85, 86, 98,
 115, 166
*Morfudd fel yr Haul* (GDG 42), 26, 52,
 82
Morgannwg, 21, 22, 104
Myrddin, 50, 117, 142, 160

Narcissus, fountain of, 74
Nest, d. of Gwrwared, 16 and n., 107
Nest, wife of Ifor Hael, 23, 24
Newcastle Emlyn, 13 and n., 14, 117
Nightingale, the, 5, 6, 81 and n., 82,
 84, 117–18
Norman boroughs, 88, 94, 99
Norman Conquest, the, 103
Nuns, 82

Odo of Cheriton, 81n.
*oed*, 65, 117
Offa's Dyke, 13
*Offeren y Llwyn* (GDG 122), 52, 77
'Old North', the, 20, 92, 141–2
Oldest Animals, the, 79
Ó Tuama, Seán, 60–1 and n., 79n.,
 97, 100, 102, 111n., 198
Ovid, 1, 2, 41, 59, 68, 70, 72, 73, 88,
 96, 117, 151, 160; *ofyddiaeth*, 2, 70
Owain Myfyr, 57
*Owl and the Nightingale*, the, 70n.

*pair dadeni*, 133 and n.

Parry, Dr Thomas, 22, 51, 52, 58–61,
    67n., 68, 69n., 78, 82, 84, 86n., 96,
    102, 114, 155, 167
Parry, R. Williams, 7, 78n.
Parcrhydderch, 108, 123, 130
*pastourelle*, 87, 96
*pencerdd*, 64; *penceirddiaid*, 20, 91, 106
Peredur, 90, 136, 150
Personification, 82
Phylip Brydydd, 64
*Philomela*, 117
'Poet's Burial for Love', the (OBWV
    no. 61), 78
Priscian, 127
Provence, Provencal, 2, 46, 68, 93,
    103; *see* Troubadours
*Prydlyfr*, the, 128 and n.
Pughe, William Owen, 1, 13n., 57

Red Book of Hergest, the, 91, 106,
    109, 111, 113 ff., 123, 129, 147, 148
Retraction (Dafydd's), *see* Edifeirwch
*Reverdie*, 79, 87 and n., 93, 100
Rheged, hall of, 90
*Rhieingerdd, rhieingerddi*, 27 and n., 46,
    67, 110–11, 121, 165
Rhosyr (Newborough), 17, 44, 94,
    133
Rhydderch ab Ieuan Llwyd, 16 and
    n., 108n., 130, 148, 149
Rhys Ieuanc, 65
Rhys Meigen, 16, 19, 48, 62, 145, 156
Rhys Goch ap Rhiccert, 57n., 96
Rhys Goch Eryri, 65n.
Rhys ap Gruffudd, Syr, 16, 107, 108,
    110, 113, 116, 117n., 123, 161, 162,
    169
Rhys ap Tewdwr, 13n., 164
Robin Nordd, 'Robert le Northern',
    28, 29
*Roman de la Rose*, 59, 71, 73, 74, 75,
    78 and n., 81, 88
Romances, the 3 Arthurian, 136–8
Rowlands, Eurys, 14, 16n., 61n., 68n.,
    82, 90, 94n., 104n., 133, 146

*Saith Doethion Rhufain*, 95, 135
*sangiad(au)*, 9, 43
Satire, 62–3, 67

Saunders Lewis, *see* Lewis, Saunders
Seagull, the, 5, 36
Seisyll Bryffwrch, 64
*Serch fel Ysgyfarnog* (GDG 46), 39, 82
*serenade*, 42, 44, 87, 96, 97, 167–8
Simwnt Fychan, 106
Siôn Tudur, 101
Siôn Cent, 54, 56n., 65n.
*siryf*, 54
Skylark, the, 6, 55
Smith, Beverly, 107, 114n.
Spears and arrows (of love), 46, 68
    and n., 74
Stanley, Sir John, 63n.
*Statute of Gruffudd ap Cynan*, the, 14
    and n.
Star, the (GDG 67), 38
Strata Florida, 11, 108

*Taith i Garu* (GDG 83), 12
Taliesin, 20, 50, 59, 64n, 89, 90, 141,
    142, 160, 164
Talley Abbey (*Talyllychau*), 11
Tegau Eurfron, 90, 99, 127, 138
Tenby, poem in praise of, 163
*tenso*, 46
*toddaid*, 14, 46, 63
*traethodl*, 87, 91, 102, 153
*Trafferth mewn Tafarn* (GDG 124), 3,
    43, 44, 66, 67n., 94
Triads, 2, 86, 115, 144, 147
*Tri Hael Ynys Prydein* (Rhydderch,
    Nudd, and Mordaf), 20, 62, 134,
    141
*Trioedd Cerdd*, 105, 127
*Tri Phorthor Eiddig* (GDG 80), 74
Troubadours (Provençal), 57n., 67,
    68, 103; Troubadour poetry, 59
    and n.
Tudur Aled, 51

*Uchel y bûm yn ochi* (GDG 129), 96
*uchelwr, uchelwyr*, 12, 107, 123, 166
Ulster Cycle of tales, 139–41
Urien Rheged, 62, 164
*ustus* (justice of peace), 54
Uwch Aeron, 32

Venus, 76, 77

*Welsh Genealogies 300–1400* (P. C. Bartrum), 13n., 16n., 28n.
Welsh Laws, 64n. *see Cyfraith Hywel*
White Book of Rhydderch, the, 89, 129–30, 148, 149
White Doe (theme of), 76 and n.
Wiliems, Thomas (Trefriw), 11n.
William of Poitiers, 93
Williams, Gruffudd Aled, 65n.
Williams, J. E. Caerwyn, 63n.
Williams, Glanmor, 49, 56n., 128
Williams, G. J., 51 and n., 57n., 91n., 106, 120, 126
Williams, Sir Ifor, 16n., 24, 28, 58, 61, 64n., 80n., 83, 87n., 96, 97, 98, 107, 113 and n., 116, 128
Woodcock, the, 37, 79

*Yr Adfail* (GDG 144), 53–4, 143
*Y Breuddwyd* (GDG 39), 76
*Y Bwa Bach*, 26, 30; *Ebowa baghan*, 29 and n.
*Y Carw* (GDG 116), 36–7
*y Cloc* (GDG 66), 76
*Y Cwt Gwyddau* (GDG 126), 44, 66, 94

*Y Don ar Afon Dyfi* (GDG 71), 72, 75, 77
*Yr Ehedydd* (GDG 114), 36
*Y Ffenestr* (GDG 64), 42
*Y Garreg Ateb* (GDG 130), 142
*Y Gwynt* (GDG 117), 32–3, 36, 37, 55, 85, 157
*Y Llwynog* (GDG 22), 38
*Y Mwdwl Gwair* (GDG 62), 55
*Y Niwl* (GDG 68), 39
*Y Pwll Mawn* (GDG 127), 3, 42
*Y Rhugl Groen* (GDG 125), 42
*Y Serch Lledrad* (GDG 74), 25
*Ymddiddan, ymddiddanion*, 78, 80, 100
*Ymddiddan Arthur a'r Eryr*, 79n.
*Ymryson* (contention) D. ap G. â Gr. Gryg, 46, 49n., 50, 63–5, 70, 86, 127n., 159
Ysgolan, 143, and n.
*Ystorya Trystan*, 137
Ystrad Fflur, *see* Strata Florida
Ystudfach, 143 and n.

Zodiac, signs of, 18